Jun 17

"Simultaneously informative, engaging and entertaining. Michael Trickey speaks to the audience of young home buyers with wit and intelligence. Get this book and then get into your own home. You will be glad you did."

-Sean Low,
President, The Business of Being Creative, and Recent Homebuyer

"Finding Home *is the most comprehensive guide to home ownership available, covering both the practical and the psychological aspects of buying and owning your piece of the American dream. A must-read for the inexperienced and the experienced alike!"*

-Steven Herrmann,
CFP, ChFC, Mass Mutual Financial Group

"Finding Home *is a powerful tool and insightful guide that is a must-have for not only millennials, but anyone who is looking for a successful transition from renting to home ownership! Michael Trickey has laid the groundwork to home ownership in a step-by-step process that is easy to read and understand. The wisdom and guidance he provides is invaluable not only to the first-time homebuyer, but to anyone who is in the process of acquiring a new home!"*

-Nathan Justice,
Mortgage Underwriting Operations Director,
Cognitive Options Group, LLC

"Few people in the mortgage business have a more complete and detailed understanding of the home buying and mortgage process than Michael Trickey, and he delivered his knowledge in an approachable format for the everyday potential home buyer. His desire to make a difference for future home buyers is clearly demonstrated. Finding Home *is a home buying and personal finance guide that people can actually read, enjoy, and continue to use as a reference. Bravo!"*

-Peter Crouchley,
Fixed Income Capital Markets,
Structured Finance Trader for Mortgage Whole Loans and
Wunderlich Securities

"Buying your first home is unfamiliar territory, and Finding Home *is the map you need. This handy guide to the players, paperwork and processes is organized so that each chapter can be read independently. Even veterans of the housing market will benefit from practical advice on finding the right home and neighborhood, saving for the down payment, and calculating how much house you can afford."*

-Richard Termuhlen,
Attorney

"Michael Trickey keys in on the fundamentals of the entire home buying process. From making sure that you are mentally ready, checking your financial wherewithal, getting your credit in order, budgeting, qualifying for a mortgage, figuring out where you want to live and what kind of home you want, making an offer and buying the home, moving in, and even having a housewarming party, this book covers it all."

-Ralph Aguirre,
Principal, RA Advisors, LLC

"It's really convenient that my dad wrote this book just when I was starting to think about buying a home for the first time. There aren't any other good guides on the market—mostly you see web pages that are biased or only deal with a specific piece of the process. This book is organized, unbiased and detailed. My friends and I are eating it up."

-Michele Trickey,
Product Manager

FINDING HOME

MICHAEL W. TRICKEY

FINDING HOME

EVERYTHING YOU NEED TO KNOW
- *AND DO* -
FOR HOME BUYING SUCCESS

NEXT CENTURY
PUBLISHING

FINDING HOME
Everything you need to know - *and do* - for home buying success

Published by Next Century Publishing
Las Vegas, Nevada
www.NextCenturyPublishing.com

ISBN: 978-1-68102-291-8
Library of Congress Control Number: 2016913211

Printed in the United States of America

Dedication

To Michele and Amanda

May this book contribute to your home buying success, and that of your friends, and your generation!

Acknowledgments

Finding Home would have been much more difficult without the support of my family, friends and colleagues. My wife, Diane, not only endured my countless hours devoted to the book, but also provided support reading, editing, and commenting on content. My longtime friend David Schiff was an all-round champion, providing encouragement, edits, insights, and suggestions. My colleague Debra Vander Weit brought years of industry experience, providing technical edits and suggestions as well. Their mastery of the English language, editing skills, and combined experience in looking for, buying and setting up homes, helped me to add tips and point out pitfalls in a straightforward, insightful manner.

My own millennial focus group, led by my daughters Michele and Amanda, and my colleague Janis Nagobads, read and reread chapters, telling me what sections needed to be clarified, expanded or nixed. Along with others in the group, they made sure I was up to date on what matters most to young people shopping for homes, while contributing significantly to resources discussed in the book and on the companion website. Amanda helped me to edit the first complete draft, and substantially helped to make it more readable and easier to understand.

The talented folks at Next Century Publishing also helped make this book possible. I worked with and benefited greatly from the contributions of Frank and Julie Ward in piecing together the early structure of the book. They helped me to bring Jack and Eva to life. Simon Presland and his editing and layout teams did a masterful job, giving both a great look and feel to the book, and fitting the multitude of questionnaires, tables, templates, checklists, charts and maps onto the pages. I thank Simon for his unwavering patience, encouragement and support, and for helping me give life to Jack's father, Mike. I also thank Rod Larrivee and Ken Dunn for their assistance and support.

Other colleagues at my consulting firm Berkshire Group LP, and its affiliates, helped me enhance the discussions about repairing credit, avoiding mortgage fraud, and details about recent changes in lending laws and regulations. My thanks also to Caroline Bowden and Craig Henderson for helping me to establish and keep the FindingHomeBook.com site running smoothly.

Many others provided feedback, comments, suggestions, insights and encouragement. Thanks to the many real estate professionals, lenders, regulators and others who strive to make the United States home buying market vibrant, safe and strong. Without you, finding home would be a much more difficult task.

CONTENTS

FINDING HOME

Introduction

Welcome! I am so glad you are here. It tells me that you are contemplating what could be the biggest transaction of your life so far, and you want to be prepared. Over the years, I have helped many people find and buy the right home for them. I have also repeatedly been down this road myself, and I look forward to helping you to successfully find and buy your home.

Buying a home involves ***preparation*** (research, savings, and soul searching), ***tools*** (websites, data, forms, checklists, and people) and ***processes*** (walk-throughs, negotiations, mortgage loan approval, and closing the deal) that will lead you to a home that meets your needs and budget. The Finding Home book will help you navigate the home buying maze by giving you guidance, answering questions, and helping you feel confident *before* you take your first steps.

In this book, you will find insights and tips for first time home buyers and seasoned investors alike. This is a guide that you can reference any time questions arise, and it incorporates new attitudes, technologies, laws, demographic trends, environmental concerns, and economic realities. Recognizing that changes in these areas are nonstop, I have created a companion website that includes updates, answers to frequently asked questions, an extensive glossary, recommended websites, calculators, downloadable forms, and more. You can find it at FindingHomeBook.com. Simply go to the site, create a user account, and access extensive content.

When you log in, you can download templates for the forms included in this book and customize them for your needs. You can add in your dreams, needs and wants, desired locations, income, budget, family size and everything else related to your home search.

I routinely receive home buying questions from people of all ages and backgrounds. Many have delayed buying a home with the belief that real estate is no longer a good investment. As you will see, if you approach the process correctly, and with the right tools and knowledge, buying a home is not only a good investment but provides a foundation for security and peace of mind.

The largest home buying group right now is comprised of adults in their twenties and thirties. The media loves labels and refers to this group as millennials, echo boomers, or Gen Y. While I address this group, the book is also perfect for anyone of any age. My goal is to guide the home buying public to make the processes fit individual needs and tastes. Many aspects to purchasing a home have nothing to do with traits, but they do follow common steps that reach a successful outcome.

Some factors unique to today's younger home buyers include:

1. You have straddled the advent and expansion of personal computers, the Internet, smartphones, and social media. These things did not exist or were not widespread in prior decades but are now commonplace. Being proficient in the use of electronic interaction and collaboration:

    a. Your attitudes on the sharing of information and intellectual property have been impacted, and also your views towards those who do not use social media.

    b. You likely have a much more diverse group of friends than previous generations, due to your frequent contact with social media.

    c. You are a better researcher than previous generations, and able to obtain information on the Internet and through social media groups.

2. You came of age during a time of increased economic distress. You have witnessed neighbors, and perhaps family members, suffer through declining home prices and foreclosures.

   a. This has impacted your views regarding risk and your attitudes towards large financial institutions.

   b. It is harder for you to obtain a home loan as lenders have stricter lending requirements.

3. You may have student loan debt burdening your balance sheet and your personal life. This may contribute to your decision to delay buying a home.

4. Certain environmental and health awareness and concerns have come of age, and:

   a. You are likely more concerned and aware of health, pollution, global warming, and other related topics.

   b. You use and understand terms like "carbon footprint."

5. Stereotypes of the term "traditional family" are being broken.

   a. The advances of civil and gay rights are changing what families "look" like.

   b. More couples are choosing to delay marriage; some are choosing a domestic partnership instead.

   c. Families are mixed; remarriages and introductions of stepchildren into households are common.

I consider these factors in each chapter as I list what is needed for your success, point you to resources, stimulate your thinking about your individual wants and needs, discuss agreements and documents you may want to use, and address other considerations.

My Qualifications

What are my qualifications and why should you trust me to guide through what seems to be a daunting process?

I am an active participant in the residential and commercial real estate markets, both as a consultant to others and for my own use and investment. I purchased my first condo thirty-two years ago. Since then, I have acquired single-family homes, duplexes, multi-unit flats, apartment buildings, and commercial buildings.

I earned my MBA in financial management from the University of Chicago and a bachelor's degree in accounting from The Ohio State University. I obtained less formal but equally enlightening education completing real estate transactions, where I made mistakes as well as had many good experiences employing tools and techniques we will explore together.

As a CPA, with thirty-five years of experience working in the financial services industry, I worked for publicly traded mortgage lending institutions for nearly fifteen years, half of which time I was a chief financial officer. In 1998, I left the big corporate world and formed a consulting firm called the Berkshire Group LP, which is based in a Chicago suburb. Berkshire Group has been providing advisory services to banks and other financial firms dealing with mortgage loans since 1998. We also manage residential real estate, invest in mortgage loans and real estate tax liens, and track and analyze monthly activity on over 100 million mortgage loans.

The following chapters are organized in a logical progression but are designed to stand on their own. To help you translate the concepts presented into real life, you will be following a young couple, Jack and Eva, through the home buying process along with some great help and advice from Mike, Jack's father. You can see how they use the tools and fill in the forms, which will give you a great example of planning, budgeting and purchasing. With that said, let us begin. Together we are going to take the right steps to help you to successfully acquire your first, or next, home.

Here's to your home buying success!

Michael Trickey

Chapter 1

Thinking about Buying a Home?

"Home is the nicest word there is."
—Laura Ingalls Wilder

Whatever prompted you to pick up or download this book, home buying is somewhere in your sights. Congratulations! You have taken a step in the right direction. So let's get going and build some momentum before you get busy again, or have second thoughts. The home buying process can seem daunting, but you have picked the right source to help you through it.

This is going to take some time to accomplish. You should anticipate the process taking many months, depending on your circumstances, needs and market conditions. Unless of course you have hordes of extra cash from your recent IPO or favorite uncle, you have to get your finances and credit in order. You have to find a place, get a contract signed, obtain a mortgage loan, close on the deal, and move in. Purchasing a home is not something you can do in a week.

Why should you purchase a home? You have more control over what you can do, and how you shape your surroundings. You can play your violin until 3 a.m. without neighbors banging on the wall. You can paint and decorate as you like without fear of losing your security deposit. You can have pets, a garden, a completely wired environment, and a place to park your car or store your bike. You might even decide to start and grow your family there. The only limits are your time, imagination, bank account, handyman and gardening skills, and of course, local laws and building codes. For most, homeownership represents a form of freedom.

Buying a home is also an opportunity to leave behind the transient lifestyle of renting, and the ever-present threat of rental payment increases. You are leaving something temporary, owned by someone else, and moving on to something permanent which you can call your own. Your home may become your biggest single investment, and if purchased properly, can add significantly to your wealth over time.

1-1 Checklist to See if You are Ready

1-1-1 Helping to Understand the Process – Introducing Jack and Eva

In a local coffee shop one Saturday morning, a newlywed couple, Jack and Eva, sit at a table, sipping on lattes. Eva has a stack of school papers in front of her, red pen in hand, while Jack taps away on his laptop. She is an elementary school teacher. He is a software developer. They dream of purchasing a home but are not sure where to start. A small stack of papers is on the right side of the table, containing some checklists, forms and questionnaires that Eva downloaded and printed that morning, and a yellow highlighter on top.

Eva sets down her red pen, then stretches her arms over her head.

"Okay, Jack, no more computer work."

Jack looks up as Eva picks up the paper and highlighter, then dutifully saves his work and closes his laptop. "It's that time?"

Eva pulled out a readiness checklist. "Yep, here's the first checklist we need to fill out together. Time to start the process of finding our first home."

Jack sighs. "You're right, and I promised. This is going to take some work, but our current apartment is getting too small. It's hard to have company stay overnight when we are using the second bedroom as an office. And I see that wistful look you get when your sister Ellie is over with her kids. We need to find a better place to live, one that fits our needs."

Jack slides his chair next to Eva and they spend the next couple of hours reviewing checklists and talking things through so they can begin to figure out what they really need and want in a home, and get a feel for the price they can afford to pay.

Jack and Eva have been busy the last few years focusing on their careers, courtship, and marriage. Now they are ready to shift their focus to include buying their first home. As we follow the couple throughout the book, you will gain a solid understanding of what your quest will be like, and what you will need to do as you search for your home. Jack and Eva will go through the process, completing helpful checklists, forms, and questionnaires along the way, giving you confidence when you begin to do the same. Blank copies of all documents are on the companion website (FindingHomeBook.com) for easy access and download. You can either fill them in on your computer, smartphone or other PDA device, or print them out and complete them by hand.

1-1-2 Assessing Your Situation – Setting the Groundwork

Now that we have met Jack and Eva, let's start thinking about you and assessing your situation. We will go into detail later, but, just to get you started, I will pose some rapid-fire questions.

Are you employed? Where do you want to live? How do you want to live? Is owning an affordable option? What is your income? How much do you have in savings? Are you ready to do this whole home buying thing: a mortgage payment, taxes, insurance, and home maintenance? You might suddenly feel overwhelmed. But don't worry; we'll look at these together so that you have a true picture of what you can do now and what you may need to do in order to fulfill your dream of buying a home. Let's look at some details of your life that will greatly impact your home buying decisions.

Work History and Income: First of all, you want to take a broad view of your employment and salary. How stable is your employment situation? How much are you making now versus last year? Is your income steady or growing? What is the nature of your job? Chances are, you have an employer and receive a paycheck. If you are an employee (not self-employed or a business owner), in general, you will need at least two years of employment history with the same employer or in the same field to qualify for a mortgage. This is important. The amount of income you earn is important as well. Lenders like to see that you are consistently earning enough to meet your debt obligations. They like to see year-over-year growth to meet expected increases in the cost of living. Technically, you can qualify for a mortgage if you have an entry-level job flipping burgers, but the amount for which you qualify will be commensurate with your income. If you are self-employed or a business owner, the guidelines are a little different. Do not worry; we will talk about that in more detail later on.

Credit History and Debt: Next, it is extremely important to understand how your credit and debt will affect your purchase of a home. Most people have some form of debt: student loan payments, car payments, credit cards, etc. If you have a very high level of debt or do not make payments on time, this will be counted against you when applying for a loan to purchase a home. However, if you are planning on using a mortgage loan to buy a home, ironically, not having any debt will also count against you. Lenders want to see you have been

> Show the mortgage lenders you use credit as a tool and you know how to use and manage that tool.

24

able to properly manage smaller amounts of debt before they give you a big loan. So get yourself a credit card or use an auto loan to buy your car, and then make sure you make all your payments on time. I recommend setting up an automatic withdrawal from your checking account to make each payment. Pay your credit card balance in full each month so you do not have to pay those high card rates. And if you can, pay off your auto loan early. Show the mortgage lenders you use credit as a tool and you know how to manage that tool.

Part of the formula a mortgage lender uses to assess your creditworthiness is your debt-to-income ratio (DTI). This is expressed as a percentage. A simple way to illustrate this is to divide your monthly debt payment obligations by your income. For example, if you make $4,000 per month (before deductions), and your monthly payment obligations are $1,500 (1,500 / 4,000 = .375), your debt-to-income ratio is 37.5 percent. The lenders have rules for different loan programs as to what is acceptable and within guidelines. Obviously, lower debt and/or higher income will lower your debt-to-income ratio, which is a good thing. We'll talk more about this later, but this illustrates the general point.

Budget Skills: Some of us are "penny pinchers", knowing where every penny we get originates and where every penny we spend goes. Others are not quite this exact but have reasonable knowledge and control of where their money goes. There are also those among us who have no clue. If you are in the first two categories, you are probably doing pretty well with your budgeting. If you are in the latter, you may need to alter your habits if you want to keep the homeownership dream alive.

Savings and Reserves: The word "savings" can conjure up anxiety in even the most financially responsible among us. Many people have plenty but never think they have enough, while others do not have any and need to start saving. It can be hard to save money. Life comes with expenses.

The good news is that there are a number of tools and automated mechanisms to help you to add to your savings account. For example, if you are an employee, your employer likely has some type of payroll deduction or direct deposit. You can send some of that paycheck right into a savings account. This means the money comes out of your check before you can spend it. Just make sure you are not raiding that account because you didn't budget well enough, and you need money three days before your next paycheck. With your new mindset, going out to see your favorite band may no longer justify a raid on your savings.

To buy a home, you will need savings sufficient to make a down payment, pay your closing costs, and cover at least three months mortgage loan payments just in case. There will be more on this topic later. I will help you figure out exactly how much you will need.

Are you mentally ready to own a home?

Homeowner Psychology: Are you mentally ready to own a home? For example, are you prepared to do (or pay for) all ongoing maintenance? Grass doesn't cut itself. Are you ready to live in one place for an extended period? You also have to be willing and disciplined enough to fix any of the shortfalls in the aforementioned categories of budgeting, savings, credit, and income. If you do have a shortfall, you will find the tools you need in the coming pages to help you along.

The following is a checklist to help you assess if you are ready to purchase a home. If you answer with the indicated response, give yourself a score of one (1) for that item, otherwise zero (0). This form, as with the others in this book, is available on the companion website for you to access and complete, or print. Let us see how Jack and Eva filled out the checklist.

Downloadable Template 1-1: Readiness Checklist

		Question	Response	Score 1 if:	Score	More Information
	Work History					
1		Has your income been reliable (stable, steady, and predictable) the last two years?	**yes**	yes	1	**Jack - 4 years at Metro-X Corp. / Eva – 4 years at Central Elementary School**
2		Have you worked at your current job for at least one year?	**yes**	yes	1	**Yes, per 1 above**
3		Have you been steadily employed for the last two years?	**yes**	yes	1	**Yes, per 1 above**
4		If you changed jobs, did your pay match or exceed the pay from your old job?	**yes**	yes	1	**N/A**
	Credit History					
5		Do you pay your bills on time?	**yes**	yes	1	
6		Do you have a big revolving balance on your credit cards?	**yes**	no	0	**$1,500 on credit cards from vacation**
7		Do you have a decent credit score?	**yes**	yes	1	**Jack 705 / Eva 712**
	Budget Skills					
8		Do you know where your money comes from and where it is going every month?	**yes**	yes	1	
9		Do you pay off your monthly expenses without going into debt?	**yes**	yes	1	**Some credit card debt due to unplanned vacation layover related to hurricane grounding flights**
10		Do you put a portion of your monthly budget into savings?	**yes**	yes	1	**At least 5%**
11		Do you have control of your debt?	**yes**	yes	1	
	Savings and Reserves					
12		Do you have a sizeable emergency fund?	**no**	yes	0	**Two months emergency savings**
13		Have you saved enough for both a down payment and closing costs?	**yes**	yes	1	**It depends on the type of loan - $15,000**

	Question	Response	Score 1 if:	Score	More Information
	Homeowner Psychology				
14	Are you ready and willing to maintain your own home, not just call a landlord?	**yes**	yes	1	
15	Are you ready to make a commitment to stay in one place?	**yes**	yes	1	**Like area, ready to start family in next two years**
16	Are you ready to make some sacrifices to fill any gaps in this questionnaire?	**yes**	yes	1	
	Total Score			14	

There are sixteen (16) questions in the checklist. If you score above 12, you are probably ready to be a homeowner (as long as the answer to number 16 is yes). Every day, there are people who buy homes who do not score above 12, but your odds of being ready improve the higher your score.

1-2 Renting versus Buying – Do You Have the Appetite to Buy?

You might be thinking, *why buy a house when I have a great apartment overlooking the city, or near work, or some other attractive feature?* Jack and Eva have discussed this question many times. Like them, you may not have the life of a TV character with a dream apartment and great view, but there are advantages to renting. You can call the landlord if something breaks. Jack and Eva like this because neither is the handyman type. You can move after your lease is up if you do not like where you live. Renting helps you gain familiarity with an area before you commit long-term.

Some apartment complexes have workout facilities and/ or swimming pools, all of which are typically maintained by the management company of the complex. It is convenient and a potential perk of being a tenant. You may not be able to afford a fully equipped gym if you become a homeowner, but you can always turn up the volume on your favorite workout video.

Renting may allow you to live in a neighborhood where no housing is for sale in your price range. Also, in your current situation, renting may be your only option because you lack the amount to cover a down payment. As a renter, you might make a deposit equal to two months' rent, but it is likely less than what lenders require as a down payment when you buy and finance a home.

There are some additional costs associated with being a homeowner. One major cost is maintenance and repairs. In their discussions, Eva has brought this up to Jack, and he has promised her that he will learn some basic skills, and that he could always call his dad for advice or watch a YouTube[1] video. As a renter, the landlord handles the costs associated with repair and maintenance. As a homeowner, the costs and responsibility are all yours. As a tenant, all you have to do is pick up the phone, say my sink is clogged and *voila*, someone will magically be there to fix it. In reality, it may be more difficult than this, but someone other than you is responsible. So why buy?

One reason is stability, of both monthly housing costs and your right to stay where you are. With regard to costs, rents usually do go up. With a home loan, you can choose one with a fixed interest rate over the life of the loan. Your payments will stay the same for the

So why buy?
One reason is stability.

entire term of the loan.[2] Your property taxes may go up (likely due to the increasing value of your home), but the loan payment will not. With regard to staying put, a landlord can ask you to move when your lease is up, even if you have made every rent payment right on time. A lender cannot ask you to move if you are current on your loan payments.

---

1   YouTube.com and some home improvement store chain websites have great online videos providing instruction for doing home maintenance projects yourself.

2   Some websites, such as zillow.com, have a rent versus buy calculator tool to help you figure out comparable costs. They calculate a price/rent ratio which serves as a quick indicator of which option is less expensive. Of course cost is only one of the factors to consider, as discussed in the text above.

There are longer-term economic benefits for homeowners. For instance:

1. Tax deductions for real estate taxes and mortgage loan interest.

2. Increases in the value of their home.

First, we will consider tax deductions. The United States tax code allows homeowners to deduct from their income the amount of real estate taxes and mortgage loan interest they pay on their homes. Rent payments, on the other hand, are not deductible.

In Jack and Eva's case, they are spending $1,500 per month in rent, or $18,000 annually, for which they receive no tax deduction. After buying a house, if they pay roughly $13,000 in mortgage loan interest and $5,000 in real estate taxes, they are eligible to take $18,000 in itemized deductions on their joint income tax return. Based on the level of their taxable income, if their tax rate is 25 percent, they will save $4,500 in income taxes. This equates to $375 per month in savings due to taxes for owning a home versus renting. The following table shows how this looks to Jack and Eva.

Table 1-1: Tax Benefits from Buying a Home

Description	Rent		Mortgage Loan Interest	Real Estate Taxes	Total Interest plus Taxes
Amount Paid	$ 18,000.00		$13,000.00	$5,000.00	$ 18,000.00
Income Tax Deduction	$ -				$ 18,000.00
Income Tax Rate	25.00%				25.00%
Income Tax Savings	$ -				$4,500.00

Second, we will look at increases in home values. Despite up and down cycles, the long-term trend for home values has been decidedly up. Increases in home values increase homeowners' net worth. And because most new home buyers use debt to fund their purchases, the increase in home values measured against their down payments can be very significant. The following table shows how Jack and Eva anticipate this will work for them.

Table 1-2: Return on Investment from Buying a Home Using a Mortgage Loan

A	Purchase price of home		$ 250,000
B	Amount of loan	90%	$ 225,000
A - B = C	Homeowner's investment (down payment)		$ 25,000
D	Increase in home value	10%	$ 25,000
D / C	Home value increase as percent of homeowner's investment		100%

Notice that a 10 percent increase in home value equates to a 100 percent return on the amount the home buyer put down as an investment in the home. This is the investment power of purchasing a home using a mortgage loan. Of course, the costs of buying and selling the home have to be factored in too, but this simple example shows you – as it did Jack and Eva – the power financial leverage can bring to you through use of a mortgage.

Increases in home values increase homeowners' net worth.

Be aware that the opposite impact can also occur as well. A 10 percent decrease in the value of the home represents a 100 percent reduction of the home buyer's investment. That said, this concept really only registers "on paper." No profit or loss is "realized" until you actually sell the home. If your home is worth 10 percent more when you sell, you will see the return depicted above. If your home is worth 10 percent less, and you do not sell, you still have a place to live with a fixed payment and you can wait until the value comes back up. Careful planning in the buying and financing process helps to mitigate this risk but cannot eliminate it. We will discuss the importance of buying strategically and not over-borrowing in later chapters.

The longer-term odds favor the home buyer. According to U.S. census data, the average home price in the U.S. has increased from $98,300 in January, 1985 to $341,500 as of April, 2015. That is nearly a 250 percent increase in value. Even with the average house price drop during the recent recession, the average home price at the low point in January 2009 was still $245,200. Prices have recovered from the 2009 levels in most markets, again increasing returns.

These prices represent the national average, but it illustrates the point. In some areas of the country the housing market struggled during the recession, while in other areas home values did not go down at all. You will want to look at the particular part of the country where you are planning to purchase a home when considering pricing trends and data.

A third reason home buying beats renting is that when you buy a house, you have much greater flexibility in what you can do with it compared to a rental. As mentioned earlier, you are much freer to decorate, paint, and create your own surroundings.

So where do you start? The following section and chapters will explain everything you need to know in qualifying, looking for, purchasing, and closing on your first home. So, start thinking about where you are going to put your turntable and vintage vinyl albums, your camping gear, and all your designer shoes. You are going to be a homeowner!

1-3 You Are Ready – So Who Will Be Involved in Your Home Purchase?

As Jack and Eva move through their home buying process, they will come into contact with the same types of people you will encounter, people who play many different roles. Some will become a part of your team, some will just be sources of information, and some will be the seller and the seller's team.

1-3-1 Who Are the Players in the Game?

Although every home and transaction is unique, the categories of participants are pretty much the same. Below are some of the categories of people (and entities) involved in the home buying process:

a. *The buyer* – You, the one who is purchasing the home. Take a bow. You are the most important.

b. *The seller* – The party selling the home you want to buy. They are also important. Figure out what motivates them, and you will increase your purchase odds.

c. *Sites and services listing properties* – Websites that provide comparative property information, such as Zillow.com, Trulia. com, Realtor.com, or that of your realtor.

d. *Real estate agent[3] or realtor* – Person who will be one of your best resources in the home buying process and an integral part of your team. Good realtors know the market in which you are looking, and yours will help you to locate properties, take you on tours through the properties, assist you with drawing up your offer, present your offer to the seller, and handle many of the details involved with coordinating the home inspection and closing of the home. Their goal is to end with a happy, satisfied client (meaning you). Being prepared will help your real estate agent do the best job for you.

e. *Real estate broker[4]* – Party who runs the business where your realtor is likely based. Brokers manage or own the business and are involved in all aspects of running the business. You may or may not meet the broker, as most of your interactions will be with your real estate agent who works for the broker.

---

3   The terminology can vary by state. In some states, the agent is instead referred to as the buyer broker representative.

4   In some states, the owner is called the managing broker. Everyone else is a broker.

f. *Title insurance company (title company)* – Company that makes sure you are buying your home from the party who actually owns it and that nobody else has any claims to it. They examine and verify ownership of your desired home through examination of property records (a title search). The title company usually prepares an abstract of title, which shows the legal owner of the property, reveals any mortgages, liens judgments, or unpaid taxes outstanding on the property, and details any existing restrictions, easements, or leases that affect the property.

g. *Real estate attorney* – Lawyer that helps with many contract and legal aspects of the purchase. They can help you understand the purchase agreement, prepare and process your legal documents, review closing documents prior to you signing them, and ensure you receive valid registered ownership of your home. In many parts of the country, it is common practice that a closing agent or title company performs some of these duties.

h. *Appraiser* – Licensed third party who gives their opinion on values. The appraiser looks at the worth of the home by examining the recent sales prices of comparable homes in the area and making adjustments for the unique aspects of the home being appraised.

i. *Mortgage broker / loan officer* – Individual or company that has access to loan products from multiple wholesale lenders. They will counsel you on what loans are available, take your application, and perform some initial processing of your loan. Once your application is processed, the mortgage broker delivers your file to the lender who underwrites your loan. It is then out of the mortgage broker's hands.

j. *Retail lender* – Entity such as a bank that offers mortgage loans directly to borrowers and funds the loans using its own sources of funds. Retail lenders only offer their own loan programs.

k. *Underwriter* – Person at your lender who examines all the data about your transaction and home to determine whether the lender should provide you with the mortgage loan for which you are applying.

l. *Fannie Mae, Freddie Mac, Ginnie Mae, FHA, VA* – U.S. government entities, or so-called government-sponsored entities, that are involved in mortgage practices and housing. The majority of mortgage loans in the country are underwritten (determined to be qualified) to the guidelines of at least one of these entities, and will either be sold to, insured by, or guaranteed by one these entities.

m. *Home inspector* – Independent party that works for you to determine if the home you are looking to buy is safe and identifies any needed repairs. The inspector looks for problems with the foundation, structure, plumbing, electrical, roofing, pavement and concrete, and other key elements of your home. They will also look for leaks, rodents, and bugs.

n. *Property insurance company* – Company (usually represented by an agent) that will issue your homeowner's property insurance policy. Property insurance provides protection against most risks to property, such as fire, theft, and some weather damage. Separately, you may also get insurance for other risks to your home, such as flood, earthquake, or required repairs that were undiscovered at the time you purchased your home (homeowner's warranty).

o. *Homeowners' Association (HOA)* – Organization existing in certain subdivisions, planned communities, and condominiums that makes and enforces rules for the properties in its jurisdiction. HOAs also collect monthly or annual dues to pay for upkeep of common areas like parks, tennis courts, elevators, and swimming pools, and can levy special assessments on homeowners when needed to pay for unexpected costs and repairs.

p. *Settlement agent* – Party responsible for placing orders for title insurance, setting the closing appointment, receiving and dispersing money, and issuing receipts for money obtained from all the parties involved. They order loan checks, determine payoff amounts, and make sure the lender's instructions are satisfactory. They administer the closing, instructing the buyers where to sign and making sure all documents are completed correctly. They record all the documents with the county in which the property is located, and report the income tax information to the IRS.

q. *Title agent* – Party that administers the issuance of title insurance policies for the benefit of the buyer and the lender.

r. *Moving company* – Company that is hired to move furniture and household items. Services range from packing and caring for small individual items to loading, moving, and unloading items.

s. *Accountant / tax advisor* – Consultant that is a financial expert. Make sure yours is specially trained in financial and tax matters related to property ownership, and can advise you on the financial impact of buying a home.

t. *Utility, cable and trash companies* – Companies that provide basic services for the function and operation of your home and household. Utilities may include telephone, electricity, water and sewer, natural gas, and heating oil.

Chapter 2

Taking Inventory - Part 1

How Much Can You Afford to Pay for Your Home?

"You cannot chart a path to where you want to go if you do not know your starting point."
—Michael Trickey

You have decided to buy a home. Now you want to determine the amount you can afford to pay for one. This does not mean that you have to push the limit and find a home costing the maximum amount that you can afford. You just want to start with a benchmark so you know your limit.

It could be that you are able to pay for the home entirely out of savings, but if you are like most people, you will borrow money to help you to buy your home. In the home purchase transaction, you will pay a certain amount of your savings toward the purchase (your down payment), and the lender will advance the remaining portion of your home's cost for you to pay to the seller. You will pay the lender back the amount borrowed, plus interest, over a designated number of months under the terms of a note and mortgage loan agreement.[5]

---

5   In some states, a deed of trust document is used rather than a mortgage loan agreement.

You will likely also have to pay various fees and costs (closing costs) to parties such as appraisers, inspectors, title insurance companies, and others involved in your home purchase.

To determine the amount you can afford to pay for a home, you will follow a six-step process. These steps involve using the downloadable "Key Home Buying Affordability Numbers" (KHBAN) template shown on the next page, filling in just five numbers, and letting the formulas in the template calculate other key numbers for you.

Jack and Eva downloaded the template and filled in the five inputs required. Using the procedures covered in this chapter, they used their current best estimates, with the idea that they would revisit the KHBAN table as they gained more information. The next page shows Jack and Eva's initial results. This chapter will help you to come up with the numbers that you will input into the KHBAN template.

We will set back the time machine, and follow Jack and Eva through the process of completing the schedules supporting the KHBAN table. As we progress, you can download templates of all tables and forms Jack and Eva used from the companion website, and use them to determine your own inputs for the KHBAN table. In later chapters you will revisit the KHBAN table and refine the inputs as you gain more information.

When you have completed this chapter, you will have an initial idea of:

1. How much you can pay for a home;

2. How much money you will need for a down payment and closing costs;

3. How big of a mortgage loan you can get if your credit profile is good;

4. How much you will pay monthly for your mortgage loan and other housing costs; and

5. How this all fits into your overall financial picture.

Downloadable Template 2-1:
Key Home Buying Affordability Numbers (KHBAN) Table

Step 1:			
Figure out the Affordable Mortgage Loan Payment Amount you can afford (AMLPA)	**$1,140.04**		INPUT *from Chapter 2 analysis*
Step 2:			
Based on your financial and credit profile, find out from your lender the following three loan terms available to you:			INPUT *from Chapter 2 & 3 analysis*
1. Interest Rate	**4.500**	%	INPUT
2. Loan-to-Value (LTV) Percent	**90.00**	%	INPUT
3. Amortization Term	**360**	months	INPUT
Step 3:			
This is the Maximum Mortgage Loan Amount (MMLA) for which you will qualify	**$225,000**		Calculated
Step 4:			
This is the Maximum Home Price Amount (MHPA) you can afford to pay, equal to MMLA divided by the LTV percent:			
Maximum Mortgage Loan Amount (MMLA)	$225,000		From Step 3
divided by: LTV Percent	90.00	%	From Step 2
equals: Maximum Home Price Amount (MHPA)	**$250,000**		Calculated
Step 5:			
Savings amount you will need for your down payment:			
Maximum Home Price Amount (MHPA)	$250,000		From Step 4
minus: Maximum Mortgage Loan Amount (MMLA)	$225,000		From Step 3
equals: Down Payment Amount (DPA)	**$25,000**		Calculated
Step 6:			
Savings amount you will need for your Closing Costs:			
Maximum Home Price Amount (MHPA)	$250,000		From Step 4
multiplied by: Approximate Closing Cost Percent	**3.00**	%	INPUT
equals: Approximate Closing Cost Amount (CCA)	**$7,500**		Calculated
Total Amount Needed for Closing (DPA + CCA)	**$32,500**		Calculated

2-1 Your Financial Foundation

◇◇◇◇◇

"Are you two ready?" asks Jack's dad, Mike, as he walks into their kitchen, then sets his laptop on their table, and fires it up.

"We sure are," Jack replies.

"It's great of you to help us plan out our finances, Dad," adds Eva, as she brings over a serving tray with hot cups of coffee.

"Great," Mike says. "I'm going to type out some notes as we talk and send them to you later." After Eva settles into her chair, Mike begins.

"To build a home, you first set down a *structural* foundation. To buy a home, you first establish your *financial* foundation. Your financial foundation is a function of your assets (what you own), obligations (what you owe), disposable income (what you earn in excess of your costs of living), and your demonstrated ability to repay your debts (credit standing). Each of these basic elements factor into how much you can afford to pay up front for your down payment and closing costs, and on an ongoing basis for your monthly mortgage payment and other housing costs. Does that make sense so far?"

Jack and Eva both nod.

"Good. Let's put aside your down payment and closing costs for a minute. First we need to figure out how much you can comfortably afford to pay each month for total housing costs. Mortgage lenders call this your '*ability to pay*' your housing costs."

To buy a home, you first establish your financial foundation.

"Keep in mind, if you plan on using a mortgage loan to buy your home, and I know you do, mortgage lenders will also look at your credit payment history and credit score as reflected in your credit report they obtain from the three credit bureaus. They will evaluate your credit standing to determine your demonstrated *'willingness to pay'* your debts."

Jack takes a sip of his coffee. "When we took out our car loan, the finance guy at the dealer said both our credit scores were excellent, Dad. Nothing much has changed since then, so we shouldn't have any problems."

Mike smiles. "That's good to hear. We can verify that later."

For the next couple of hours, Jack and Eva carefully listen to Mike as he guides them through basic finances for home buying. They download financial templates from the companion website, and complete them right on Jack's computer.

Like Jack and Eva, you too need to evaluate your *financial* foundation so that you can figure out your ability to pay your mortgage and determine ways to strengthen your position. As we go through this chapter, we will focus on your ability to pay. In the next chapter we will address your credit standing and how to get that into good shape.

2-2 "Ability to Pay" Self-Assessment

You will need money from your savings[6] to cover your down payment, closing costs, and moving. If you do not have enough savings, the analysis in this chapter and Chapter 4 will help you to identify money you may be able to put into your savings account.

> **You will need money from your savings to cover your down payment, closing costs, and moving.**

Once you buy your home, you will need money each month for mortgage payments, real estate taxes, homeowner's insurance,

---

6   Some home buyers may have other sources of money for their down payment such as gifts from relatives and cash credits from sellers. Lenders put limits on the amount of a down payment that may come from these sources.

maintenance, home improvements and other costs. It can seem a little daunting at first, but with some effort expended in this analysis you will figure out how much you can afford monthly after buying your home. You will get some help from Uncle Sam, who allows you tax deductions for mortgage interest and real estate taxes.[7]

As you can see in the KHBAN table, determining a monthly mortgage loan payment amount that you can afford is the "Step 1" starting point in determining the price you can afford to pay for a home. To do this, you need to look at your monthly cash inflows (revenues) and outflows (debt costs and expenses). As part of this process, you will first assess your current assets and liabilities to see how much you have in reserves to fall back on if you experience disruptions in your revenues or encounter unexpected debt costs or expenses. Doing this will also allow you to see how much you have available for your down payment and closing costs, which factors into Steps 5 and 6 of the KHBAN process.

2-2-1 Your Financial Foundation Cornerstone - Your Balance Sheet

Assets are what you own, liabilities are how much you owe, and the difference between the two is your net worth. Assets, liabilities, and net worth are typically set out in the form of a balance sheet. On the next page is a sample balance sheet template, filled in for Jack and Eva.

---

[7]   Note: you do not get these type of tax deductions for rent.

Downloadable Template 2-2: Balance Sheet

	Current Situation Total	After Purchase Total	Comments
ASSETS			
Bank Accts:			
Checking	$1,600	$1,600	
Savings	30,950	1,250	*Current* includes gift from parents. *After* deducts down payment & closing costs
Total Liquid Assets	32,550	2,850	
Retirement accounts	-	-	
401K	1,425	1,425	
Roth IRA	2,200	2,200	
Other Assets:	-	-	
NEW HOME!	-	250,000	Purchased home.
Clothes	12,000	12,000	
Autos	21,000	21,000	
Computer	1,400	1,400	
Other Assets:			
Smartphone	600	600	
Other assets	-	-	
Household goods	12,300	12,300	
TOTAL ASSETS	**$83,475**	**$303,775**	
LIABILITIES			
Mortgage	-	225,000	Mortgage on purchased home.
Student loan	42,000	42,000	
Auto loan	13,434	13,434	
Credit card 1	1,200	1,200	
Credit card 2	-	-	
Other debt	-	-	
TOTAL LIABILITIES	**$56,634**	**$281,634**	
NET WORTH	**$26,841**	**$22,141**	
TOTAL LIABILITIES + NET WORTH	**$83,475**	**$303,775**	

This form may look a little scary, but it is really helpful. Take just a minute to study it and you will see it contains information you can easily fill in. There is a blank version of this template on the companion website that you can download, edit, and input your own numbers. In Chapter 4, I will very briefly introduce you to simple-to-use personal accounting software (such as Quicken and Moneydance) that will help you track your financial position on an ongoing basis.

Your balance sheet tells the lender how many resources you can draw upon to meet your obligations. It empowers you to take charge of your financial picture. A lender considers your total net worth, but is also looking at *liquid assets* that you could access in times of temporary distress, such as loss of job or illness. Liquid assets are comprised of cash and "near cash" assets, such as marketable securities (i.e., stocks and bonds). They are called liquid because they can be converted quickly into cash, like water moving from a measuring cup into a bowl.

Although retirement accounts usually contain some liquid assets, in general they can only be accessed if a penalty is paid (unless you are over 59 1/2), so lenders do not give them as much credit in the liquid asset analysis. There are exceptions to this rule if you have a Roth IRA, but most lenders will not consider retirement assets. We will discuss borrowing against some employer sponsored retirement plans in Chapter 4.

The cash value of life insurance policies can be very liquid, but you should exercise extreme care drawing on this asset. Any amount you would withdraw needs to be paid back with interest, and if you should die before it is paid back, that amount would be

> **Your balance sheet empowers you to take charge of your financial picture.**

deducted from your death benefit payout. Just remember that you obtained the policy for a purpose and you do not want to dilute its impact.

Hard assets such as clothing, automobiles, and electronics are generally less liquid and require a discounted price for quick sale. Lenders give little or no value or liquidity consideration to these assets.

Amounts you owe are claims against your current assets and your future income. Those claims will be competing for your dollars with any new mortgage loan you obtain to buy your home. Your mortgage lender does not like to have too much competition, and will look to see that your balance sheet is not too loaded with debt.

Later on, when we get to the goals section, one of your primary goals will likely be to strengthen your balance sheet by increasing liquid assets, reducing debt, and thereby increasing your net worth. In the budget section we will talk about some actions you can take to achieve these goals.

Notice that in the balance sheet template provided, there are two sets of columns (Current Situation and After Purchase). Your liquid assets will likely be lower after the purchase because you had to use some of your money for the down payment and closing costs on your new home. You will add your new home to the "Other assets" section of the balance sheet, and your new mortgage to the "Liabilities" section.

2-3 Determine What You Can Afford

In a later chapter we will discuss how to find a lender and secure a loan for your home. However, it is very important for you to understand that a lender can only tell you if you *qualify* for a loan; you need to decide for yourself *what you can comfortably afford* based on the monthly payment that would be required on the loan and your disposable income.

This section is going to help you figure out how much you can afford to pay each month for total housing costs, including the monthly payment required on your mortgage loan. We are going to take two approaches. I call the first the Quick and Easy Home Affordability Calculation Method; it only looks at what you are paying for housing now and assumes that is what you can afford for monthly home ownership costs. It then backs out expected costs for property taxes,

> **You need to decide for yourself what you can comfortably afford.**

insurance, and other non-mortgage loan housing costs to arrive at the amount available for the monthly mortgage payment. Using this amount, we can fill in the Step 1 amount on the KHBAN table and start determining the other key amounts on the schedule.

The second method looks in detail at your revenues coming in and your costs and expenses going out. It helps you to see the whole picture and decide what has to stay and what can change, providing you with some flexibility in determining the mortgage loan payment you can afford, and, as a result, in perhaps getting a bigger or better home.

As Mike goes through Jack and Eva's finances with them, he asks some questions that will also help you to define what the word "affordable" means to you.

1. What is the most you feel comfortable with having your mortgage, taxes, insurance, and housing expenses comprise of your total income and total ***disposable*** income (free cash after all expenses)?

2. What is more important to you – having a bigger house and associated bigger mortgage, or having more money available for other things?

3. How much cash over monthly housing expenses do you need to budget for costs and other expenses such as tuition, commuting expenses, and personal items, and want to budget for discretionary items and savings?

2-4 Method 1: The Quick and Easy Home Affordability Calculation Method

For the Quick and Easy Home Affordability Calculation Method, you assume that you can afford to pay at least what you are paying for rent plus renter's insurance. You start with that amount, then add a monthly amount you are currently putting aside for your down payment, and expected tax benefits from the new deductions for mortgage interest and property taxes (for ease, estimated at 15 percent of your current rent amount). Then you deduct incremental home ownership costs, and arrive at a net amount available for a mortgage payment. Below in Downloadable Template 2-3 is Jack and Eva's completed Quick and Easy analysis:

Downloadable Template 2-3: Quick and Easy Affordable Mortgage Loan Payment Amount (AMLPA) Calculation

	Quick and Easy Affordability Calculation		Assumption
	Monthly rent	$1,500.00	Goes away, put towards mortgage payment
+	Monthly renter's insurance	40.00	Goes away, put towards mortgage payment
+	Amount currently being saved for down payment /closing costs	500.00	Goes away, put towards mortgage payment
+	Income tax benefits - estimate 15% of current rent amount	225.00	Mortgage interest and property tax deduction benefit put towards mortgage payment
=	Total amount you can afford for new housing costs	$2,265.00	
	Less: Monthly Incremental Costs of Homeownership:		Extra and new expenses which take away from amount available for mortgage payment
-	Property taxes	$416.67	estimated new, $5,000 per year / 12
-	Homeowner's insurance	104.17	estimated new, $1,250 per year / 12
-	Natural gas for heating	70.00	estimated extra
-	Electric	15.00	estimated extra
-	Water and sewer	40.00	estimated extra
-	Garbage collection	35.00	estimated extra
-	Commuting cost	20.00	estimated extra
-	Cleaning supplies	15.00	estimated extra
-	Yard maintenance	50.00	estimated new
-	Maintenance and repairs	100.00	estimated new
-	Appliances	50.00	estimated new
-	Home security	30.00	estimated new
-	Home improvements	70.00	estimated new
-	Home furnishings	50.00	estimated new
-	Contingency reserve	59.12	estimated new
=	Total Affordable Mortgage Loan Payment Amount (AMLPA)	$1140.04	

Notice the detail line items under the Monthly Incremental Costs of Homeownership section of the schedule. This is a sampling of some the new types of expenses you will encounter as a homeowner. You will have different amounts and perhaps line items, but you get the picture. You have to do a little research and estimating, but the bottom line number gets you started at a reasonable level.

When you buy a home using mortgage financing, your lender will likely require you to pay, in addition to your monthly mortgage payment, one-twelfth (1/12) of your annual property taxes and homeowner's insurance each month into an escrow account. The lender then pays the tax and insurance bills from your escrow account as the amounts become due.

Think of an escrow account as a forced savings account, requiring you to put aside a little bit each month to avoid having to pay big amounts all at once. The lender collects money monthly and holds it on your behalf until it is needed to pay taxes or insurance.

While it is possible for Jack and Eva to pay these separately from their own savings account, doing so is not the wisest action. For most people, unless they are disciplined with their finances, an escrow account is the easiest way to make sure taxes and insurance are paid on time. I recommend the same course of action for you.

You may hear your lender talking about P-I-T-I ("PITI"). This stands for principal, interest, taxes, and insurance. It is the sum total of your mortgage payment (monthly **P**rincipal and **I**nterest) and the amount your lender escrows monthly for real estate **T**axes and homeowner's **I**nsurance. Smiling, Mike tells Jack and Eva, "It is a PITY you have to pay these, but you do."

The property taxes you are required to pay help fund your local and county government and school systems. The better the services and schools, the more you will likely find yourself paying in property taxes, all other things being equal.

You may also have homeowners' association fees and other types of insurance such as flood, hurricane, or earthquake that have to be paid. Typically the lender will not escrow these other costs. You will either need to pay them directly each month, or put aside a sufficient amount in your own savings account each month to pay these costs as lump sums when they become due.

2-4-1 Transferring the Quick and Easy Estimate to the KHBAN Table

Using the calculated Quick and Easy Affordable Mortgage Loan Payment Amount, fill in the Step 1 AMLPA number on the KHBAN table. Jack and Eva fill in their payment amount on the table.

Step 1:		
Figure out your monthly Affordable Mortgage Loan Payment Amount (AMLPA)	$1,140.04	INPUT *from Chapter 2 analysis*

Step 2 on the KHBAN table asks for the interest rate, LTV, and loan amortization term your lender offers to you based on your financial and credit profile. At this point, you are going to just put best guesses for these values on the KHBAN table. You will update them later after reading Chapter 3, then again after you actually get preapproved for a loan as described in Chapter 5, and maybe again, as Jack and Eva do in Chapter 7, when they start looking at houses and want to evaluate their options.

To put in best guesses for now, you need to have some idea of what reasonable values are for these three items. Go online and search for "current mortgage rates." Click on a few of the links. You will see rates for various "loan types" such as 30-year fixed, 15-year fixed, 5/1 ARM, and others. In Chapter 5, we will discuss loan types, but for now, pick the rate for the 30-year fixed loan and input it in the proper cell in the KHBAN table. Then input the amortization term as 360 (which is 30 years expressed in months). Jack and Eva fill in the two numbers under Step 2, lines 1 and 3.

Step 2:			
Based on your financial and credit profile, find out from your lender the following three loan terms available to you:			*From Chapters 2 & 3 analysis*
1. Interest rate	4.50	%	INPUT
2. Loan-to-Value (LTV) percent			INPUT
3. Amortization term	360	months	INPUT

You will likely discover that different lenders offer different rates for the same loan type. Do not worry about being precise right now. They are competing for your business and advertising their best rate. As a new borrower, you may not qualify for their best rates. Be conservative and pick one of the slightly higher rate offerings.

For the LTV field on the KHBAN table, start with 90 percent, meaning you will borrow 90 percent of the cost of your home. You can adjust that later too. Jack and Eva fill in 90 percent under Step 2, line 2.

Step 2:			
Based on your financial and credit profile, find out from your lender the following three loan terms available to you:			*From Chapters 2 & 3 analysis*
1. Interest rate	4.50	%	INPUT
2. Loan-to-Value (LTV) percent	90.00	%	INPUT
3. Amortization term	360	months	INPUT

When Jack and Eva do this, as will happen for you, the KHBAN table automatically calculates the Maximum Mortgage Loan Amount (MMLA) for which they may qualify given the inputted values for mortgage payment amount, interest rate, LTV, and amortization term. They see under Step 3 in the table that this amount is $225,000 for them.

Step 3:		
This is the Maximum Mortgage Loan Amount (MMLA) for which you will qualify:	**$225,000**	**Calculated**

The table also calculates and displays the Maximum Home Price Amount (MHPA) that the couple can afford and the resulting down payment money they will need. Jack and Eva see under Step 4 in the table that, based on their preliminary inputs for payment amount, LTV, interest rate, and amortization term, the Maximum Home Price Amount they can afford is $250,000. After later analysis, they will see if their excess disposable income will allow them to increase the price they can afford, but $250,000 is their starting point for analysis.

Step 4:		
This is the Maximum Home Price Amount (MHPA) you can afford to pay, equal to the MMLA divided by the LTV percent:		
Maximum Mortgage Loan Amount (MMLA)	$225,000	From Step 3
divided by: LTV Percent	90.00%	From Step 2
equals: Maximum Home Price Amount (MHPA)	**$250,000**	**Calculated**

The couple sees under Step 5 in the table the resulting down payment they will need is $25,000.

Step 5:		
This is how much savings you need for your down payment:		
Maximum Home Price Amount (MHPA)	$250,000	From Step 4
minus: Maximum Mortgage Loan Amount (MMLA)	$225,000	From Step 3
equals: Down Payment Amount (DPA)	**$25,000**	**Calculated**

Finally, for now, under Step 6, Jack and Eva enter "3 percent" in the Approximate Closing Cost Percent input cell, and an Approximate Closing Cost Amount of $7,500 also appears for them.

Step 6:		
This is how much savings you need for your closing costs:		
Maximum Home Price Amount (MHPA)	$250,000	From Step 4
multiplied by: Approximate Closing Cost Percent	3.00 %	INPUT
equals: Approximate Closing Cost Amount (CCA)	**$7,500**	**Calculated**
Total amount needed for closing (DPA + CCA)	**$32,500**	**Calculated**

Jack and Eva will revisit the KHBAN table later to refine their inputs as they gain more information. I suggest that you "play" with the input numbers a little to see how changing them affects the loan amount, home price, down payment, and closing costs, and how simple the KHBAN template is to use. Later, you will likely revisit the table too, when you gain more information and can refine your inputs. The next section shows you the type of information you can obtain by experimenting with inputs in the KHBAN template

2-4-2 A Quick Look at How Mortgage Payment Amounts Relate to the Mortgage Terms Your Lender Offers

The following table shows how the affordable level of home prices change under seven different lending scenarios, assuming that Jack and Eva's affordable payment amount cannot be changed from $1,140.04. The couple examines various combinations of LTV, amortization term, and interest rate. You can quickly see the importance of loan terms. See how the loan amount, home price, down payment, and closing cost numbers significantly change as the input assumptions change.

These are examples of typical options you will have:

Table 2-1: Monthly Mortgage Payment Scenarios – Payment Held Constant

Scenario	1	2	3	4	5	6	7
Scenario Description	Base Case	20% down	5% down	240 month term	180 month term	6.00 % rate	3.50 % rate
Max Home Price Amt (MHPA)	$250,000	$281,250	$236,842	$200,223	$165,585	$211,277	$282,090
LTV %	90.00%	80.00%	95.00%	90.00%	90.00%	90.00%	90.00%
Max Mtg Loan Amt (MMLA)	$225,000	$225,000	$225,000	$180,201	$149,027	$190,149	$253,881
$ Down Payment	$25,000	$56,250	$11,842	$20,022	$16,559	$21,128	$28,209
Closing Costs	$7,500	$8,438	$7,105	$6,007	$4,968	$6,338	$8,463
Amort Term (months)	360	360	360	240	180	360	360
Interest Rate %	4.50%	4.50%	4.50%	4.50%	4.50%	6.00%	3.50%
Affordable Mtg Loan Pmt Amt (AMLPA)	$1,140.04	$1,140.04	$1,140.04	$1,140.04	$1,140.04	$1,140.04	$1,140.04

Note, in the table above, any assumption change from the prior column scenario is shaded dark grey. Abbreviations used: Amt = Amount; Pmt = Payment; Mtg = Mortgage

In Table 2-2 below, Jack and Eva want to hold the home price constant at $250,000. They do some defined combinations of LTV, amortization term, and interest rate, and through trial and error find the payment amount that brings them back to the $250,000 home price amount. Notice how the payment amount varies widely in the different cases. This gives the couple an idea of how much their required payment could vary based on their loan terms.

In the next section we examine the couple's revenues and expenses to determine how much leeway they have to increase the mortgage payment amount they can afford based on their disposable income.

Table 2-2: Monthly Mortgage Payment Scenarios – Cost of Home Held Constant

Scenario	1	2	3	4	5	6	7
Scenario Description	Base Case	20% down	5% down	240 month term	180 month term	6.00 % rate	3.50 % rate
Max Home Price Amt (MHPA)	$250,000	$250,000	$250,000	$250,000	$250,000	$250,000	$250,000
LTV %	90.00%	80.00%	95.00%	90.00%	90.00%	90.00%	90.00%
Max Mtg Loan Amt (MMLA)	$225,000	$200,000	$237,500	$225,000	$225,000	$225,000	$225,000
$ Down Payment	$25,000	$50,000	$12,500	$25,000	$25,000	$25,000	$25,000
Closing Costs	$7,500	$7,500	$7,500	$7,500	$7,500	$7,500	$7,500
Amort Term (months)	360	360	360	240	180	360	360
Interest Rate %	4.50%	4.50%	4.50%	4.50%	4.50%	6.00%	3.50%
Affordable Mtg Loan Pmt Amt (AMLPA)	$1,140.04	$1,013.37	$1,203.38	$1,423.46	$1,721.23	$1,348.99	$1,010.35

Note, in the table above, any assumption change from the prior column scenario is shaded dark grey. Abbreviations used: Amt = Amount; Pmt = Payment; Mtg = Mortgage

2-4-3 The Impact of Lending Terms on Payments and What You Can Afford

We will discuss mortgage loan terms in detail in Chapter 5, but make just a few observations here.

You can quickly see from Table 2-2 that the longer the term of the loan, the lower the payment. The lower the interest rate, the lower the payment. The less money borrowed, the lower the payment. Look at scenarios with similar monthly payments (e.g., 2 and 7) and you will get a feel for the trade-offs and sensitivity that payments are to each of these three factors.

The table below summarizes the payment amount and interest impact of changing each of the three factors. Note that a lower interest rate or amount borrowed will both lower the payment, and benefit the borrower (you) in the long run. A longer maturity term lowers the payment, but, in the long run, costs the borrower much more money.

Table 2-3 Key Factors Impacting Mortgage Loan Payment Amounts

Factor	Result	All else being equal…
Longer **term**	Lower payment	More of each payment goes to interest, less to pay down the loan.
Lower **interest rate**	Lower payment	Less of each payment goes to interest.
Lower **amount borrowed**	Lower payment	Less of each payment goes to interest.

2-5 Method 2: Breaking Down Income and Expenses to See Your Affordable Payment Options

Method 2 of your monthly payment "affordability" quest is a bit more detailed, but gives you added insight into your financial situation and options. You will fill in a more detailed schedule (Downloadable Template 2.4) broken into several "bite-sized" Income, Housing Expense, Debt Payment, Withholding Tax, and Other Expense sections for ease of understanding and data input. These sections are spread across the next few pages.

A blank, editable version of the schedule (all sections) is available for download from the website. You can fill it in with your numbers as we go along. The schedule automatically calculates any additions and percentages for you.

As we progress, you will note that there are two columns in the schedule, one for your "Current Situation" and one to reflect your estimated situation "After Purchase" of your home. Your situation may change due to other expected changes in your life, such as a new job, pregnancy, or other factors which may actually be contributing to your decision to buy a new home.

Within the schedule, you will go through seven steps, as summarized below.

1. Determine your income.

2. Determine your housing expenses. Start by using your Quick and Easy Home Affordability Calculation Method number and then adjust it in later iterations.

3. Determine the cash you need to service non-housing-related other debt.

4. Determine your other monthly expenses.

5. Figure out how much excess monthly cash (disposable income) you have left over.

6. Examine key ratios lenders use.

7. Go back and "play" with your housing expenses numbers. Hone in on more refined numbers that reflect how much you can afford to pay for monthly housing expenses.

2-5-1 Filling in the Schedule for Jack and Eva

At the top of the first section of Template 2-4, Jack and Eva fill in their salaries. They assume these numbers will not change after they purchase their home. They know they want to start a family and may at least temporarily lose one income in the future, but they ignore that fact for now. Jack makes $6,500 per month as a software developer. Eva makes $3,200 as a fifth grade teacher. They earn $5.00 per month in interest on their savings.

The next few lines show their "Current Situation" and "After Purchase" housing expenses. Here they can clearly see the difference in costs of being a renter versus being a homeowner with a mortgage. The first section of the schedule does not show tax benefits, housing maintenance expenses, or contingency reserve costs. Those benefits and costs are shown later in the schedules.

Downloadable Template 2-4: Detailed Housing Cost Affordability Calculator

	Monthly Income, Debt Service & Expenses	Monthly Average Amounts		Comments
		Current Situation	After Purchase	
	Income before taxes:			
	Salary or wages			
	Job 1	**$6,500.00**	**$ 6,500.00**	
	Job 2	**3,200.00**	**3,200.00**	
	Tips			
	Bonuses	-	-	
	Interest and dividends	**5.00**	**5.00**	
	Other:			
A	**TOTAL INCOME BEFORE TAXES**	**$9,705.00**	**$9,705.00**	
	HOUSING EXPENSES:			
	Rent	**$1,500.00**		Goes away
	Mortgage		**$1,140.04**	New mortgage
	Property taxes	-	**416.67**	Housing expense estimated $5,000 per year / 12
	Renter's insurance	**40.00**		Goes away
	Homeowner's insurance		**104.17**	Housing expense estimated $1,250 per year / 12
	Flood / earthquake insurance			
	Association fees			
B	*SUBTOTAL HOUSING EXPENSES*	**$1,540.00**	**$1,660.88**	Comparable pre-tax numbers
B / A	*Housing Expense to Income Ratio (front-end ratio)*	**15.87%**	**17.11%**	First ratio mortgage lenders examine

We can see that Jack and Eva are currently paying about 15.87 percent of their gross incomes in housing expenses, and that will go up to 17.11 percent after they buy their house. This is the first important ratio lenders consider. It is called the front-end ratio. 28 percent is a common front-end ratio upper limit guideline imposed by lenders, but many will accept a higher front-end ratio if the borrower has mitigating factors such as strong credit, reliable income and large cash reserves. Also FHA lenders allow up 31 percent (33 percent for energy efficient homes).

Downloadable Template 2-4: Detailed Housing Cost Affordability Calculator (continued)

| | Monthly Income, Debt Service & Expenses | Monthly Average Amounts | | |
		Current Situation	After Purchase	
A	**TOTAL INCOME BEFORE TAXES**	$9,705.00	$9,705.00	
B	**SUBTOTAL HOUSING EXPENSES**	$1,540.00	$1,660.88	Comparable pre-tax numbers
	OTHER DEBT PAYMENTS:			
	Student loan	$400.00	$400.00	
	Auto loan 1	250.00	250.00	
	Auto loan 2			
	Credit card 1	300.00	300.00	
	Credit card 2			
	Other debt			
C	**SUBTOTAL OTHER DEBT PAYMENTS**	$950.00	$950.00	
D = B + C	**TOTAL DEBT PAYMENTS** (housing expenses plus other debt payments)	$2,490.00	$2,610.88	
D / A	**DEBT-TO-INCOME (DTI) RATIO** (*back-end ratio*)	25.66%	26.90%	Second ratio mortgage lenders examine

They now look at their other debt payments: Jack's student loan, Eva's car loan, and the amount they need to pay down the balance they have on their credit card. You may have other types of debt payments to add here as well. The schedule adds these monthly other debt payments to the housing expenses calculated above to arrive at total monthly debt payments. The schedule then divides that total monthly debt payments by gross income to arrive at the second important ratio mortgage lenders consider. It is called the back-end ratio, or debt-to-income (DTI) ratio.

Note that Jack and Eva's back-end ratio is projected to be 26.90 percent after buying their home. Most lenders like to see this ratio at 36 percent or less. FHA lenders allow up to 43 percent (45 percent for energy efficient homes). As with the front-end ratio, lenders will make exceptions, some for ratios up to 50 percent, for borrowers with strong mitigating factors.

At the top on the next page, Jack and Eva figure out how much they have to pay to the federal and state governments for income taxes, as well as amounts paid for FICA and Medicare tax. After entering those amounts, the schedule subtracts them from the gross amount of income Eva and Jack earned to arrive at total income after tax.

The schedule then divides the total monthly housing expenses and other debt payments by the after-tax income to arrive at a ratio mortgage lenders do not use, but which is important to you. It is called the debt to after-tax income ratio. I call it your debt-to-take-home-pay ratio. Simply put, this percent of your take-home pay is going for housing and other debt service costs.

If you are not comfortable with the percent of your take-home pay projected to go towards housing expenses and other debt service, it does not necessarily mean you cannot buy a home. It just means you might have to put more money towards your down payment, find a loan with a lower interest rate, take out a longer-term loan, or buy a less expensive house. If you have the funds, you could also pay off some of your other debts to eliminate the associated monthly payments.

**Downloadable Template 2-4: Detailed Housing Cost
Affordability Calculator (continued)**

	Monthly Income, Debt Service & Expenses	Monthly Average Amounts		
		Current Situation	After Purchase	
	Income tax withholdings:			
	Federal	$2,015.00	$1,703.66	
	State	$873.45	$733.35	
	Local			
	FICA	$630.83	$630.83	
	Medicare	$140.72	$140.72	
E	SUBTOTAL WITHHOLDING TAXES	$3,660.00	$3,208.55	
F = A – E	TOTAL INCOME AFTER TAXES	$6,045.00	$6,496.45	
D / F	DEBT TO AFTER-TAX INCOME RATIO (*debt-to-take-home-pay ratio*)	41.19%	40.19%	Ratio to help you judge affordability

Next, Jack and Eva need to see how much income they have left over for everyday expenses after deducting taxes, housing costs, and other debt payments from their income. Line G of the schedule shows they will have $3,885.57 available After Purchase.

Figuring out everyday expenses may be the hardest part for some. If need be, jump to the section in Chapter 4 on budgeting. The first part of that section helps you figure out everyday expenses.

The couple fills in their everyday other expense amounts. The schedule then deducts the everyday other expenses from total income after deducting taxes, housing expenses, and other debt payments. This is their net excess monthly cash, or disposable income available for savings.

Downloadable Template 2-4: Detailed Housing Cost Affordability Calculator (continued)

	Monthly Income, Debt Service & Expenses	Monthly Average Amounts		
		Current Situation	After Purchase	
F	TOTAL INCOME AFTER TAXES	$6,045.00	$6,496.45	
D	TOTAL DEBT PAYMENTS	$2,490.00	$2,610.88	
G = F − D	TOTAL INCOME AFTER TAXES minus TOTAL DEBT PAYMENTS	$3,555.00	$3,885.57	
H	Less TOTAL OTHER EXPENSES from next page	$2,595.00	$2,947.00	
I = G − H	NET EXCESS MONTHLY CASH	$960.00	$938.57	Amount available to Jack and Eva for savings

After expenses, Jack and Eva have just over $938 available for savings each month, or about 9 to 10 percent of their monthly gross income of $9,705.

The schedule on the next page shows the detail of the monthly expenses that is summarized in line H in the schedule above. Note that Jack and Eva decided that they would cut back a little in entertainment and travel expenses to make sure they will have enough left over for savings after they buy their home.

Based on this analysis, it appears that a $250,000 home is affordable for Eva and Jack to buy, as long as they can borrow 90 percent or more of the purchase price under terms that would result in a payment of about $1,140 per month. The mortgage payment calculation Table 2-2 in the Quick and Easy payment section shows they would need an interest rate 4.5 percent or less.

Downloadable Template 2-4: Detailed Housing Cost Affordability Calculator (continued) Detail of Expenses Comprising Amount Summarized on Line H in the Table above

| Other Monthly Expenses: | Monthly Avg. Amounts | | Comments |
	Current Situation	After Purchase	
Utilities:			
Telephone	$40.00	$40.00	
Gas	30.00	100.00	More costs
Electricity	35.00	50.00	More costs
Water & Sewer	-	40.00	New costs
Trash Collection	-	35.00	
Cable Television	80.00	80.00	
Cellular Phone	100.00	100.00	
Internet Service	60.00	60.00	
Other Insurance:			
Medical	250.00	250.00	
Life	50.00	50.00	
Auto(s)	80.00	80.00	
Rec. Vehicle	-	-	
Transportation:			
Gasoline	55.00	55.00	
Commuting	10.00	10.00	
Vehicle Maint	60.00	60.00	
Licenses	5.00	5.00	
Public Transport	80.00	100.00	
Food:			
Groceries	275.00	275.00	
Take-out Food	50.00	50.00	
Restaurants	150.00	150.00	
School Lunches			

| Other Monthly Expenses: | Monthly Avg. Amounts | | Comments |
	Current Situation	After Purchase	
Household Expenses:			
Cleaning Supplies	$10.00	$15.00	
Yard Maint.		50.00	New costs
Home Maint.		100.00	New costs
Contingency		57.00	New costs
Home Security		30.00	New costs
Home Improvements		100.00	New costs
Computer	40.00	40.00	
Home Furnishings	50.00	50.00	
Appliances		50.00	New costs
Personal Expenses:			
Clothing	100.00	100.00	
Accessories	25.00	25.00	
Personal Care	20.00	20.00	
Jewelry	30.00	30.00	
Entertainment	420.00	300.00	Cut-back
Travel	300.00	200.00	Cut-back
Gifts	40.00	40.00	
Hobbies			
Babysitting			
Pet-care Costs	100.00	100.00	
Donations	50.00	50.00	
Other			
Other			

		Current	After	
G	**TOTAL OTHER EXPENSES**	$2,595.00	$2,947.00	

Note that Jack and Eva can still fund savings at this purchase amount. Also, they have some discretionary expenses on which they can cut back further. This means that they may have flexibility to go higher in price if they can afford the resulting larger down payment requirement. This will become important to them later in their home buying process.

Take whatever time you need and go through this process. It can be very instructional and eye opening.

Jack and Eva need to consider that at some point they want to start a family. This means their combined income could be impacted, at least for a while, and additional costs associated with children would need to be added to the analysis. This may prompt the couple to look for a lower-priced home, or perhaps delay their plans for children a little while until their salaries increase or their financial situation otherwise improves. You likewise may need to consider life plans and expected changes in your analysis.

Now that you have an idea of what you can afford, we will look at your credit report and make sure your lender will see that you are serious about paying your bills.

Chapter 3

Taking Inventory – Part 2

Your Credit History and Score, and How They Impact Your Mortgage Loan Costs and Terms

"Credit is not a competition, but you will be scored."
—**Michael Trickey**

3-1 Your Credit Report

Mike joins Jack and Eva for an early evening scrumptious meal of lasagna, salad, apple pie, and ice cream, followed by large cups of coffee. After a few minutes of stretching their legs and small chit-chat, the trio settle at the kitchen table again, and Mike fires up his computer.

"What we are about to discuss is of utmost importance to your financial future. So we are going to spend the next couple of hours discussing it." After a few keystrokes, Mike turns his computer so that the young couple can see the screen. "The next thing on your to-do list is to obtain a copy of your credit report."

"We hear advertisements on the radio all the time, touting credit bureau websites," says Eva.

"I'm sure you do. The federal government requires the three major bureaus to provide a free report every twelve months. The key word is free, so don't get roped into any payments." Mike points to the computer screen. "This website, AnnualCreditReport.com, allows you to obtain your free report. This site offers facts and advice to improve your credit score and protect you from identity theft. It is valid information, free from advertisements and spam, so you will not be confused by false or misleading items."

The young couple nods and both write down the website on their pads of paper.

"When you get your credit report, be sure to review it carefully. Simple errors, as well as fraud and identity theft may have impacted your report."

Mike goes on to explain that each credit report contains the following main sections:

1. **Identifying information** – your name, current and previous addresses, Social Security number, birth year, employment income and history, and home ownership.

2. **Credit information** – information for each credit account you hold, including date opened, credit limit or loan amount, balance, monthly payment, and recent payment history. This information is obtained from a large number of sources, including lenders (banks, credit unions, credit card issuers, and mortgage and loan companies), landlords, insurance companies, professional service organizations, and others.

3. **Public record information** – governmental agency and court information, including federal district bankruptcy records, state and county court records, tax liens, monetary judgments, and (in some states) overdue child support, for the last seven years (sometimes ten years for bankruptcies).

4. **Inquiries** – the identity of anyone who has requested a copy of your credit report within the past year (or the past two years for employment-related inquiries).

5. **Credit score** –a numeric predictor of your credit worthiness. (We will discuss this in greater detail a little later.)

Mike looks up at Jack and Eva. "Do either of you notice what is not included on your credit report?"

After looking over the information, Jack looks at Eva and nods. "There is no race, gender, or salary included," he says. "Nor are there any bank account balances or information about personal assets."

"And there isn't any personal information listed, such as lifestyle, religion, or pets," adds Eva.

"You are both correct. That means you don't have to worry about not getting a loan because you named your goldfish Willie Nelson."

The three laugh, then Mike continues to explain the credit reporting process.

◇◇◇◇◇

3-1-1 The Process for Fixing Errors on Your Credit Report

Mike tells the young couple that if they find any inaccurate information on their credit reports, they should take *immediate* steps to get it corrected. Adverse items can negatively impact credit and their ability to obtain a mortgage loan.

If you dispute an item, you should contact both the credit bureau and the company that provided the information to the credit bureau. You should clearly identify each mistake, state the facts, and provide an explanation of why you think each is wrong. You should provide copies of documents, if needed, supporting why certain information

> **Adverse items can negatively impact credit and ability to obtain a mortgage loan.**

is inaccurate. ***Do not include originals of the documents you use to support your dispute***. Always send photocopies or images.

You can file disputes online at the credit bureau websites.

For creditors, you may have to submit your dispute by certified mail. Your dispute letter should contain:

1. Your full name;

2. Your address;

3. Your telephone number;

4. The report confirmation number, if available; and

5. The account number for any account with them you are disputing.

In this letter, you should also enclose a copy of the portion of your credit report that contains the disputed items and circle or highlight the disputed items. Ask the post office for a return receipt, so that you will have a record that your letter was received.

The credit bureaus and companies are required by law to investigate disputed items, with some exceptions. There are some types of disputes that companies do not have to investigate, including the following:

1. Information that identifies you (generally at the beginning of the credit report) such as your name, date of birth, Social Security number, telephone number, or address;

2. The identity of past or present employers;

3. Inquiries or requests for a consumer report;

4. Information derived from public records, such as judgments, bankruptcies, liens, and other legal matters (unless provided by a furnisher with an account or other relationship with you);

5. Information related to fraud alerts or active duty alerts;

6. Information some other creditor or furnishing institution (company that furnishes credit information on behalf of creditors) gave to the credit reporting company.

Mike explains to Jack and Eva that, in general, when disputes are filed directly, creditors and furnishing institutions investigate:

1. Your liability for a specific credit account or debt with the reporting entity (i.e., is it your account at all?);

2. The amount or terms of your credit account or debt with that entity (e.g., how much you owe);

3. Your performance or other conduct or relationship on an account with that entity (e.g., whether you are paying on a timely basis);

4. Other information about your relationship or account with that entity relevant to a credit report (e.g., your creditworthiness).

If the company corrects your information as a result of your dispute, it must notify all of the credit reporting companies to which it provided the inaccurate information, so they can update their reports with the correct information.

The credit bureau will have thirty days to investigate and correct any mistakes. If the individual creditor does not respond within thirty days, the disputed item is automatically removed from your credit report, which is a fast way to raise your credit score.

Mike tells the couple that if they think that an error on their report is the result of identity theft, the federal government has set up a website for "federal trade fighting back against identity theft" with information about identity theft and steps to take if Jack and/or Eva feel they have been victimized. This includes filing a fraud alert, as well as possibly filing a security freeze.

Negative items, except bankruptcy, should only appear on your credit report for seven years – bankruptcy can remain for ten. If you have negative entries that are correct but are older than seven years, you should dispute them purely based on age.

Credit bureaus do not take the time to verify the information they receive from creditors, so it is up to you to stay on top of your credit history. In some cases, a single error can drop your credit score by 20 points or more. Having negative items removed can quickly raise your credit score. We will discuss credit scores next.

> **It is up to you to stay on top of your credit history.**

The FindingHomeBook.com website contains current links for companies providing credit monitoring services. You will also find links to sign up directly with any of the three credit reporting agencies for reporting services if you wish. They will charge for the service.

3-2 Your Credit Score

◇◇◇◇◇

Mike stretches his arms over his head. "Now we get to the interesting part," he says. "Your credit score. It is mysterious. It is serious. It is a statistically derived number that essentially is a score of how well a person has managed credit. It is used by lenders to assess the likelihood that a person will repay their debts. The higher the number, the better the score, and the more creditworthy the person is judged to be."

Jack grins at Eva. "We've been studying this a little, Dad. We know that a FICO score is the most widely used credit scoring system. It is an acronym for Fair Isaac Corporation, the name of the company that has been the primary provider of credit scores to financial institutions since 1958."

"FICO scores range from 350 to 850," adds Eva. "There are other providers of credit scoring systems as well with similar scoring ranges. For instance, the three major credit bureaus created the Vantage score to compete with the FICO. The Vantage score also ranges from 350 to 850. Consumers can keep their credit scores high by maintaining a long history of always paying their bills on time and not having too much debt."

Mike chuckles. "You two really have been doing your homework. Here's a little more information. A credit score plays a large role in a lender's decision to extend credit or not and, if so, under what terms. There are no sharp lines in the sand, but take a look at this table I found online that gives some indication as to how lenders judge your credit based on your FICO score."

Table 3-1: FICO Score Ranges

Quality of Credit	FICO Range	
	Low	High
Excellent	810	850
Very Good	760	809
Good	710	759
OK	680	709
Borderline	640	679
Not so Good	580	639
Bad	500	579
Awful	350	499
No History - no score	0	0

Mike explains that "borrowers with a FICO score under 680 will be unable to receive a prime (lower interest rate, better terms) mortgage loan and will typically need to go to a lender offering alternative lending products which will typically have a higher interest rate. Borrowers who qualify for a prime mortgage loan are referred to as prime borrowers; those who do not are referred to as non-prime or subprime borrowers."

"There are three national credit bureaus responsible for FICO scores: Equifax, Experian and Transunion. Your credit score will be slightly different with each of these three, because the information each bureau collects varies slightly."

Mike smiles. "Unfortunately with credit, there are no participation trophies. You do not get to go out for ice cream, and sometimes pizza, if you make a good effort at paying your bills but somehow do not get around to doing it on a timely basis. You must actually pay your bills to get credit gain. Every time you show you can manage credit, your credit score improves. Every time you do not, it worsens."

A credit score is calculated based on items tracked on your credit report. The graph below and the following description illustrate generally how your score breaks down into five major categories, both positive and negative, based on items contained in your credit report. As will be discussed later, some variations in these weighting occur based on your individual circumstances.

Table 3-2: FICO Score Component Weightings

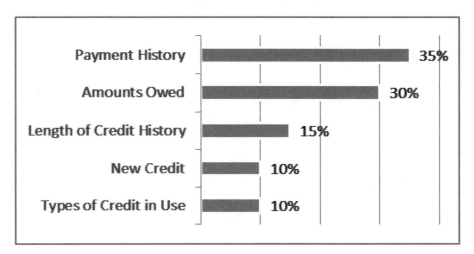

Credit scores are designed to measure the risk of default, which is the risk that the borrower will not pay his obligations, by taking into account various factors in a person's financial history. The precise formulas for calculating credit scores are proprietary, but FICO has made some information known. The following five paragraphs provide some insights into what is considered for each of the categories in Table 3-2.

Your payment history – 35 percent: Do you pay your credit accounts on time? The existence or absence of derogatory information such as late payments, bankruptcies, liens, judgments, settlements, charge-offs, repossessions, and foreclosures determine this portion of the score. Your payment history is the primary indicator of your willingness to pay your debts when due.

> **Your payment history is the primary indicator of your willingness to pay your debts when due.**

Your debt burden (amounts owed) – 30 percent: The FICO score uses several debt-specific measurements for the debt burden portion of its scoring model. Some items it considers are:

1. Your credit card debt-to-limit available (utilization) ratio (total credit utilized versus available);

2. The number of accounts you have with balances;

3. The amount you owe across various types of accounts; and

4. The amount that has been paid down from the original balance on installment loans.

Length of your credit history – 15 percent: All else being equal, the longer the recorded credit history you have, the more positive of an impact it has on your FICO score. This is because you have a more established track record encompassing the ups and downs in your life. The two measurements in this category are the average age of the accounts on your report and the age of the oldest account.

> **The longer the recorded credit history you have, the more positive of an impact it has on your FICO score.**

Types of credit you use – 10 percent: There are several types of loans. Installment loans have a set amount of payments, such as a car or student loan. Revolving lines of credit such as credit cards allow you to repeatedly draw down and pay back funds. Secured credit cards require a cash account held by the creditor that is tapped if the borrower does not pay. And last, but not least, there is the mortgage category. These include mortgage installment loans and home equity lines of credit (HELOCs, which are another type of revolving line, but are secured by your home). Be aware, there can be a benefit to building a history demonstrating proper management of different types of credit.

Recent searches for your credit – 10 percent: When you (the consumer) apply for a credit card or a loan and the lender checks your credit, it is registered as a ***hard*** credit inquiry. Hard inquiries can have a negative impact on your score if there are a high number of inquiries between forty-five days and twelve months old, because lenders will worry that you are applying for and being turned down on lots of loans. However, individuals who are "rate shopping" for a mortgage, auto loan, or student loan over a short period will likely not experience a meaningful decrease in their scores as a result of these types of inquiries. The FICO scoring model calculates these types of hard inquiries as only one. In addition, mortgage, auto, and student loan inquiries do not count into your FICO score if they are less than thirty days old. Credit inquiries are recorded and displayed on personal credit reports for two years. They have no effect on scoring after the first year.

Do not interpret this to mean that you will be penalized for checking your own credit score. Some credit inquiries are not considered hard. So-called ***soft*** inquiries are not considered by credit scoring systems. Soft inquiries include those made by:

1. You (the consumer), such as when you request your credit report for personal use;

2. An employer (for employee verification); and

3. By companies prescreening consumers for offers of credit and insurance.

Although soft inquiries are captured by the credit bureaus, they do not appear on the credit report that lenders utilize. They do, however, appear on your personal report.

Variations

The weighting percentages shown above indicate the importance assigned to the categories. For some groups, the relative importance of these categories may be different. For example, for those who have a shorter period of using credit, the other categories will weigh heavier in the formula. Your score considers both positive and negative information in your credit report. Late payments will lower your FICO scores, but establishing or re-establishing a history of making payments on time will raise your score.

Your score considers both positive and negative information in your credit report.

3-3 Improving Your Score and Keeping It High

◇◇◇◇◇

"Okay, I need a break," says Eva.

"Me, too," adds Jack.

Together, Jack and Eva clear the dessert dishes from the table. Jack loads the dishwasher, while Eva makes fresh cups of coffee. A few minutes later, the three meet back at the kitchen table.

"Are you still okay to continue?" asks Mike.

"Sure, this is interesting," says Jack.

"And important," adds Eva.

"Great, but it is getting late, so I just want to explain one last point. Knowing what goes into your score allows you to manage your affairs to increase the score and maintain it at a high level. What you want to show is that you take your obligations seriously, you pay back what you owe on time, and that you do not overextend yourself."

Mike pulled out a list of items and they went over these together:

1. Make sure you are paying your bills on time. You may want to set up automatic withdrawals from your checking account to make sure you do not forget to make a payment on time.

2. Lower your credit card utilization ratio. Either pay off your balances due in full each month, or keep your balances as low as possible. You may also request a higher limit on your cards and then not use the extra amount available.

3. Do not run up big new balances on accounts that you do not immediately pay down again; lenders will interpret new big balances that are being paid over time as an indication you are relying more on borrowed money for your daily living.

4. Do not close existing accounts, even if you are not using them (as long as you are not paying fees to have them open). Your credit report will show zero utilization for these accounts, boosting your score.

5. Do not apply for a whole bunch of new credit. Avoid hard inquiries to whatever extent you can.

3-4 Reaping the Benefits of a High Credit Score

Mike powers down his laptop. "That's it for tonight. But let me leave you with three things you should bear in mind."

"If you have a stellar score, you will likely qualify for a prime mortgage loan with a lower interest rate and better terms. That translates into lower monthly payments on your mortgage loan, meaning more money left in your pocket after paying housing costs that you can use for savings or other expenditures."

"Alternatively, you may be able to borrow a higher percentage of the cost of your home. Lenders call the percentage they lend divided by the cost of your home the loan-to-value (LTV) ratio. Borrowers with a good track record of credit management often qualify for a higher

LTV loan. This means you would not need to make as large of a down payment as borrowers with lower credit scores if you do not so desire."

"Finally, if you can afford a bigger down payment, the lower interest rates available to you on a prime loan could allow you to obtain a larger loan and buy a more expensive home. A prime borrower pays the same amount in monthly payment for a bigger loan that a non-prime borrower pays for a smaller loan. This is because the prime borrower pays a lower interest rate and interest comprises the biggest part of monthly payments on new mortgage loans."

Eva says, "That beats a participation award any day of the week. Even though I do love ice cream."

"And pizza, too," Jack adds.

"With better loan terms, you'll be able to afford more of both." Mike smiles. "On your own, without the need for the award."

As we will discuss in the next chapter, these are examples of how a great credit score affords you the opportunity to increase your financial leverage.

Chapter 4

Saving Enough for Your Down Payment and Closing Costs

"The speed of your success is limited only by your dedication and what you are willing to sacrifice."
—Nathan W. Morris

4-1 Financial Leverage

At some point in your life you have probably used a lever. Perhaps you used a jack to raise your car to change a tire; or lifted a child up in the air at the other end of a teeter-totter; or used a pair of pliers to get a better grip on something; or squeezed the brake lever on a bicycle or motorcycle. Each of these is an example of a lever being used to transmit, magnify, and modify force.

A mechanical lever involves a rigid bar and a pivot point or axis (the fulcrum). The length of the bar and where along it you place the fulcrum cause a variation in how much can be lifted, and moved.

Diagram 4-1: Leverage

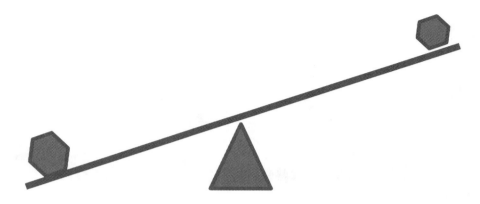

As I will explain next, a similar concept holds true in the purchase of your home. When you use a mortgage loan, you are using financial leverage.

By using financial leverage, you are able to buy a bigger and better home. The amount of money you can put as a down payment determines the height and placement of the financial fulcrum. The loan-to-value (LTV) ratio[8] that your lender gives you for your loan determines the angle of the lever. Working together, they can magnify the amount of your buying power to allow you to obtain a bigger mortgage loan and higher-priced home. The drawing below displays the concept of financial leverage.

---

8   As we discussed in Chapter 3, your LTV ratio is the amount your lender lends as a percentage of the value of your home. For instance, if your home is worth $100,000 and the lender lends your $80,000, your LTV ratio is 80 percent.

Diagram 4-2: Financial Leverage

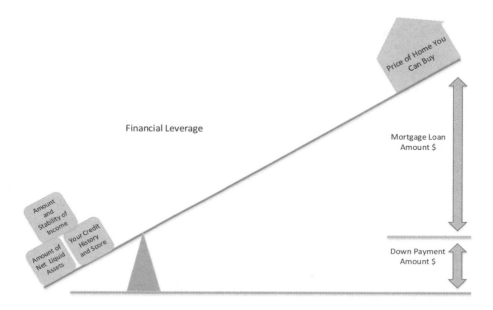

As you can see, the combination of your down payment plus the size of your mortgage determines the price of the home you can buy. The size of your mortgage depends on the monthly payment amount you can afford to pay based on your income and liquid assets, and the LTV your lender grants you based on your financial and credit profile (financial foundation).

To fully realize the power of financial leverage and to optimize the size and quality of home you can buy, you should strive to make your down payment as large as possible. We will spend time in this chapter helping you to find and implement ways to save money towards your down payment.

4-2 Set Savings Goals

4-2-1 Determine Your Savings Needs

We will start with the basics. Do you currently have any money that you designate as savings?

You may say, "Well, I have some, but I am not sure if it is enough."

No need to worry. Let us talk first about what it means to have "enough." Not considering what you will need to have for a down payment, your core savings should be an amount that could reasonably carry you through an unexpected disruption in your life, such as a loss of job or diminished income due to sickness, injury, or other life event. Some advisors recommend the amount be equal to three months of your income to deal with such unexpected events.

You should also have additional amounts above that to cover emergencies, such as your car breaking down, or the extra costs of being stranded on a trip due to transportation delays, or other situations like that. A typical emergency may cost less than $1,000, but without savings, this might be enough to push some into a downward spiral.

We will not go into it much now, but if you have children you may want to be saving for future education expenses. And then there is your retirement. Both types of events may be far off, but building little by little towards the eventual costs is easier for most than lump sum funding them later on.

In addition to your core savings for contingencies, education, and retirement, you need savings to fund the down payment and closing cost amounts required to buy your home. I suggest that you establish a separate savings account just for that purpose. Segregating the home buying savings account helps you to focus on it and make sure you do not raid your core savings for your down payment. The amount you need for a down payment is dependent on the price of the home you want to buy and the amount you can borrow (financial leverage) to fund the purchase.

For example, say you figured out in Chapter 2 that you can afford the monthly payments on a $225,000 mortgage loan. Then in Chapter 3 you figured out you were a prime borrower, and as such your bank will give you a 90 percent LTV loan. That means the bank will lend you nine dollars for every one dollar of down payment you make.

To figure out how much you can pay for a house, you divide the mortgage amount you can afford by the LTV ratio the bank will allow you. For instance:

$225,000 loan / 90 percent LTV = $250,000 home price

In this example, the amount you need to save for a down payment is the home price minus the loan amount, or $25,000.

$250,000 home price - $225,000 loan = $25,000 down payment required

In addition to the down payment, you will need to save for the costs of obtaining your loan, often called "closing costs." We will examine these in greater detail in Chapter 10, but for now we will assume they will equal 3 percent of the cost of your home, or $7,500 in this example. So in total, you will need to save $32,500 for your down payment and closing costs.

4-2-2 Establish a Savings Plan and Establish Formal Savings Accounts

Saving is easier if you establish a plan. Many people save a designated percentage of their income each month. The percentage depends on your income and expenses, which determine how much disposable income is available. Some advisors suggest that saving ten percent of pre-tax income is a good rule of thumb. If you are living

Saving is easier if you establish a plan.

with your parents rent free or have minimal or no rent expense, try to save more. This will allow you to realize your dream of homeownership—and your parents' dream of having you out of their home—more quickly.

While some folks may stuff their savings in a mattress or bury them in a coffee can under the rose bush, many people opt to keep their savings at a bank or other type of financial institution. At banks, your money is insured up to pretty high limits, and you do not have to worry about your dog, Rover, digging it up and scattering it all over the yard.

Also, many employers and payroll services will allow you to directly deposit a portion of your paycheck into an account at your bank or another financial institution. This is a great way to save, because you get used to living on the net amount you receive in your check, and your savings grow at a regular pace. What you do not see you do not miss. Accounts at financial institutions also pay you interest on your money. Your mattress and coffee can do not.

Online savings accounts offered by major financial institutions may be a good alternative to an account at your local bank. Many times these accounts offer a higher interest rate than most local banks. This might also appeal to your techy side. Your goal with any savings is to put your money to work making more money for you.

But you need to do this in a way that maximizes earnings while avoiding fees. One month of fees can wipe out many months of interest earnings. Make sure you will not fall victim to fees. Pay attention to whether fees will be charged if your balance falls below a certain dollar level, or your account activity exceeds certain limits, and avoid letting these events happen.

Also, make it inconvenient for you to raid your savings. If you have to put in some effort, you will be less likely to make withdrawals for spur of the moment purchases and other reasons not in line with your savings goals. Put some distance between you and the temptation to make a withdrawal with your bank ATM card by not even getting an ATM card for the account holding your savings.

Money market accounts are another savings option and typically pay higher interest on your money. However, most require a minimum balance. Another benefit to your saving strategy, money market accounts have limits on the number of times per month you may withdraw money from the account without penalty, making you think twice before compulsively buying something that you really do not need.

If your employer offers access to a credit union, consider taking advantage of this. Credit unions are owned by their customers. They generally offer higher interest rates on savings accounts and lower rates on loans than banks do.

Another great savings/investment tool is a CD or Certificate of Deposit. A CD offers a higher interest rate than a traditional savings account. The money is locked in for a period of time; the longer the period, the higher the rate of return. You will not have access to this money for several months to several years. If you have a longer timeframe for saving, CDs may be a good option. You will sacrifice all interest earned and may incur a penalty for withdrawal before the expiration date.

4-2-3 The Retirement Portion of Your Saving Plan – Help from Your Employer and Uncle Sam

◇◇◇◇◇

"Dad, since you've retired, you and Mom seem to be doing pretty well," Jack says one evening as he and Eva meet with Mike for what has become their weekly homeownership session.

Employer-Sponsored Retirement Plans

Pre-tax deductions, employer matches, and tax-deferred earnings help your savings grow faster.

"Thanks for the coffee, Eva." Mike sips from his mug. "You're right, Jack. We are doing okay. Not rich, mind you, but we can pay our bills and take a couple of vacations—and I can afford my golf addiction."

Jack laughs. "I know that for sure. I still can't match your scores."

"You keep practicing like you've been doing, and you'll be beating me soon," Mike says. "The big reason Mom and I are living the lifestyle we want is because we learned the value of saving for retirement."

"As I told you when you first started working full-time, it is important to make use of employer-provided retirement savings plans to the maximum extent you can. These plans have labels such as 401(k) or 403(b), which are just the names of the sections of the U.S. income tax code governing the taxation of retirement plans. Dollars you earn that you put into these plans are contributed pre-tax, meaning that they go in before your employer figures out how much to withhold from your paycheck. Furthermore, while your dollars are in the plan, earnings on them are not subject to current taxation, allowing your account to grow faster."

Eva slips her hand into Jack's. "Dad, when Jack and I were first married, we discussed your advice and we've been following it ever since."

"That's great! You are now planning for the present *and* the future. As you both know, most employers will match all or a portion of up to 5 percent of the amounts you contribute. That matching is like receiving 100 percent interest in your first year. Keep taking advantage of this. It's free money, and about the only place you can earn 100 percent on savings in the first year. Some companies will only match the money after you are fully vested, which means you have worked at your place of employment for a required amount of time. Check out the rules with your employer."

"Have you been taking advantage of the fact that your contribution can come directly out of your paycheck and into your retirement account?"

The young couple nods.

"Excellent. Because your contribution comes out pre-tax, for every dollar you put in, the amount of your net paycheck is only about seventy cents less."

"Sometimes there is an option to borrow against your 401(k) to purchase your first home. This may be the best of both worlds. Of course, you have to pay it back to your account, but this is paying yourself back, literally. Note that many plans have a five-year time limit to pay the money back, so the payment can be on the higher side."

◇◇◇◇◇

4-2-4 Some Other Tips to Help You on Your Savings Journey

Mike tells Jack and Eva about some other great tips to help them save. Here is a list.

Save 100 percent of any windfalls: Will you be receiving a $3,000 tax refund or a nice year-end bonus? While you could be tempted to splurge a little as you have a fixed savings plan, building up a down payment for a home requires a lot of discipline. This applies both to your daily expenses, as well as one-time infusions of cash. After all, if you have built a good budget, then you do not really "need" any of those funds. The extra money is perfect for saving.

Find bigger amounts to save: You can save a few bucks each week by eating store-brand peanut butter instead of Jif or Skippy. But you may also have higher dollar savings opportunities available. You can make the biggest impact by cutting out the biggest expenses. Canceling or cutting back on unused subscriptions, being a little less extravagant in your vacation selection, and driving that fully paid for car a couple more years may be good areas to start. Forgoing big expenditures where you can, rather than just pinching pennies, is an effective way to build up savings quickly.

Downsize before you upsize: Moving to a one-bedroom apartment from a two-bedroom apartment can drop your rent by 20 to 30 percent in most areas. If you do not have kids, it may be a smart move to live small before you move into your new home and reallocate the unused rent into your housing fund. An added bonus is that a smaller place will mean fewer boxes to move once you finally do find your dream home.

Alternatively, you can effectively downsize your living space without moving by taking on a roommate. Sharing space has certain drawbacks and you need to exercise care in your roommate selection, but your roommate's contributions towards rent, utilities, and other fixed costs can greatly accelerate your savings plan.

Work more hours: Spending less is the obvious way to save, but working more and *bringing home more money* is also a great way to boost your savings. If you are eligible for overtime or additional work, take every opportunity that comes your way. And if you are not, consider taking a second job on the side even if it is only a few days or a few projects each month. The effort you are putting in may convince your boss to give you a raise, which will help your savings efforts even more.

Ask for help: Much like going on a diet, staying on a strict savings plan is much easier with the support of the people around you. If your buddies are always inviting you to happy hour or your girlfriend invites you shopping each weekend, the temptation and stress are going to be an issue. Make sure your friends and family know that you are changing your behavior so they can meet you halfway.

Do not stress yourself: The math of saving for a house may be straightforward, but the emotions of saving are very complicated. If saving feels painful or frustrating every single day, it is going to be difficult to be successful at it. So, rather than letting the frustration build up by denying yourself every discretionary expense, take comfort in a simple pleasure once in a while. Reduce your dining out budget, but maybe consider cooking a nice dinner once a week at home with premium ingredients. You can cut down on going to the movies and perhaps subscribe to Netflix and Amazon Prime instead. The idea is to save money, not to spend zero. You will find it much easier to save if you are enjoying your life while doing so.

> **The idea is to save money, not to spend zero.**

4-3 Creating a Budget - Taming the "Fuzz and Blur"

4-3-1 Everyday Expenses

Whether it is formal or not, you probably have at least some form of budget. Like Jack and Eva, you know that you need to have enough set aside to pay the rent, cable bill, utilities, maybe a student loan bill, and to buy some food. After that it may get a little fuzzy, or maybe a total blur. In the fuzz and blur lies opportunity, and you need to start formally grabbing some of it and diverting it to your down payment savings account.

How do you figure out how much of the fuzz and blur you can divert? To start, you need to bring it into focus, and to figure out where the money is going. You do this by spending (no pun intended) just a little time figuring out your "everyday expenses."

The good news is that this may be easier than you think. So much today is paid for with ACH transfers, debit cards, and credit cards that it is likely you have a lot of records from which to draw. Even the portion of expenses you pay in cash can be estimated pretty well. The harder piece of this is being honest with yourself about where your money is going.

We are going to start by listing just three bits of information for each of your electronic payments over the course of a month: date, amount, and vendor. You may be able to download these onto a spreadsheet or into Quicken, Moneydance, or other accounting software package. It does not matter how you do it, just list those three fields for every one of your electronic payments for the last thirty days. If you made any ATM or other withdrawals, put them on your list and list the vendor as "cash."

Now, to the best of your ability, categorize each payment. At the end of Chapter 2 is a schedule called "**Detail of expenses comprising amount summarized on line H in the table above.**" You can use the expense line items on that schedule as category names. I have summarized them for you again in the Monthly

Budget Worksheet at the end of this chapter. You may have more to add based on your circumstances, and you may be able to drop a lot of the non-applicable categories listed as well. You can download a template from the companion website to get you started if you like.

If you are using a spreadsheet, create a column for each of these expense categories and input the dollar amount of each expenditure in the appropriate expense category column. If you are using an accounting software program, assign the appropriate expense category to each expenditure. If you are using paper and pencil, write the appropriate expense category name next to each amount.

You may need to subdivide cash payments across multiple expense categories. If you withdrew $100 from the ATM, think hard about what you used it for. Find any cash receipts you may have saved to help you. Do your best, and estimate where you have to.

When you are done, tally the totals for each expense category. A cutout of your analysis may look something like this:

Downloadable Template 4-1: Budget Category Monthly Expense Log

Date	Vendor	Amount	Utilities: Electricity	Other Insurance: Medical	Transportation Exp.: Gasoline	Public Transportation	Food: Groceries	Take-out Food	Restaurants	Hsehold Expenses: Computer	Clothing	Personal Care	Entertainment	Gifts
6/1/2015	The Gap	$78.50									$78.50			
6/1/2015	Cash	120.00			1.50		20.00	21.00	42.25			17.25	18.00	
6/2/2015	Shell Gasoline	31.00			31.00									
6/3/2015	Ben's Diner	12.53							12.53					
6/5/2015	NewEgg	23.75								23.75				
6/5/2015	MetroTransit	80.00				80.00								
6/6/2015	Comedy Shop	25.00											25.00	
Details of multiple dates left out in order to fit on page		272.60			75.25		85.00	15.00	54.22	10.00				33.13
6/15/2015	Cash	60.00											60.00	
6/15/2015	Walgreens	21.50		21.50										
6/16/2015	Valley Optical	73.25		73.25										
Details of multiple dates left out in order to fit on page		358.00		80.00	22.50		170.00	14.00	41.00	6.25	21.50	2.75		
6/29/2015	Kay's Hallmark	6.87												6.87
6/30/2015	Valley Electric	35.00	35.00											
	Totals	$2,535.00	$35.00	$250.00	$55.00	$80.00	$275.00	$50.00	$150.00	$40.00	$100.00	$20.00	$370.00	$40.00

88

Many line items for dates and columns for expenses are left out of this cutout, but you get the picture.

Study your results. Is the fuzz and blur coming into better focus? Are you surprised by how much you are spending on any category? Are any opportunities to divert cash into your home down payment savings jumping out at you?

Again, if you go to the schedule at the end of Chapter 2, you will see some of the line items where Jack and Eva determined they could cut out expenses. You can do the same.

4-3-2 Budgeting Savings into Your Everyday Expenses

Eva and Jack were fortunate enough to be exposed early in life to the value of saving and budgeting, so they were well ahead of many people their age when they got married. Because the couple was already saving and budgeting, Mike only needed to go over this briefly with them. I highly encourage you to follow the same path.

After completing your expense analysis, you are now in a position to construct a simple budget. A formal budget is a must have for some, and for others, a confining nuisance. Many people take the "tree falling in the forest" approach to money management. You know the question: if a tree falls in the forest and no one is there to hear it, does it make a sound? The lack of money management equivalent seems to be, if I do not look at where I spend my money, will things just fall into place?

I cannot answer the tree question, but I assure you that if you go too long without managing money, things will not just fall into place. Perhaps instead the tree will fall on your head, metaphorically speaking, and you will feel it even if you do not hear it. Time will go by and you will wonder one day where all your money went and why you did not accomplish more.

Putting your budget guidelines down on paper is a powerful subconscious tool that will help you to achieve your savings goals faster.

I am not suggesting you stop having fun. Simply use the spending analysis you just created as a basis for making a formal budget that will provide some guidance and motivation for managing your money a little more in line with your goal to buy a home. The first step will be to identify that portion of your money that is still leaking out for some no-longer-useful purpose due to habit, fear of missing out, or simply your failure to make a phone call to cancel something, and divert it to your down payment savings account. Make a line item on your budget for "savings" and send the money there instead.

You may be familiar with Disney's "Pirates of the Caribbean" movie series. There is a line in one of the movies in the series about the "Pirate's Code", which says, "The Code is more of what you'd call **guidelines** than actual **rules**." That sentiment applies to budgets as well. The budget you put together will be guidelines, not rules. No one from the "budget police" will be watching your every move and expenditure.

The following page has a sample budget, which Jack and Eva filled out. The Internet has a wealth of printable budget worksheet examples. You could make your own Excel spreadsheet as well. You can add childcare, pet care, hobbies, gym memberships, etc. Putting your budget guidelines down on paper is a powerful subconscious tool that will help you to achieve your savings goals faster.

Note the budget can have columns for each cohabitant, so expenses are split separately according to individual income and expenses.

Downloadable Template 4-2: Monthly Budget Worksheet

Monthly Budget			
Monthly Amount:	**Cohabitant No. 1**	**Cohabitant No. 2**	**Total**
Income:			
Salaries / Wages / Commissions / Bonuses	$6,500.00	$3,200.00	$9,700.00
Taxes withheld	(2,150.06)	(1,058.49)	(3,208.55)
Interest and Dividend		5.00	5.00
Total Income net of W/H taxes	**$4,349.94**	**$2,146.51**	**$6,496.45**
Housing Expense:			
Rent or Mortgage	$570.02	$570.02	$1,140.04
Property Taxes	208.34	208.33	416.67
Renter's / Homeowner's Insurance	52.08	52.09	104.17
Debt Payments:			
Vehicle # 1	125.00	125.00	250.00
Student Loans	400.00		400.00
Credit Card #1	250.00	50.00	300.00
Utilities:			
Telephone	20.00	20.00	40.00
Gas	50.00	50.00	100.00
Electricity	25.00	25.00	50.00
Water & Sewer	20.00	20.00	40.00
Garbage Collection	17.50	17.50	35.00
Cable Television	40.00	40.00	80.00
Cellular Phone	50.00	50.00	100.00
Internet Service	30.00	30.00	60.00
Insurance:			
Medical	200.00	50.00	250.00
Life	25.00	25.00	50.00
Auto(s)	40.00	40.00	80.00
Transportation Expenses:			
Gasoline		55.00	55.00
Commuting		10.00	10.00
Vehicle Maintenance	30.00	30.00	60.00
Licenses		5.00	5.00
Public Transport	100.00		100.00
Food:			
Groceries	200.00	75.00	275.00
Take-out Food	40.00	10.00	50.00
Restaurants	60.00	90.00	150.00

Monthly Budget			
Monthly Amount:	Cohabitant No. 1	Cohabitant No. 2	Total
Household Expenses:			
Cleaning Supplies	7.50	7.50	15.00
Yard Maintenance	50.00		50.00
Home Maintenance	100.00		100.00
Contingency	57.00		57.00
Home Security	15.00	15.00	30.00
Home Improvements	50.00	50.00	100.00
Computer	20.00	20.00	40.00
Home Furnishings	25.00	25.00	50.00
Appliances	25.00	25.00	50.00
Personal Expenses:			
Clothing	25.00	75.00	100.00
Accessories		25.00	25.00
Make-up, Personal Care		20.00	20.00
Jewelry		30.00	30.00
Entertainment	275.00	25.00	300.00
Travel	150.00	50.00	200.00
Gifts	10.00	30.00	40.00
Pet-care Costs	75.00	25.00	100.00
Donations	10.00	40.00	50.00
TOTAL EXPENSES	$3,447.44	$2,110.44	$5,557.88
DISPOSABLE INCOME (Total Income net of W/H taxes minus Total Expenses = amount available for savings)	$902.50	$36.07	$938.57

4-4 Track Finances with Personal Accounting Software such as Quicken or Moneydance

Money software programs take a little bit of time to set up, but the benefits you reap from taking the time are tremendous. Once downloaded, you can set up these programs to pull in information from your various online financial accounts. You can categorize your expenses, and clearly see what your bottom line is. Programs such as Quicken and Moneydance are great tools. You can find other good ones by searching online. Some services offer a free trial, so you can get the feel of the program to see if it is right for you. When looking for a program, consider the ease of entering information, and if you can, connect to it via an app so you can manually enter expenses throughout the day. Most programs also sync with your bank accounts automatically once you set them up.

The charts and graphs in these programs show clearly the breakdown of income versus expenses. Your expense categories show you where your money is going, which gives you a clearer idea of what might be a problem area for you. For example, if your entertainment expenses take up 90 percent of your spending, you may be able to trim to 50 percent and save 40 percent or start paying off your credit cards, thus helping with your debt-to-income ratio.

There is an added bonus if you choose Quicken. Quicken will link directly with TurboTax. This means big time savings during tax season. TurboTax (or another tax software program) may also let you upload from other accounting software programs, so do your homework.

A short list of key questions you should consider when looking for accounting / budgeting software is as follows:

1. Does the program generate reports?

2. Will the software connect with a mobile app?

3. Does the program import your accounts directly or do you have to manually enter everything?

4. Is it easy to use? Do they offer clear instructions?

5. Is there a helpline, blog, knowledge base, tutorials, or even a chat line for when you get stuck on a problem?

6. Are common reports included, such as:

    a. Spending by category;

    b. Income vs. expenses; and

    c. Budget reports?

Chapter 5

Borrowing to Buy Your Home

"One does not simply obtain a mortgage."
—Mortgage meme of a quote by the character Boromir in
the 2001 movie The Lord of the Rings

You have completed your financial and credit self-assessments, figured out how much you can afford in monthly financing and housing costs, saved for a down payment, and learned who the players are and some of the basics the game. Now it is time to get your mortgage loan financing in order. This chapter is divided into three related parts:

> **Part 1 – Getting Preapproved or Prequalified for a Mortgage Loan,**

> **Part 2 – Determining the Right Kind of Mortgage Loan for You, and**

> **Part 3 – Applying for a Mortgage Loan to Finance the Purchase of a Specific Property**.

Each part of Chapter 5 can stand alone. They are all related, but pertain to different points in your home buying process. I placed them in the same chapter for ease of cross-reference, but broke them out as separate parts for you to read when the time is right.

You should read and begin doing the steps set forth in Part 1 right away, well before you begin meeting with sellers and realtors and doing walk-throughs. You need to establish your credentials, both for yourself and for those with whom you will be dealing, so they know you are a serious buyer. Getting prequalified will help you to do that.

You should read Part 2 either simultaneously with Part 1, or shortly thereafter. It is the "everything you need to know about mortgages" summary course. You need to figure out what type of mortgage loan (yes, there are many types) and features are right for you and your situation. Do this before you begin applying for your loan as described in Part 3.

Part 3 you should read after you have been looking at homes and think you are getting close to making an offer.

5-0 It is a Brave New World in Lending since the 2007 to 2011 Crisis

"It's chilly out today," says Mike as he closes the apartment door, then hangs up his coat in the nearby closet.

"Thanks for coming over, Dad," says Jack.

Eva takes hold of Mike's arm. "Mom told me you ate at home, so I have some homemade cookies and coffee waiting for us all in the kitchen. And I had to threaten Jack to leave them until you came over."

"That's why I'm so glad you are here, Dad," says Jack. They all laugh.

After the three sit in their chairs, Jack is the first to reach for the cookies, but after getting "the look" from Eva, he withdraws his hand and waits for Mike, who smiles at him.

Mike munches on an oatmeal raisin cookie. "Wow, these are good, Eva, and they go great with hot coffee."

"Thanks, Dad, it's the least I could do considering the time you're spending with us."

"Okay, down to business," says Mike. "You saw what happened to housing prices in 2007 to 2011. After a huge multi-year run-up to unsustainable levels, housing prices corrected starting in 2006."

"It's a good thing Eva and I were still at home when this happened," replies Jack, his plate sporting three oversized cookies.

"That's true, Son. Some blamed lenders for giving 'easy' credit, some blamed the Federal Reserve for flooding the market with liquidity, and the federal government for encouraging lenders to go after lower credit borrowers to meet national home ownership goals. Others blamed consumers for borrowing recklessly, investment bankers for creating overly risky mortgage-backed securities (MBS), and MBS buyers for not understanding what they were buying. Still others think the rating agencies and bond insurers were asleep at the switch, and that fraud increased among borrowers, mortgage brokers, appraisers, and others in the mortgage loan origination process. I think there was plenty of blame to go around."

"The result of all this is that home prices increased to unaffordable levels that eventually came crashing down, leading many borrowers to owe more on their loans than their homes were worth. Many borrowers lost their homes as a chain reaction caused unemployment to grow rapidly. Underwater borrowers could not afford to pay their loans and could not refinance them because the home values had declined significantly."

"What you may not know is that the vast majority of borrowers did not default on their loans throughout the crisis. When loans are properly underwritten and borrowers do not borrow more than they can pay back, they can usually withstand economic downturns. But enough borrowers did default to cause a problem across the whole system."

"Lending is highly regulated in the United States. Mortgage lenders must be licensed or be a regulated bank, credit union, savings bank, or other regulated entity. During this crisis, federal and state lawmakers and agencies took steps to try to prevent a similar financial crisis in the future. The result was a new agency called the Consumer Finance Protection Bureau, or CFPB, whose mission is to protect consumers in financial transactions, and a host of new laws, regulations, and disclosures."

"So I'm going to talk about the new government disclosure requirements."

5-0-1 New Mortgage Loan Disclosure Requirements

Mike opens his laptop and opens a document he had created with his loan disclosure notes. He then explains that for over thirty years, federal law required lenders to provide two different disclosure forms to consumers applying for a mortgage (GFE and initial TIL as described below). The law also generally required two different forms at the time of, or shortly before, closing on the loan (HUD-1 and final TIL, also described below). Two different federal agencies had developed these forms separately, under two federal statutes:

1. The Truth in Lending Act (TILA); and

2. The Real Estate Settlement Procedures Act of 1974 (RESPA).

The information on these forms was overlapping and the language was inconsistent. Consumers often found the forms confusing, and lenders and settlement agents found the forms burdensome to provide and explain.

During the 2007 to 2011 financial crisis, which resulted in widespread mortgage loan delinquencies and homes lost in foreclosure, Congress passed the Dodd-Frank Wall Street Reform and Consumer Protection Act (Dodd-Frank Act, or the DFA). The DFA directed the Consumer Financial Protection Bureau to integrate the TILA and RESPA mortgage loan disclosures into a comprehensive, easy-to-understand format.

The Bureau finalized a new rule entitled Integrated Mortgage Disclosures Under the Real Estate Settlement Procedures Act (Regulation X) and the Truth in Lending Act (Regulation Z)(78 FR 7973, Dec. 31, 2013)(TILA-RESPA rule). The TILA-RESPA rule set forth new integrated disclosure forms and provided a detailed explanation of how the forms should be filled out and used. You can find these explanations on the CFPB website at ConsumerFinance.gov.

First, the Good Faith Estimate (GFE) and the initial Truth in Lending disclosure (initial TIL) have been combined into a new form, the Loan Estimate (LE). The new LE form provides disclosures to consumers to help them in understanding the key features, costs, and risks of the mortgage loan for which they are applying. The LE must be provided to consumers no later than the third business day *after* they submit a loan application.

Second, the HUD-1 and final Truth in Lending disclosure (final TIL) have been combined into another new form, the Closing Disclosure (CD). The CD provides disclosures to consumers to help them understand all of the costs of the transaction. The CD must be provided to consumers at least three business days *before* consummation (closing) of the loan.

Mortgage lenders commonly refer to the new documents as TILA-RESPA Integrated Disclosures or TRID. The forms use clear language and are designed to make it easier for consumers to locate key information, such as interest rate, costs to close the loan, and monthly payments. The forms provide information to help consumers determine if they can afford the loan, and to make it easier to compare the costs of different loan offers, including the costs of the loans over time.

The TILA-RESPA rule applies to most closed-end consumer mortgages. It does not apply to home equity lines of credit (HELOCs), reverse mortgages, or mortgages secured by a mobile home or by a dwelling that is not attached to real property (i.e., land). The final rule also does not apply to loans made by persons who are not considered creditors.

The TILA-RESPA rule became effective October 3, 2015. Below is a table summarizing changes in rules, disclosures, and terminology. You do not need to master it, but if you do, you will most certainly impress (or intimidate) your lender and realtor.

Table 5-1: TILA-RESPA Terminology

TILA-RESPA Terminology	
New Agency	**Description**
Consumer Financial Protection Bureau (CFPB)	A federal government agency set up to look out for the interests of consumers seeking financial services.

Old Disclosures	New Disclosures	Description of New Disclosures
Good Faith Estimate (GFE) Initial Truth-in-Lending Disclosure (Initial TIL)	Loan Estimate (LE)	A form that the consumer receives within three days of applying for a mortgage. It details everything you need to know about the loan you have applied for, including the estimated interest rate, monthly payment, closing costs, and any other fees. It will also inform you of any special features in the loan, such as a prepayment penalty.
HUD-1 Settlement Statement Final Truth-in-Lending Disclosure (Final TIL)	Closing Disclosure (CD)	A form that the consumer receives at least three days before closing on a mortgage. This form includes loan terms, projected monthly payments, and what closing costs will be involved. The three-day window allows you to compare these terms and costs to the ones estimated in your LE, and to ask your lender any questions you may have about your loan before closing.
	TILA-RESPA Integrated Disclosures (TRID)	A new disclosure rule which applies to most residential mortgage transactions. It combines the Good Faith Estimate, the Truth in Lending statement, and the HUD-1 into two new forms: the Loan Estimate and the Closing Disclosure. Therefore, TRID is the integration of the TILA and RESPA disclosures.

Old Terms	New Terms	Description of Terms
Lender	Creditor	This is the financial institution supplying the funds for the loan, and instituting the terms and conditions of the loan.
Borrower	Consumer	The person(s) taking out the loan.
Closing date	Consummation	The date on which the consumer becomes contractually obligated to the creditor on the loan.

Laws	Laws with New Rules	Description of Laws and Rules
Truth in Lending Act (TILA)	Truth in Lending Act (TILA)	This law requires mortgage companies and other lending institutions to disclose all costs and fees associated with a borrower's transaction.
Real Estate Settlement Procedures Act (RESPA)	Real Estate Settlement Procedures Act (RESPA)	This law requires lenders, loan servicers, and brokers to provide borrowers with disclosures regarding the costs associated with real estate settlements. RESPA also prohibits anti-competitive practices that can inflate the costs of real estate transactions, such as kickbacks.
	TILA-RESPA rules	The purpose of these changes is to improve the mortgage loan settlement process for consumers. They were implemented by regulations issued by the Consumer Financial Protection Bureau (CFPB).

Mike closes his laptop. "That's more than enough information for one night. As always, I'll email you my notes so you can review them together. It's time for me to get going; your mom is waiting up for me and we have a movie to watch."

After Mike leaves, the young couple sits at their kitchen table, absorbed in their own thoughts.

"Well, what do you think?" Jack finally asks.

Eva glances up at him. "Well, all of this is a little overwhelming. But we will figure things out and I'm determined to have a plan in place."

Jack smiles and reaches for Eva's hand. "That's just one more thing I love about you—you're never-say-die attitude. You're right; we can do this." He leans over and kisses her.

Chapter 5

Part 1

Getting Preapproved or Prequalified for a Mortgage Loan

5-1 Getting Started

Before you begin picking out the home of your dreams and contacting sellers and realtors, it is time to get preapproved or prequalified for your financing. By doing this, when you get to Chapter 7 and start walking through houses, you will have figured out what you can afford, and taken the preliminary steps to put your financing in place.

As you begin the process, take some time to visit the website of the Consumer Financial Protection Bureau (CFPB). The section on mortgage loans is very well-designed and easy to read and navigate. Go to ConsumerFinance.gov and under the Consumer Tools tab, click on the "Know before You Owe: Mortgage" link.

5-1-1 Lender Comparison Shopping

Although you may not end up getting your loan from the same lender who preapproves you, it makes sense for you to do your preliminary lender comparison shopping prior to getting preapproved. Then you can try to get preapproved by a lender with some likelihood of being the one you will ultimately select to provide your mortgage loan.

Nearly half of borrowers seriously consider only one lender or broker before deciding where to apply for a mortgage. However, as Mike told Jack and Eva, do not let yourself be a part of this group. It is common for rates to vary by more than half a percent among lenders. Shopping around can save you lots of money on your mortgage.

Some of the differences you will find among lenders are as follows:

a. Type of entity: Banks versus mortgage companies;

b. The way they source loans: In-house loan officers, mortgage brokers, online, or some combination of these;

c. Timelines for application processing and loan completion;

d. The amount of effort and stress they put you through with document requirements;

e. Types of loans offered:

    i. Fixed rate, adjustable rate, hybrid;

    ii. 30-year, 20-year, 15-year, 10-year term;

    iii. Down payment requirements;

    iv. Government programs;

f. Interest rates charged on loans;

g. Fees charged;

h. Requirements for escrowing taxes and insurance;

i. Online options for payments and account management;

j. Other relationships offered:

    v. Deposit products;

    vi. HELOCs.

A blank checklist form to help you compare lenders is included on the companion website for you to download and complete. Jack and Eva went through the comparison process, and their completed Lender Comparison checklist form is shown on Downloadable Template 5-1 below.

Downloadable Template 5-1: Lender Comparison

Description	Lender 1	Lender 2	Lender 3	Lender 4
a. Name	Ready Mortgage	1st National	Top Notch Mortgage	Speedy Loans
b. Type of entity	Mortgage Broker	Bank	Mortgage Company	Online Mortgage Company
c. The way they source loans	Realtors, referrals	In-house loan officers	Mortgage brokers & in-house loan officers	Online application
d. Timelines for application processing and loan completion	30- 60 days	45 days	30 days	25 days
e. Conservative vs. aggressive underwriting	Various	Conservative	Moderate	Moderate
f. Loans offered:				
1. Rate Type: Fixed rate (FRM), adjustable rate (ARM), hybrid (HRM)	FRM, ARM, HRM (3/27, 5/25)	FRM, ARM, HRM (2/28, 3/27, 5/25)	FRM, ARM, HRM (2/28, 3/27, 5/25, 10/20)	FRM, HRM (2/28, 3/27, 5/25, 10/20)
2. Amortization Term (months)	360, 300, 240, 180, 120	360, 180, 120	360, 240, 180, 120	360, 300, 240, 180, 120
3. Down payment requirements	Programs down to 3.5%	Programs down to 3.5%	Programs down to 3.5%	Programs down to 3.5%
4. Government programs	FHA, VA	FHA, VA, HARP	FHA, VA	FHA, VA, HARP
g. Fees charged:				
1. Application	$300.00	$600.00	$300.00	$250.00
2. Appraisal	$250.00	$250.00	$250.00	$250.00
3. Processing	$200.00	$200.00	$100.00	$100.00
4. Credit at closing		($400.00)		
5. Other				
h. Requirements for escrowing taxes and insurance	Required Taxes and Insurance	Required Taxes and Insurance unless LTV < 80%	Required Taxes and Insurance	Required Taxes and Insurance
i. Online options for payments and account management	Yes	Yes	Yes	Yes
j. Other relationships offered:				
1. Deposit products	No	Yes	No	No

5-1-2 Where to Begin?

In order to compare lenders, you need to identify a few to include in the comparison. The question is how to do that? You want to make sure you are working with reputable lenders offering good loan programs for borrowers like you.

Begin with current banking relationships. Assuming you are satisfied with the relationships, start with them. They will likely be a good benchmark for comparisons, and may offer existing customers some sort of discount on rates or fees.

You should also talk with family and friends who own homes and may have recently obtained mortgage loans or refinanced existing ones. Learn about their experiences. Because he was retired, Mike was a great help to Jack and Eva in researching various lending institutions. He let them know that different lenders have various requirements (although core elements are likely the same or very similar), take different amounts of time to process your documents, charge different amounts of fees, and have other variables.

Make sure you are working with reputable lenders offering good loan programs for borrowers like you.

Mike also showed Jack and Eva several forums on the Internet that discuss mortgage lenders. He warned them not to reveal personal details, and to be wary because it is possible that some forum participants have an ax to grind or are even lenders themselves. But the couple could still pick up useful information. I suggest you follow Mike's advice.

If you have already been talking to a real estate agent, they will generally have a list of mortgage brokers and lenders with whom they like to work. It says a lot about the mortgage broker. Real estate agents like things to be streamlined like most normal humans. Finding an appropriate lender and going through the loan application process takes many weeks. There will be many questions to answer and much more documentation (sometimes the same information more than once) required than you thought was humanly possible, so you want someone who will be available. If you like your real estate agent, you will probably work well with the mortgage broker they recommend.

Buy a Sunday newspaper (I know, I know; just recycle it when you are done and you will feel better) and search the real estate section. See which lenders are advertising and what sorts of rates and terms they are offering. Be aware that the rate advertised may not be the rate you would ultimately get, but it is a starting point.

Search for online mortgage lenders. Start by searching "50 biggest mortgage lenders." Also, qualify the search with your location (e.g., "50 biggest mortgage lenders in Boston"). You will find some good leads for lending institutions that you can research further.

Pay attention to TV and radio ads. Some of the nation's largest online lenders routinely advertise on TV. One or more of these lenders may offer programs that are suitable for you.

Once you have good leads, prepare a formal lender comparison checklist.

5-2 Prequalification versus Preapproval

"Dad, Eva and I have looked into the prequalification and preapproval process at a couple of different lending institutions," says Jack as the three eat some leftovers from the big batch of Eva's homemade cookies and sip coffee at the couple's kitchen table. "But I am confused; aren't prequalification and preapproval the same thing?"

"Great question, Jack. It depends on the terminology used by a given lender, but technically, no, they are different. Preapproval is better."

Mike drains the last of his coffee and sets the cup down on the table. "Although the terms 'preapproved' and 'prequalified' are often used interchangeably in the mortgage lending world, prequalification typically involves finding an estimate of how much a lender is willing to loan you to purchase a home. The lender determines whether a prospective borrower has the ability (meaning the sufficient assets and income) to repay a loan. Prequalification is subject to verification of the information provided by the applicant and is short of approval because it does not take into account the credit history of the borrower. Prequalified borrowers may ultimately be turned down because, while they may have demonstrated the ability to repay, a poor credit history suggests that they may not have the willingness to pay."

Mike explains, "A preapproval carries more weight, because this means the lender essentially runs you through a full loan application process. The lender checks your credit, and verifies your employment and employment history, your income, the amount of money in your bank accounts to see if it covers the down payment you plan to make, the amount of your other assets, and other factors pertinent to getting a loan. To check your credit, the lender runs a hard inquiry on your credit. Remember that hard inquiries do have an effect on your credit score. This is another reason for making sure you pick a lender you have researched and like for the preapproval process."

"A preapproval is an actual document saying you are tentatively approved (assuming circumstances do not change and the assumptions used are correct) for a particular loan amount for a particular time frame, typically ninety days. Preapproval can take as little as a week or up to several months. Once you have been preapproved, you will receive a tentative preapproval letter. This carries more weight than a prequalification letter, because it lets the seller know that you are likely to get financing."

Exhibit 5-1 on the following page includes a sample prequalification worksheet. It is filled in with Jack and Eva's information.

Exhibit 5-2 on the subsequent page shows a preapproval checklist to get an idea of what documents and information you should gather ahead of time. You may be asked for more or less information depending on the lender. It is not necessary to get prequalified before you get preapproved; you can dive in headfirst and go right for the preapproval, should you choose.

Exhibit 5-1: Mortgage Prequalification Checklist

Borrower's Name: *Jack D. Barnes*   Date of Birth: *7-1-1985*

Current Address: *237 North St. Apt. C, Chicago, IL*

Phone Number: *(312) 555-1234*   Email Address: *Jack.D.Barnes@MetroXCorp.com*

Monthly Rent/Mortgage Payment: *$1,500*

Current Employer: *Metro-X Corp*   Current Position: *Software Developer*

How long have you worked with your current employer?: *4 years*

Co-borrower's Name: *Eva A. Brandt*   Date of Birth: *5-15-1985*

Current Address: *Same as borrower*

Phone Number: *(312) 555-1234*   Email Address: *Eva.A.Brandt@CentElemSchool.edu*

Rent/Mortgage Payment: *$1,500.00, included in borrower amount above*

Current Employer: *Central Elementary School*   Current Position: *5th Grade Teacher*

How long have you worked with your current employer? *4 years, 2 months*

Source of Down Payment: *Savings*

Required Documentation for Prequalification:

- Last two paystubs from borrower and co-borrower
- W-2s from the last two years
- Last 401(k) statement
- Last two months of bank statements from checking and savings
- Any debts, such as loans

Exhibit 5-2: Preapproval Checklist

- Name of borrower and co-borrower.

- Address for the past two years.

- Social Security number.

- Driver's licenses.

- Landlords for the past two years; if you rented, proof of paying rent on time.

- Two year work history.

- Pay stubs and/or W-2s for past one to two years.

- Credit report (will be pulled by the lender or broker).

- Bank statements for past one to two months of all savings and checking accounts.

- Real estate holdings; this includes addresses, income if you are receiving rent, current market value, your lender, and balance owed.

- Gift letter if you will be receiving a gift or grant to assist with down payment. You may be required to prove funds.

- Tax returns, especially if you are self-employed.

- Assets IRAs, stocks, bonds, securities. Any assets you might use for your down payment.

- Retirement account statements.

- Debts that do not appear on your credit report (e.g., auto, mortgage, student, or personal loans). You will be asked for the account number, name, monthly payment, and balance of your loans.

5-2-1 Hints about the Prequalification and Preapproval Process

Here are some hints for the prequalification and preapproval process:

1. Comparison shop to find a lender with programs appropriate to your needs:

    a. This may or may not be the lender from whom you ultimately get your mortgage loan, but you are better off with this approach.

2. Apply for the loan by completing the application as completely and accurately as you can.

3. Assemble all the documents you need (e.g., W-2s, tax returns, bank statements, paystubs.)

4. Respond to any and all inquiries from the lender:

    a. Do not procrastinate.

    b. Provide complete and accurate information. The lender will find out if you are guessing at the dates you lived in your last apartment or that you worked at your employer for fourteen months, not two years. Do not give them any reason to doubt your application's integrity.

5. After all of this hard work, if you are approved, you will receive a letter that looks similar to the one in Exhibit 5-3. Take this to your realtor and say, "Let's get serious. I'm going to be a homeowner!"

6. If you are declined, do not despair. Find out why so you can take actions to improve your chances of approval:

    a. Ask the lender why you were declined. Was it due to income, or was your credit score too low, or your debt load too high?

Do not procrastinate. Provide complete and accurate information.

b. Request a copy of the credit score the lender used. If the lender used your credit score to deny your preapproval request, they are required by law to send you a notice with the credit score they used to make the decision and instructions on how to get a free copy of your credit report.

c. If there are errors in your credit report, get them fixed, as described in Chapter 3.

Exhibit 5-3 shows a copy of the preapproval letter that Jack and Eva received from a lender to which they applied.

Exhibit 5-3: Your Prospective Mortgage Company Preapproval Letter

Date: **6/22/20xx**

Borrower: **Jack D. Barnes and Eva A. Brandt**

Address: **237 North St. Apt. C, Chicago, IL**

Dear: Jack and Eva,

After analyzing your credit history, employment, income, and assets, we believe you qualify for the following:

Loan Program: Type of loan **15 or 30 year fixed rate**

Loan Amount: Maximum amount of loan you qualify for is **$270,000**

Expiration Date: How long the preapproval is good for, usually **90 days**

Down Payment: **10 percent of loan amount**

State: **IL**

This letter is not a guarantee of specifics rates or terms. Your loan will have to be given final approval when the following conditions are met:

- A purchase agreement

- An approved appraisal

- A clear title of the property

- Proof of funds to close

- Final underwriting

For further information, contact:

George Jones

Prospective Mortgage

(312) 555-5555

GJonesmanager@homeloan.com

It is tempting to get really excited about your upcoming home purchase after you hear you are preapproved. You are going to find a house and actually be able to buy it! Excitement is good. But slow down a little. There are a few things you need to know. The lender who ultimately provides your mortgage is going to underwrite your loan application again at the time you make an offer on a home and apply for the loan on that specific home. Do not mess up your financial and credit situation between now and then.

Here are the "Ten Commandments of Buying a Home." Read them. Absorb them. Emblazon them in your memory, because one minuscule misstep can bring your dream of home ownership crashing down.

Exhibit 5-4: Ten Commandments of Buying a Home[9]

1. Do not change jobs, become self-employed, or quit your job.

2. Do not buy a car, truck, or van (or you may be living in it!).

3. Do not use credit cards excessively or let current accounts fall behind.

4. Do not spend money you have set aside for closing.

5. Do not omit debts or liabilities from your loan application.

6. Do not buy furniture on credit.

7. Do not originate any inquiries into your credit.

8. Do not make large deposits without checking with your loan officer.

9. Do not change bank accounts.

10. Do not co-sign a loan for anyone.

---

9   From http://lightersideofrealestate.com/

Chapter 5

Part 2

Determining the Right Kind of Mortgage Loan for You

5-3 Financing the Purchase of Your Home

You have been answering questions, filling out applications, and potentially providing documentation if you have gone through the preapproval process. But there are still some more formalities and considerations before actually committing to a home loan and getting that mortgage. Of course, actually finding your dream home is a critical step, but you should be aware of the following information, as it will help you to work better with your loan officer when choosing which type of loan best fits your circumstances.

Unless you have amassed substantial liquid assets (cash and near-cash investments), you will likely have to borrow most of the purchase price of your new home. The lender will generally require you to put some of your own money towards the purchase price (this is called your down payment or equity), and lend you the difference. The standard for a conventional mortgage is traditionally a 20 percent down payment. However, there are loan programs that allow for 10 percent, 5 percent, or 0 percent down, depending on the borrower's qualifications.

When you get a mortgage loan, the lender will require you to sign 1) a "note" evidencing the debt and your obligation to repay it, and 2) a "mortgage" through which the lender obtains a security interest in your property until the note is paid in full. A security interest means that if you stop paying on the note, under the terms of the mortgage the lender can foreclose on your property and take your home away in full or partial satisfaction of the note.

Neither you nor the lender wants you to lose your home to foreclosure. Both of you will lose if foreclosure becomes necessary. The decrease in value of a neglected house, combined with property taxes, insurance, legal, and other costs involved in foreclosure, take so much money out of the transaction that both the borrower and lender are left worse off. As with so many adverse situations, only the lawyers profit from this scenario.

To minimize the chance of a default of payments, the lender will require you to go through an underwriting (evaluation) process to determine your ability and willingness to repay under the terms of the note. You will have to fill out a loan application and provide supporting documents to the lender. This process can prove frustrating to new and seasoned borrowers alike. But you can minimize frustration and delays by being prepared and understanding the process. This chapter is designed to prepare you and provide you with that understanding.

5-3-1 Understanding Home Financing

It's a warm evening when Mike arrives at Jack and Eva's apartment. Eva meets him at the door with a smile and hug, and takes his spring jacket. The three enjoy a great dinner of hamburgers with all the fixings, salad, and a Coke to wash all the food down. As Jack clears the plates, Eva spoons out vanilla fudge ice cream into three bowls, and Mike starts his computer. After the three finish their dessert, Mike begins.

"Before discussing the process for obtaining a mortgage loan, let us talk about the costs. There are upfront and ongoing expenses involved. These expenses to you make up part of the lender's profit, as well as fees paid to an appraiser, home inspector, closing agent, title company, and other service providers." Mike was glad to see Jack and Eva had their laptops open and were busy tapping on the keys.

"Lenders, such as banks and mortgage companies, earn revenue by making loans to customers. They charge their customers fees and interest on the money they lend. Depending on the type of loan you obtain, how long you have to repay it, and market conditions, the lender will charge you differing amounts of fees and interest over the life of your loan."

"There are some basic loan concepts you need to understand so you can choose the right loan for you and make sure you do not get yourself in financial trouble down the road."

5-3-2 Loan Features and Costs

In this section, we will address loan features and costs. Throughout this section are tables summarizing key concepts with explanatory comments. The typical choices you will face are identified and pro and con points are presented for each choice. More detailed explanations are provided in addition to the tables.

5-3-2-1 Interest Rate Types

As Mike explains to Jack and Eva, the first thing to consider is what type of loan you will get. There are two main types; fixed rate and adjustable rate (ARM). A third type is just a combination of the two, where the loan is fixed rate for some initial number of months and then changes to adjustable rate.

Fixed rate means that each month's loan payment will always be calculated using the same interest rate for the life of the loan. Adjustable rate means that at set intervals the interest rate on your loan can change to reflect changes in the market rate of interest, and as a result your payment can change. The magnitude of these changes often shock borrowers, and can lead to the borrower being unable to afford the full monthly payment due. This is called payment shock risk. Make sure you fully understand the terms before you accept an ARM loan, including the pattern your payments will follow if you experience the maximum possible rate increase at each reset date.

ARM loans generally start at a lower rate, and there are usually limits on how much the rate can change each time it adjusts. If you want certainty for your budget, a fixed rate loan is the way to go. If you think interest rates will stay low a long time, or if you think you will be moving and therefore paying off your loan in relatively short period of time, a lower starting rate ARM loan may be a better choice for you.

You can obtain a loan that starts off as a fixed rate loan, then after a predefined number of months will switch to being an adjustable rate loan. This type of loan is called a hybrid loan. Hybrid loans provide the benefit of predictable payments during the fixed rate period, and usually have a lower beginning interest rate than pure fixed rate loans. Many borrowers who think that they will be refinancing or moving and paying off their loans before the fixed portion of the hybrid loan term ends choose these loans for that reason.

Table 5-2: Type of Loan

Choices	Pros	Cons
Fixed Rate (FRM)	No payment shock risk	Higher starting payment
Adjustable Rate (ARM)	Lower starting payment than FRM	Payment shock risk
Fixed Rate Changing to Adjustable Rate (Hybrid)	Somewhat lower starting payment	Eventual payment shock risk

Next to consider is the absolute level of the initial interest rate charged on the loan, and, if it is an ARM or hybrid loan, the subsequent interest rates that will be charged on the loan. This is what the lender earns for your use of their money. The interest rate on your mortgage is dependent upon general market interest rates at the time you obtain your loan (or when each ARM rate adjustment occurs), your credit history and score (more on this in Chapter 3), and other features of your loan that we discuss in this section (loan type, LTV ratio, term, IO period, etc.).

All else being equal, the lower your rate, the lower your payment for any given size loan. The table below shows payment amounts per $100,000 of original loan balance at different interest rates for a 360 month loan.

Table 5-3: Monthly payment per $100,000 of loan balance for a 360 month loan

Interest Rate	Monthly Payment Per $100,000 of Loan Balance
8.00%	**$733.76**
7.00%	$665.30
6.00%	$599.55
5.00%	$536.82
4.00%	**$477.42**
3.00%	$421.60
2.00%	$369.62

Think about what this means while considering Jack and Eva's (and your) situation. Let's say the couple can afford a monthly payment of $1,500. If rates go down, they can buy a more expensive house, because their $1,500 payment can cover the interest charged on a bigger loan at the new, lower rate. Let us explore what this means using Table 5-3 above. Note that if Jack and Eva's loan rate was 8.00%, their $1,500 payment could only support a loan balance of about $200,000 (2 x $733.76 = $1,467.52). However, if their loan rate was only 4.00%, they could support a loan of about $300,000 (3 x $477.42 = $1,432.26). So market rates of

The interest rate on your mortgage is dependent upon general market interest rates at the time you obtain your loan, your credit history and score, and other features of your loan.

interest play a big role in the price they (and you) can afford to pay for a home.

Let's extend this concept and consider the content of each of your mortgage payments. Each month when you make a mortgage payment, the amount you pay includes a portion for interest on the loan and a portion to reduce the remaining principal balance owed on the loan. The principal component of each payment is said to be "amortizing" the balance of the loan. Your payment size is calculated such that the principal component of all monthly payments, when summed together, will fully amortize (fully pay off) the original balance of your loan.

Table 5-4 below demonstrates this very important point. It shows the principal and interest component for each monthly payment for the first 24 months of a 360-month term, 4.50% fixed rate mortgage loan with an initial balance of $250,000. The fixed monthly payment on this loan is $1,140.04.

Take a moment to study this table because it will teach you much about how mortgage loans work. The interest component (Column E) of each month's payment is equal to the prior period remaining balance (Column C) of the loan times the annual interest rate divided by 12 (to convert the interest rate to monthly instead of annual). The difference between the monthly payment (Column D) and the interest portion (Column E) is the principal (Column F) portion of the monthly payment. This portion pays down (amortizes) the remaining balance of the loan.

The interest portion of the next payment is therefore less, because the smaller remaining balance is then multiplied by the interest rate divided by twelve. As you make each mortgage payment, a bigger and bigger portion of each payment goes towards principal and a smaller and smaller portion of each payment goes towards interest.

Table 5-4: Mortgage Loan Amortization Table: First 24 Months of 360 Month Fixed Rate Loan

Original Balance: \$250,000; Interest Rate: 4.50%; Monthly Payment \$1,140.04

	A	B	C	D	E	F
			C = prior month C - F		E = 4.5% / 12 * prior month C	F = D - E
Loan Amortization Table	Remaining Loan Term	End of Month Number	End of Month Remaining Balance	Payment Amount	Interest Amount	Principal Amount
	360	0	\$ 225,000.00			
	359	1	\$ 224,703.70	\$ 1,140.04	\$ 843.75	\$ 296.29
	358	2	\$ 224,406.30	\$ 1,140.04	\$ 842.64	\$ 297.40
	357	3	\$ 224,107.78	\$ 1,140.04	\$ 841.52	\$ 298.52
	356	4	\$ 223,808.14	\$ 1,140.04	\$ 840.40	\$ 299.64
	355	5	\$ 223,507.38	\$ 1,140.04	\$ 839.28	\$ 300.76
	354	6	\$ 223,205.49	\$ 1,140.04	\$ 838.15	\$ 301.89
	353	7	\$ 222,902.47	\$ 1,140.04	\$ 837.02	\$ 303.02
	352	8	\$ 222,598.32	\$ 1,140.04	\$ 835.88	\$ 304.16
	351	9	\$ 222,293.02	\$ 1,140.04	\$ 834.74	\$ 305.30
	350	10	\$ 221,986.57	\$ 1,140.04	\$ 833.60	\$ 306.44
First 24 Months of 360 month mortgage loan	349	11	\$ 221,678.98	\$ 1,140.04	\$ 832.45	\$ 307.59
	348	12	\$ 221,370.24	\$ 1,140.04	\$ 831.30	\$ 308.75
	347	13	\$ 221,060.33	\$ 1,140.04	\$ 830.14	\$ 309.90
	346	14	\$ 220,749.27	\$ 1,140.04	\$ 828.98	\$ 311.07
	345	15	\$ 220,437.03	\$ 1,140.04	\$ 827.81	\$ 312.23
	344	16	\$ 220,123.63	\$ 1,140.04	\$ 826.64	\$ 313.40
	343	17	\$ 219,809.05	\$ 1,140.04	\$ 825.46	\$ 314.58
	342	18	\$ 219,493.30	\$ 1,140.04	\$ 824.28	\$ 315.76
	341	19	\$ 219,176.35	\$ 1,140.04	\$ 823.10	\$ 316.94
	340	20	\$ 218,858.22	\$ 1,140.04	\$ 821.91	\$ 318.13
	339	21	\$ 218,538.90	\$ 1,140.04	\$ 820.72	\$ 319.32
	338	22	\$ 218,218.38	\$ 1,140.04	\$ 819.52	\$ 320.52
	337	23	\$ 217,896.65	\$ 1,140.04	\$ 818.32	\$ 321.72
	336	24	\$ 217,573.73	\$ 1,140.04	\$ 817.11	\$ 322.93

Table 5-5 below assumes for the same loan that you have timely made the first 336 monthly payments over the last 28 years, and only 24 payments remain. Notice that now nearly 100 percent of each of your payments goes towards principal. The monthly payment is still \$1,140.04 (Column D), but the remaining balance is very small so the calculated interest portion of each payment (Column E) is likewise small, and thus the principal portion (Column F) of each payment is big.

The monthly payment on your loan is calculated to perfectly amortize the principal balance of your loan through this process.

Note in Table 5-5, the principal portion of the payment in month 360 is exactly equal to the remaining loan balance at the end of month 359. Thus the payment in month 360 fully pays off (amortizes) the mortgage loan.

Table 5-5: Mortgage Loan Amortization Table: Last 24 Months of 360 Month Fixed Rate Loan

Original Balance: $250,000; Interest Rate: 4.50%; Monthly Payment $1,140.04

	A	B	C	D	E	F
Loan Amortization Table			C = prior month C - F		E = 4.5% / 12 * prior month D	F = D - E
	Remaining Loan Term	End of Month Number	End of Month Remaining Balance	Payment Amount	Interest Amount	Principal Amount
	23	337	$ 25,077.01	$ 1,140.04	$ 97.95	$ 1,042.10
	22	338	$ 24,031.01	$ 1,140.04	$ 94.04	$ 1,046.00
	21	339	$ 22,981.08	$ 1,140.04	$ 90.12	$ 1,049.93
	20	340	$ 21,927.22	$ 1,140.04	$ 86.18	$ 1,053.86
	19	341	$ 20,869.41	$ 1,140.04	$ 82.23	$ 1,057.81
	18	342	$ 19,807.63	$ 1,140.04	$ 78.26	$ 1,061.78
	17	343	$ 18,741.86	$ 1,140.04	$ 74.28	$ 1,065.76
	16	344	$ 17,672.10	$ 1,140.04	$ 70.28	$ 1,069.76
	15	345	$ 16,598.33	$ 1,140.04	$ 66.27	$ 1,073.77
	14	346	$ 15,520.53	$ 1,140.04	$ 62.24	$ 1,077.80
Last 24 Months of 360 month mortgage loan	13	347	$ 14,438.69	$ 1,140.04	$ 58.20	$ 1,081.84
	12	348	$ 13,352.80	$ 1,140.04	$ 54.15	$ 1,085.90
	11	349	$ 12,262.83	$ 1,140.04	$ 50.07	$ 1,089.97
	10	350	$ 11,168.77	$ 1,140.04	$ 45.99	$ 1,094.06
	9	351	$ 10,070.61	$ 1,140.04	$ 41.88	$ 1,098.16
	8	352	$ 8,968.33	$ 1,140.04	$ 37.76	$ 1,102.28
	7	353	$ 7,861.92	$ 1,140.04	$ 33.63	$ 1,106.41
	6	354	$ 6,751.36	$ 1,140.04	$ 29.48	$ 1,110.56
	5	355	$ 5,636.64	$ 1,140.04	$ 25.32	$ 1,114.72
	4	356	$ 4,517.73	$ 1,140.04	$ 21.14	$ 1,118.90
	3	357	$ 3,394.63	$ 1,140.04	$ 16.94	$ 1,123.10
	2	358	$ 2,267.32	$ 1,140.04	$ 12.73	$ 1,127.31
	1	359	$ 1,135.78	$ 1,140.04	$ 8.50	$ 1,131.54
	0	360	$ -	$ 1,140.04	$ 4.26	$ 1,135.78

At the beginning of a loan's life, most of each payment goes towards interest. But as the balance of the loan is methodically paid down over time, less and less of each payment is covering interest and more and more of each payment further reduces principal. The rate of amortization thereby increases as the loan grows older.

Many financial advisors will tell you to send an extra amount over your scheduled payment (in this case an amount in excess of $1,140.04) each month. The reason is that the extra amount is treated entirely as principal. After studying tables 5-4 and 5-5 you will quickly see the wisdom of doing this. The quicker the remaining balance goes down, the less of each subsequent payment goes toward interest and the more towards principal. You can significantly reduce the life of your mortgage loan and save thousands of dollars in interest over the life of the loan just by paying an extra $100 in principal each month.

5-3-2-2 Interest Only Loans

To lower your payment on the mortgage for an initial number of months, some loans allow you to just include the interest component of the payment for that initial period. These loans are said to have an interest only (IO) period component to them. During the IO period, the principal balance on the loan is not being reduced at all (no amortization).

When the IO period ends, the payment increases to such an extent that the principal component of each remaining payment will cause the loan to fully amortize over its remaining life. The increase in payment may cause a bit of a financial shock to you if you are not expecting it. The expression, "there is no such thing as a free lunch" rings true in this case. Since you paid down no principal in the first months' payments, you now have less remaining months to fully amortize your loan. So each remaining payment has to cover a regular principal pay down amount plus a "catch-up" pay down amount as well.

5-3-2-3 Negatively Amortizing Loans

An even more extreme technique for early payment reduction that results in subsequent higher monthly payments is found in a so-called negative amortization (NegAm) loan. The initial payments on NegAm loans are not even sufficient enough to pay the monthly interest due, much less any principal. The interest shortfall is added to the loan balance due each month, effectively negatively amortizing your balance. The payment shock occurring at the end of the negative amortization period can be substantial. If you obtain a negatively amortizing loan, your eventual payment not only has to be big enough to amortize the original loan amount with less remaining payments, but also pay off the additional balance resulting from the negative amortization.

You should only consider a NegAm loan to get a lower initial payment in times of rapid home value increases in the market, or if you expect a substantial increase in your income in the coming months and you are trying to buy a house you currently cannot really afford but will be "growing into" from an income standpoint in a very short timeframe. NegAm loans are extremely risky. If your anticipated income increase fails to materialize, the increased payment at the end of the NegAm period may be far more than you can afford and you risk losing your home in foreclosure. I advise you to avoid NegAm loans altogether.

Tables 5-6 and 5-7 below summarize the variations in payment content and payment size for fully amortizing, IO and NegAm loans.

Table 5-6: Content of each Monthly Payment

Description	Payment Content Variations	Pros	Cons
Fully Amortizing	From beginning of loan, each payment includes both a principal and interest component.	Balance starts declining immediately.	Higher starting payment.
Interest Only, or IO	At beginning of loan, a set number of payments will be for interest only.	Lower initial payment and no negative amortization.	Loan balance does not decline during IO period; payment shock when IO period ends.
Negative Amortization, or NegAm	At beginning of loan, a set number of payments will not even cover all interest due, and each monthly shortfall is added to the loan balance.	Lowest starting payment.	Loan amount increases initially, payment shock when NegAm period ends.

Table 5-7: Monthly Payment Size Variations - Fixed Rate Loan

Description	Payment Size Variations	Pros	Cons
Fully Amortizing	Level payment throughout life of loan.	No risk of payment shock.	Highest initial payment.
Interest Only, or IO	One payment change at end of IO period, sufficient to amortize initial balance of loan over remaining non-IO period.	Lower initial payment than fully amortizing loan.	Potential payment shock at end of IO period.
Negative Amortization, or NegAm	One payment change at end of NegAm period, sufficient to amortize initial balance of loan plus deferred interest over remaining non-negative amortization period.	Lowest initial payment.	Potential very large payment shock when negative amortization period ends.

5-3-2-4 Percentage of Your Home Value That You Borrow (LTV)

The next loan question is how much of your home's value are you going to borrow? Lenders call the ratio of loan amount to property value the Loan-to-Value, or LTV ratio. The higher the LTV ratio, the bigger your loan, and the bigger your resulting monthly payment, all else being equal.

Home buyers often seek the highest LTV ratio loan they can get for which they can still afford the monthly payment. Why? Because for a given amount of money they have available for a down payment, the higher the LTV ratio loan they can get, the bigger the loan and the bigger or better the home they can get.

Let us revisit Table 5-3 that we reviewed in the interest rate discussion. This time we will vary LTV ratio as well as rate. Table 5-8 shows for each combination of interest rate and LTV, the amount you can afford to pay for a home if you have the indicated down payment amount and can afford to pay a monthly mortgage loan payment of $2,000. You can use the KHBAN table from Chapter 2 to recreate any cell of Table 5-8 and add more combinations as well.

Table 5-8: Affordable Home Value by Rate and LTV Ratio, if you have the Down Payment Amount

Payment you can afford: $2,000.00 per month

Loan term: 360 months

Interest Rate	Loan Size you can afford	Affordable Home Value by Rate and LTV Ratio, If you have the Down Payment Amount							
		97.50%		90%		80%		70%	
		Home Value	Down Payment	Home Value	Down Payment	Home Value	Down Payment	Home Value	Down Payment
8.00%	$204,425	$209,667	$5,242	$227,139	$22,714	$255,532	$51,106	$292,036	$87,611
7.00%	$225,461	$231,242	$5,781	$250,513	$25,051	$281,827	$56,365	$322,088	$96,626
6.00%	$250,187	$256,602	$6,415	$277,986	$27,799	$312,734	$62,547	$357,411	$107,223
5.00%	$279,422	$286,587	$7,165	$310,469	$31,047	$349,278	$69,856	$399,175	$119,752
4.00%	$314,192	$322,248	$8,056	$349,102	$34,910	$392,740	$78,548	$448,846	$134,654
3.00%	$355,784	$364,907	$9,123	$395,316	$39,532	$444,730	$88,946	$508,263	$152,479
2.00%	$405,823	$416,228	$10,406	$450,914	$45,091	$507,278	$101,456	$579,747	$173,924

Again, no matter what LTV you choose, lower LTV loans require bigger down payments, all else being equal. Table 5-9 below provides some of the pros and cons of high and low LTV loans.

Table 5-9: Loan-to-Value Ratio (LTV)

Choices	Pros	Cons
LTV more than 80 percent	Lower down payment for any given house. Ability to buy more expensive home limited only by absolute down payment you can fund.	Higher fees and interest rates, higher payments, greater chance of default.
LTV equal to 80 percent	Standard program for most lenders, more straightforward approval process.	20 percent down payment is difficult for some borrowers.
LTV less than 80 percent	Lower fees and interest rates, lower payments, lower chance of default.	Higher down payment for any given house. Reduces ability to buy more expensive houses, limited by absolute down payment you can fund.

5-3-2-5 Amortization Term of Loan

The next thing to consider is the number of months over which you will pay down your loan. This is called the amortization term. Lenders usually have options for 120 months (ten years), 180 months (fifteen years), 240 months (twenty years), 300 months (twenty-five years), and 360 months (thirty years). Some will even lend more than thirty years, but I do not advise you to take them up on it.

The more months over which your loan amortizes, the lower your monthly payment, but the longer the amortization term, the more months you are going to be paying interest, and the more total interest you are going to pay over the life of the loan.

People buying their first home often choose the longest amortization term loan the lender offers. Why? Because the longer amortization term allows them to obtain a bigger loan all other things being equal. This in turn allows them to pay more for a home, and get a bigger or better home in a better location.

People buying subsequent homes may be "moving up" to a bigger or better home and will again choose a thirty-year amortization term loan to maximize their buying power. But at some point, people moving or refinancing typically will attempt to shorten the amortization term of the new loan they are getting. The shorter the term, the more of each payment that goes to principal amortization, thereby allowing them to build "equity[10]" in their home more quickly. This is because the payments are going less to pay interest and more to amortize the principal.

The following table provides payment amounts for every $100,000 of your loan at various combinations of interest rates and terms. Note that for a 5.00 percent fixed rate loan with a $100,000 initial balance, the monthly payment over 360 months is $536.82; over 120 months it is $1,060.66. The extra amount paid on the 120-month loan is all going towards principal, amortizing the loan balance twenty years faster.

---

10   Equity is the amount your home is worth less the amount you owe on your mortgage loan. Just like net worth on a balance sheet, it is the asset minus the liability.

Table 5-10: Monthly Payments Based on Rate and Amortization Term

Interest Rate	120	180	240	300	360
8.00%	$1,213.28	$955.65	$836.44	$771.82	$733.76
7.00%	$1,161.08	$898.83	$775.30	$706.78	$665.30
6.00%	$1,110.21	$843.86	$716.43	$644.30	$599.55
5.00%	$1,060.66	$790.79	$659.96	$584.59	$536.82
4.00%	$1,012.45	$739.69	$605.98	$527.84	$477.42
3.00%	$965.61	$690.58	$554.60	$474.21	$421.60
2.00%	$920.13	$643.51	$505.88	$423.85	$369.62

If you paid both 5.00 percent fixed rate loans out exactly as scheduled, the total amounts paid on each loan would be as follows:

Table 5-11: Summary of Total Payments Made Based on Rate and Amortization Term

120 Month Loan	360 Month Loan	Difference
$127,278.62	$193,255.78	$65,977.17

Even though payments on the 360-month amortization term loan are smaller, there are three times as many. In both loans you pay the exact same amount of principal back over the respective terms, but with the 360-month loan you pay $65,977.17 more in interest over the life of the loan. Most people find the lower monthly payment and ability to buy a bigger or better home an acceptable trade-off. Given that most loans are paid off well before maturity due to home sales or refinancing, the full difference in lifetime interest is seldom realized.

With the 360-month loan you pay $65,977.17 more in interest over the life of the loan.

For all amortization terms, if you have additional income in a given month and can afford to make an additional principal payment, you will reduce your remaining principal balance outstanding and the amount of interest calculated for each future amortization period.

Table 5-12: Loan Amortization Term

Choices	Pros	Cons
More than 360 months	Lower monthly payment.	Greatest amount of interest paid over the life of the loan.
360 months	Lower monthly payment.	Greater amount of interest paid over the life of loan.
Less than 360 months	Much lower amount of interest paid over life of loan.	Higher monthly payment.

Be aware that the amortization term may not always equal the term in which the loan must be paid in full (maturity term). If the loan has an initial IO period, its amortization term is less than its maturity term. Contrarily, some loans have what is known as a balloon term. That means that on a date (the balloon date) before the loan is fully amortized,

> **The amortization term may not always equal the term in which the loan must be paid in full (maturity term).**

the borrower must pay off any remaining balance in full. So with a balloon loan, the amortization term is longer than the maturity term.

5-3-2-6 Monthly Escrow Payments for Real Estate Taxes and Homeowner's Insurance

We will now focus on an amount called an escrow payment that you may have to pay monthly in excess of your mortgage interest and principal payment. When you own a home, you will be responsible for paying property taxes and homeowner's insurance on your home. Often the lender will collect from you monthly one-twelfth (1/12) of the annual amount you will owe and holds it in escrow. The lender then pays the tax and insurance bills from the escrow account as they come due.

Table 5-13: Property Taxes and Insurance Collected and Escrowed Monthly

Choices	Pros	Cons
Escrowed	Easier to budget for these amounts.	Each monthly payment is higher.
Not Escrowed	Monthly payment is unaffected.	Harder to budget. Significant, concentrated payment once or twice a year.

5-3-2-7 Other Mortgage Loan Features

Often a lender will allow you a few days after your monthly payment is due before you are considered late. This is called a grace period. Once the grace period expires, you will probably be charged a late fee. The amount of the late fee is set forth in your loan documents.

If your loan continues unpaid for thirty days or more, the lender will consider you delinquent, begin collection activities, and report you as delinquent to the credit bureaus.

Table 5-14: Grace Period

Variations	Pros	Cons
The greater the number of days the better. Ten and fifteen days are both common grace periods.	Gives you a little "wiggle room" for bumps in cash flow.	Wiggle room sometimes contributes to forgetfulness.

Table 5-15: Late Fees

Variations	Pros	Cons
5 percent of late payment is most common. 10 percent or more of late payment is very unfavorable.	Existence of penalty helps keep you focused.	Can be quite expensive if you are late.

Although it is not as common with mortgage loans as with consumer loans, some mortgage loans allow your interest rate to be substantially increased if you are late making a payment. You need to be aware of the increased interest rate you will incur if you do not make your payments on time.

Table 5-16: Penalty Interest Rate If You Are Late Making Payments

Variations	Pros	Cons
Common for unsecured loans (e.g., credit cards), less common for mortgage loans.	There are no pros.	If you become late, penalty interest rates will make it nearly impossible for you to catch up.

5-3-3 Matching the Proper Loan Type to Your Situation and Needs

After interlocking his fingers, Mike stretches his arms in front of him. He then glances at his watch.

"Are you two getting tired?" he asks Jack and Eva. "After all, you have to get up for work—and I don't!" He smiles at the young couple.

Jack looks at Eva who smiles to let him know she was okay. "Thanks for the reminder, Dad, but we are okay. We don't get a lot of time with you, so this mortgage class you're giving us is very rewarding."

"Okay then, in order to determine which loan option is best for you, you need to answer a few basic questions." He began to read from a list:

1. "Will you be staying in the loan for many years?

2. Do you expect mortgage interest rates to increase or decrease in the coming years?

3. Will a lower starting interest rate allow you to buy a better-suited home for you?

4. What is the risk versus benefit of each loan type for your situation?"

Setting the list down, Mike says, "Once you have answered these questions, the type of loan you choose will become clearer. If in doubt, it is probably better to go with a fixed rate, more conventional type of loan. That way, you will know what your payment will always be and can plan and budget for it."

5-4 Other Important Loan Vocabulary

Although it is not essential for you to know the specialized vocabulary of the mortgage industry beyond that pertaining to your loan, there are a few terms that you may hear, of which you should be aware.

5-4-1 Government Agencies and Government-Sponsored Entities

The government, regulators, and many government agencies and government-sponsored entities are active participants in the mortgage market. Many create and enforce rules, while others actually buy loans from lenders and place them into investment structures called mortgage-backed securities (MBS). When loans are placed in MBS structures, they are said to be securitized.

You may be aware of two government-sponsored entities that purchase the majority of the loans created and sold in this country. They are the Federal National Mortgage Association, often referred to as Fannie Mae, and the Federal Home Loan Mortgage Corporation, known as Freddie Mac. The loans they buy are generally securitized and the MBS are sold to institutional investors.

One direct governmental agency also buys and securitizes loans. It is the Government National Mortgage Association, referred to a Ginnie Mae. The loans it buys and securitizes are either insured by the Federal Housing Administration (FHA) or guaranteed by the U.S. Department of Veterans Affairs (VA).

Collectively, Fannie Mae, Freddie Mac, and Ginnie Mae are referred to by mortgage market participants as the "Agencies." Their activities very much dictate the types and quantities of loans originated in the United States.

5-4-2 Terms Used to Categorize Loans

Conventional (conforming or nonconforming)

A conventional mortgage loan is not insured by the federal government. This loan may be either adjustable or a fixed rate, conforming or nonconforming (see definitions below). This loan is ideal for those borrowers who have good credit scores and can afford a minimum down payment of 5 percent.

Conforming

This is a loan that meets guidelines set down by Freddie Mac or Fannie Mae. There is a limit as to the size a conforming loan can be; at the time of this writing the limit is $417,000. In more expensive areas of the country the conforming limits may be higher. Your lender will know the limits.

Nonconforming

These loans are offered to those who do not qualify for a conforming loan. They usually have higher interest rates, higher fees upfront, and insurance requirements. There are a few reasons that a buyer may have to go with a nonconforming loan such as recent bankruptcy, total debt, credit history, credit score, or documentation problems.

Jumbo

A jumbo loan is a loan that is over the conforming loan limit. Generally there are stricter underwriting criteria to qualifying for a jumbo loan. You may need a more established credit history or to put more money down on the property to qualify.

FHA or Federal Housing Administration Loans

An FHA insured loan is the most popular amongst first time home buyers due to the low down payment requirement of as little as 3.5 percent of the purchase price of the property. The other benefit of an FHA loan is relatively low closing costs.

The FHA is not a mortgage institution; rather it insures loans approved by private lenders. The downside to an FHA loan is you have to pay a small insurance premium in order for the FHA to provide this insurance protection. An amount is added to each of your mortgage loan payments to cover this insurance.

VA Loans

A VA guaranteed mortgage loan is available only to ex-servicemen and women as well as those on active duty. VA loans have no down payment requirement. The lender is guaranteed against loss, up to limits, by the U.S. Department of Veterans Affairs. As with an FHA loan, a charge will be added to each of your monthly payments to cover the cost of the guarantee.

Chapter 5

Part 3

Applying for a Mortgage Loan to Finance the Purchase of a Specific Property

5-5 Apply for the Loan

You have made it through Chapter 8 and have submitted an offer for a home and, after a little haggling, it has been accepted. In that offer is a financing contingency. You have a limited number of days to be approved for your loan or your contract lapses, the deal is off, and you potentially lose your opportunity to buy the home. Time is wasting, so you need to start working on getting your mortgage loan.

5-5-1 Obtain a Loan Estimate (LE) from at Least Three Lenders

The CFPB (Consumer Financial Protection Bureau) mandated that any loan application submitted on or after October 3, 2015, be subject to new TILA-RESPA Integrated Disclosure (TRID) rules. One of those rules requires lenders to provide you with a disclosure document called a Loan Estimate, or LE, spelling out costs and terms of the loan for which you may be applying. A LE is a great tool to help you shop around to find the best deal on your mortgage.

You should obtain a LE from at least three lenders and compare them to find the loan that is best for your circumstances. Remember, you are in control of the process and can choose the best loan for you. The design of the LE form makes it easier to determine which lender is making the best offer.

A Loan Estimate (LE) is a great tool to help you shop around to find the best deal on your mortgage.

Requesting a Loan Estimate from multiple lenders is easy. You only have to provide the six key pieces of information:

1. Your name;

2. Your income;

3. Your Social Security number (so the lender can pull a credit report);

4. The property address;

5. An estimate of the value of the property;

6. The loan amount you want to borrow.

You are not required to provide additional financial documents in order to get a Loan Estimate, but you may want to share what you have with the lender. The more information the lender has, the more accurate your Loan Estimate will be.

The CFPB provides resources to assist you with comparing Loan Estimates. Go to ConsumerFinance.gov/know-before-you-owe for these additional resources.

5-5-2 Complete the Application

Once you have selected a lender, you will need to fill out an application. Most lenders require you to complete a document called the Uniform Residential Loan Application. Appendix B contains images of the five pages contained in this application. A full size version is on the companion website.

The sections of the application are summarized as follows:

I.   Type of Mortgage and Terms of Loan;

II.   Property Information and Purpose of Loan;

III.   Borrower Information;

IV.   Employment Information;

V.   Monthly Income and Combined Housing Expense Information;

VI.   Assets and Liabilities;

VII. Details of Transaction;

VIII. Declarations;

IX.   Acknowledgement and Agreement;

X.   Information for Government Monitoring Process.

You should review the application template in detail before working with the lender to complete it.

5-5-3 Do Not Facilitate or Become a Victim of Fraud or Identity Theft

"Be thorough and complete when filling out your application," Mike tells Jack and Eva.

The three had decided to meet at a local restaurant after a late evening at work for the young couple.

Mike sips his after-dinner coffee, then continues. "If you are not, you will have to take time later to correct or explain errors, delaying an already lengthy process. Represent your situation as accurately as you can. Doing otherwise may lead to significant problems down the road." He reaches into his briefcase, pulls out a sample application, and turns it towards Jack and Eva.

"Be sure not to leave major sections blank based on the understanding that the mortgage broker or others will fill in the information later." Jack and Eva nod. "And do not, I repeat, do not sign the application until it is filled in completely. Doing so leaves your application open to mortgage fraud, a very serious and unfortunately not infrequent crime in this country."

"I was discussing mortgage fraud and identity theft with a coworker yesterday," says Eva. "As I thought about Jack's and my pending mortgage application, I realized that we needed to keep strict control of the application and all the documents that go with it. They contain key data that can be used by identity thieves."

"That's wise, Eva. Also, do not email images of the application or forms unless you have established a secure email link with the recipient and have encrypted the data. Do not let anyone else email your forms or documents over open email in an unencrypted format either. If you cannot establish a secure link and encrypt the data, only fax or personally deliver copies of all the forms and documents to your mortgage broker or lender. Make sure they follow the same protocols."

> **Do not email images of the application or forms unless you have established a secure email link with the recipient and have encrypted the data.**

"Do not in any way neglect or overlook the security of your forms and documents. If your identity is stolen, your credit could be ruined, and it will take you a very long time and a lot of expense to recover it. Your home buying plans will suffer a major set-back."

Mike, Jack, and Eva sit back in their chairs for a few moments as they digest the reality of what they've just discussed.

"Thanks for the somber advice, Dad. We really appreciate it," says Jack. "So what documents do we need as we begin to prepare our application?"

Mike reaches into his briefcase and pulled out another sheet of paper. "I had anticipated your questions, so here is a list of documents."

5-5-4 Assemble the Documents You Need

Here is a list of documents you will need, the same list that Mike gave our young couple:

W-2s from past two years of employment, unless you are self-employed;

Recent paystubs (usually for the last two pay periods);

Last two years' tax returns;

A current list of debts (e.g., loans, child support payments), along with your minimum required monthly payments;

If applicable, a letter describing any of your down payment money coming from a gift rather than your savings;

Business license if self-employed and statements of past two years of income;

Proof of rental payment history, preferably twelve months;

Bank statements;

Letters of explanation—if you have had derogatory marks against your credit, a letter of explanation may be required;

Permission to obtain tax returns – Form 4506:

o   This form allows lenders to obtain copies of your prior year tax returns;

o   Many lenders will ask you to sign this form in blank; do not do so; at a minimum, fill in the dates of prior year returns that they may request;

o   See an example of Form 4506 in Exhibit 5-5.

Exhibit 5-5: Form 4506 – Request for Copy of Tax Return

Form **4506**	**Request for Copy of Tax Return**	
(Rev. September 2013)		OMB No. 1545-0429
Department of the Treasury Internal Revenue Service	▶ **Request may be rejected if the form is incomplete or illegible.**	

Tip. You may be able to get your tax return or return information from other sources. If you had your tax return completed by a paid preparer, they should be able to provide you a copy of the return. The IRS can provide a **Tax Return Transcript** for many returns free of charge. The transcript provides most of the line entries from the original tax return and usually contains the information that a third party (such as a mortgage company) requires. See **Form 4506-T, Request for Transcript of Tax Return,** or you can quickly request transcripts by using our automated self-help service tools. Please visit us at IRS.gov and click on "Order a Return or Account Transcript" or call 1-800-908-9946.

1a Name shown on tax return. If a joint return, enter the name shown first.	1b First social security number on tax return, individual taxpayer identification number, or employer identification number (see instructions)
2a If a joint return, enter spouse's name shown on tax return.	2b Second social security number or individual taxpayer identification number if joint tax return

3 Current name, address (including apt., room, or suite no.), city, state, and ZIP code (see instructions)

4 Previous address shown on the last return filed if different from line 3 (see instructions)

5 If the tax return is to be mailed to a third party (such as a mortgage company), enter the third party's name, address, and telephone number.

Caution. *If the tax return is being mailed to a third party, ensure that you have filled in lines 6 and 7 before signing. Sign and date the form once you have filled in these lines. Completing these steps helps to protect your privacy. Once the IRS discloses your tax return to the third party listed on line 5, the IRS has no control over what the third party does with the information. If you would like to limit the third party's authority to disclose your return information, you can specify this limitation in your written agreement with the third party.*

6 **Tax return requested.** Form 1040, 1120, 941, etc. and all attachments as originally submitted to the IRS, including Form(s) W-2, schedules, or amended returns. Copies of Forms 1040, 1040A, and 1040EZ are generally available for 7 years from filing before they are destroyed by law. Other returns may be available for a longer period of time. Enter only one return number. If you need more than one type of return, you must complete another Form 4506. ▶

    Note. *If the copies must be certified for court or administrative proceedings, check here* . . . . ▢

7 **Year or period requested.** Enter the ending date of the year or period, using the mm/dd/yyyy format. If you are requesting more than eight years or periods, you must attach another Form 4506.

8	Fee. There is a $50 fee for each return requested. **Full payment must be included with your request or it will be rejected. Make your check or money order payable to "United States Treasury." Enter your SSN, ITIN, or EIN and "Form 4506 request" on your check or money order.**		
a	Cost for each return	$	50.00
b	Number of returns requested on line 7		
c	Total cost. Multiply line 8a by line 8b	$	
9	If we cannot find the tax return, we will refund the fee. If the refund should go to the third party listed on line 5, check here . . . . . ▢		

Caution. Do not sign this form unless all applicable lines have been completed.

Signature of taxpayer(s). I declare that I am either the taxpayer whose name is shown on line 1a or 2a, or a person authorized to obtain the tax return requested. If the request applies to a joint return, at least one spouse must sign. If signed by a corporate officer, partner, guardian, tax matters partner, executor, receiver, administrator, trustee, or party other than the taxpayer, I certify that I have the authority to execute Form 4506 on behalf of the taxpayer. **Note.** *For tax returns being sent to a third party, this form must be received within 120 days of the signature date.*

Phone number of taxpayer on line 1a or 2a

Sign Here	▶ Signature (see instructions)	Date
	▶ Title (if line 1a above is a corporation, partnership, estate, or trust)	
	▶ Spouse's signature	Date

For Privacy Act and Paperwork Reduction Act Notice, see page 2.   Cat. No. 41721E   Form **4506** (Rev. 9-2013)

-5-5 Some Lenders Require an Application Fee

Many lenders require you to pay a non-refundable loan application fee. Mike tells Jack and Eva that some lenders will apply this fee to your closing costs, while others will not. This fee may range from $150 to $600 or more.

> **You may have to pay a separate fee for a professional appraisal of the home value as well.**

Mike tells them that the purpose of an application fee is to reimburse the lender for some of the costs of reviewing your application. The lender incurs these costs regardless of what eventually happens with your loan. A fee helps to discourage you from submitting an application if you are not serious. It also discourages you from submitting multiple applications simultaneously to other lenders.

You may have to pay a separate fee for a professional appraisal of the home value as well. Depending on the type of property and the market, this fee could range from $175 to $500.

5-5-6 Be Proactive

A home loan can take one to two months (or more) for approval, so get a jump on it as soon as possible. Recent changes in consumer lending laws have added to this timeframe.

Mortgage rates change daily, and sometimes during the day. Once you have completed the application process to a certain extent, your lender may be able to "lock in" a rate. This will protect you for a designated timeframe against an increase in your rate due to market changes.

Rate locks are discussed in greater detail later in this chapter.

5-5-7 Respond to All Inquiries

Do not procrastinate responding to requests for information; it also could cause you to lose your home if the time limit on your financing contingency runs out (more on this later). Sometimes you may need to do some digging for a long-lost document, write a letter of explanation, or obtain copies of statements from your bank or employer. Whatever comes up, complete it right away. A pinch of sacrifice can make things go much smoother in the long run.

5-5-8 Read the Loan Estimate (LE) Disclosure Document the Lender Sends You

"It's getting late for you two and I know you've had a long day," Mike says to Jack and Eva. They both nod, and Jack glances at his watch.

"Yes, morning comes early, that's for sure," Jack says.

"If you can just bear with me for a few more minutes, there are some important things I'd like to share with you." The young couple nods. "Great. I'll send you this info in summary form to your email addresses."

"You will receive an updated LE when you submit your full application. It is a legally required disclosure document that must be sent to you within three days of submitting your loan application. It contains vital information about the costs and terms of the loan being offered to you. Make sure you understand all costs and terms disclosed. Let your attorney review it. Remember, your attorney is the only party in your home buying transaction who is completely obligated to look out for your best interests, including helping explain any covenants that may apply to your home."

An example of the LE is on the companion website at FindingHomeBook.com, as well as the Consumer Financial Protection Bureau's website at ConsumerFinance.gov, and in Appendix C.

-6 Additional Documents Obtained by Third Parties

Among the dozens of documents that are required to complete a real estate transaction, the following paragraphs in this section contain a list of those provided by third parties that your lender will order and for which you will probably be charged. The lender uses these documents to verify that you did not somehow forget to tell them you changed jobs or that you just bought a new car, for example. They also use this information to make sure the property has no other unexpected liens or owners, verify the property's value, and make sure it is insured. Basically, by ordering these documents, they are dotting every "i" and crossing every "t" in order to make sure that the money they are lending for your home has a high probability of being paid back.

5-6-1 Credit Report

As mentioned earlier, the credit report is a detailed report of each applicant's credit history that is prepared by a credit bureau and used by a lender to determine a loan applicant's creditworthiness. See Chapter 3 for details.

Your credit history must demonstrate that you are willing to repay the loan for which you are applying. The lender will evaluate the credit history for each applicant who will be party to the note, so if you are applying jointly with a spouse, partner, or other party, both of you will have your creditworthiness evaluated.

The lender assesses each applicant's overall credit management skills, including repayment patterns, credit utilization, level of experience using credit, and the existence of delinquent credit accounts, charge-off judgments, and other aspects of credit history.

Each applicant's credit record does not have to be perfect to be eligible for a loan. But each credit score can affect the loan amount for which you will qualify and the

> **Each applicant's credit record does not have to be perfect to be eligible for a loan.**

interest rate of your mortgage. Isolated incidences of credit mishaps such as late payments, etc. may need to be explained in a letter and supported with documentation. A few instances of credit problems may be acceptable, if the lender determines that each applicant's overall credit record demonstrates willingness to repay their obligations.

Applicants with weak credit scores may try to obtain a co-signer on their loan. For instance, a parent with a high credit score may co-sign on a loan for a son or daughter. By co-signing, the parent is effectively putting their credit standing on the line, saying if the borrowing child does not pay, the parent will. If neither party pays, the credit of both will be damaged. For this reason, you should be very cautious about ever co-signing on someone else's loan.

5-6-2 Home Appraisal

A home appraisal is an estimate of the market value of a home by a professional appraiser. In most cases, an appraisal is done for a bank on the home serving as collateral for a loan being approved the home buyer. The home appraisal is a detailed report that looks at items such as the condition of the home, the neighborhood, the price at which similar nearby homes are selling, and how quickly similar homes sell. This is called a sales comparison approach to value.

> **Important Note:** An appraisal is not a home inspection. Appraisers only look for major concerns; they do not examine the home's full condition, like examination of the roof, appliances, mechanical systems and structural issues. For this reason, you also need to obtain a home inspection before purchasing the home!

The appraiser also provides a cost/replacement opinion of value. Under this approach the appraiser considers what it would cost to replace the home if destroyed. This is more commonly used for new homes lacking in sales price comparisons to similar homes.

6-3 Preliminary Title Report

As soon as a purchase agreement is signed, the buyer and lender want to make sure the seller actually owns the property, that no other parties have claim to the property, and that no other parties are entitled to use a portion of the property for access to another property. They also want to know who has monetary claims against the property. All of this information is compiled in a preliminary title report.

The preliminary title report is compiled by either a title insurance company or an attorney. Information in the report comes from a search of government records, usually at a county recorder's office.

The preliminary title report contains the property's legal description—the literal description of where the property is located and the boundaries of the property in relation to the nearby streets and intersections or landmarks. It also shows in what legal form the title is held (vesting) and details regarding anything that is recorded against the property such as various liens, encroachments, easements,[11] and other items.[12]

Here's an example of a legal description from a preliminary title report of a property:

> *"Beginning at a point on the Westerly line of Second Avenue, distant thereon 250 feet Southerly from the Southerly line of First Street; running thence Southerly along the Westerly line of Second Avenue 25 feet; thence at a right angle Westerly 120 feet,"* and so on.

Legalese? Absolutely. But it is precise, and necessary.

---

11   If there's an easement recorded against the property and another owner has access to the property via the easement, it will be recorded against the title report. This stays with the report until both parties agree to remove it.

12   In the case of a condo or planned urban development ("PUD"), there are Covenants, Conditions, and Restrictions (CC&Rs), which are recorded against the property. Any new buyer is buying the condo subject to the rules and regulations documented in the CC&Rs. This is why it is important for potential buyers to pull these from the report and review them. Once you are the owner, you are subject to those rules.

Property taxes always show up as the primary "lien" on a preliminary title report. A property cannot be transferred to a new owner when any outstanding property taxes are due to the city, county, or town. As the top lien, they will indicate whether taxes are due or paid in full. Taxes must be settled before any debt holder gets paid.

Mortgage liens are generally listed directly below property taxes and they are always ordered first, second, and third. The largest lien holder generally takes first position, though there are certain conditions where a secondary lien holder will be in first position. When a sale closes, the liens must be paid in the order that they appear on the title report.

This list is in no way exclusive. There are a variety of other things that less frequently could show up on a preliminary title report outside of items discussed so far. These include items such as restrictions, historic oversights, and planning requirements.

If the home is located in a historic district and therefore subject to the rules and restrictions of that district, it will show up on the title. In this case, if there are restrictions about changing the facade of a house, or requirements that facade alterations comply with a local historical oversight committee led by the local planning department, a potential buyer needs to know this.

As a potential buyer, you and/or your real estate agent or attorney should scrutinize the preliminary title report. You want the title to be delivered as clean as possible. If the property is subject to special items, or there are issues on the title that would affect your homeownership, you need to know and understand them thoroughly before you close.

Just before closing, the preliminary title report should be updated to make sure that no other items have been added as claims against the property. This final report will serve as the basis for title insurance, which is discussed in a later section.

5-4 Verification of Income (VOI)

Your lender will already have collected from you paystubs and W-2 forms identifying you as an employee and showing the amount earned for the period of time covered by employment. To obtain another verification, the lender may also get a signed and dated form or letter from your employer specifying the amount earned per pay period and the length of each pay period. They may also do this by phone, getting a verbal statement, likely from your company's payroll or human resources department representative, specifying the amount to be earned per pay period.

5-6-5 Verification of Employment (VOE)

Most lenders use both written and verbal VOEs. They require a complete VOE form declaring all positions held for the last two years of employment history. This is to verify employment history, determine the borrower's job stability, and cross-reference income history with that stated on the loan application. Once a lender receives the initial loan application, a written Verification of Employment (Form 1005) is sent to all current and previous employers within the last two years provided on the application. This form is completed by an authorized representative of the employer and includes dates of employment, positions held, and a breakdown of compensation received. The information is compared to both the loan application and the other income documentation, such as W-2s and paystubs, to verify the information is accurate.

Once the borrowers have signed their mortgage documents, an updated verbal Verification of Employment may be conducted with all current employers prior to funding the loan. This is to ensure that the borrower did not stop working since the application was submitted, which would have an impact on the terms on the loan.

Self-employed borrower guidelines are different as a VOE is not completed by the loan applicant. Self-employed borrowers are usually asked to provide either a current business license and/or a letter from their Certified Public Accountant (CPA) indicating that the CPA, as the borrower's tax preparer, has firsthand knowledge of their previous and continued employment.

5-6-6 Verification of Rental Payments (VOR)

This verification form is used to confirm that the buyer has paid their rent on time for the last twelve to twenty-four months. Typically, the form is mailed to the landlord to fill out the section under "Rental Account." This tells how long the borrower has been renting, what the monthly rental payment was, and if the borrower has any late rent payments. Your lender may instead accept twelve to twenty-four months of canceled checks showing you have paid rent on time.

5-6-7 Insurance Certification – (A Binder from Insurance Company)

Your mortgage lender will require that you purchase homeowner's insurance for your new home and pay the first year's premium in full. You will need to obtain this insurance prior to closing and provide the lender with an insurance binder naming your lender as a secondarily insured party. The insurance binder is a legal agreement issued by either an agent or an insurer to provide temporary evidence of insurance until a policy can be issued. The binder will contain definite time limits and clearly designate the name of the insurer with which the risk is bound.

5-6-8 Verification of Deposit (VOD)

In addition to copies of your bank statements, your lender may require a Verification of Deposit. This is a document prepared by your bank or credit union stating that you have a certain amount of funds on deposit in the bank, such as in a checking or savings account. Obtaining this verification may require making a visit or phone call to the bank to request the letter. The bank or credit union may send the verification directly to the lender.

5-7 Lock Your Rate

⬦⬦⬦⬦⬦

"Wow, that's a lot of information," Jack says.

"Yes, you're amazing, Dad," Eva adds.

Mike chuckles. "Thanks, Eva. With age comes experience." He reaches for his briefcase and closes the latches. "Here's the last thing I'd like to tell you for tonight. When you are approved for a loan, the lender may give you the ability to lock in the rate on your loan at levels prevailing in the market at the time. Market interest rates are constantly changing and will likely change between your application date and the date you close. If the rates go up, you may end up having to pay a higher monthly payment than you anticipated or for which you budgeted."

"Under a so-called rate lock, the creditor and borrower are committed to those terms, regardless of what happens between the rate lock date and the closing date. The creditor provides a written statement verifying that the price and other terms of a loan have been locked. If you lock through a mortgage broker, ask to see the lock commitment letter."

"A variation of a rate lock is called a 'float-down' whereby the rates and points cannot rise from their initial levels, but they can decline if market rates decline. In either case, the protection only runs for a specified lock period. If the loan is not closed within that period, the protection expires and the borrower will either have to accept the terms quoted by the creditor on new loans at that time, or start the shopping process anew."

⬦⬦⬦⬦⬦

Mike explains that the number of days for which a lock or float-down holds is called the lock period. The creditor may charge you for the rate lock. The longer the rate lock period, the higher the price the creditor may charge you.

Under the TRID rules, your creditor will need to issue a revised Loan Estimate (LE) if your rate is locked after the initial LE was provided. If the interest rate, points, or lender credits for the mortgage loan differ from those on the original LE, the creditor is required to provide you with a revised Loan Estimate no later than three business days after the date the interest rate is locked. This may have an impact on the time it takes you to close.

Chapter 6

Starting Your Home Search – Finding the Right Location

"You may not get everything you want, but with a little planning and effort, you can get what you need."
—Michael Trickey

6-1 Where Should You Buy Your Home?

The logical first step before buying a home is figuring out where that home is going to be located. This may seem obvious, but my point is that, in your home search, you are going to have location options, and the choices you make regarding those options are going to involve trade-offs. You can greatly reduce the time of your search and improve your results if you set priorities up front and identify areas that best address those priorities. Then you can restrict your search to homes located in just those areas.

You probably learned about Robert Maslow's Hierarchy of Needs Pyramid in school. Maslow identified five levels of human needs as follows:

Self-Actualization
(Creativity, Problem Solving,
Authenticity, Spontaneity)
Esteem
(Self-Esteem, Confidence, Achievement)
Social needs
(Friendship, Family)
Safety and Security
Physiological needs (survival)
(Air, Shelter, Water, Food, Sleep, Sex)

He theorized that humans focus on getting lower level needs satisfied before they worry about higher level needs. It is difficult to disagree with Maslow. If you are starving and living on the street, self-actualization is probably not on your mind; getting some food and finding a safe place to sleep are likely higher priorities.

A similar hierarchy of needs and wants will be present in your home buying decisions, starting with the locations you consider, and then in your choice of homes within that location. I call it the Location Choice Hierarchy (LCH). It is presented in Table 6-1. The LCH is not a simple pyramid, because it has too many levels and interactions (based on individual priorities) to neatly present in a pyramid format.[13] But you will see after looking at it for a minute that it is pretty easy to understand.

The horizontal geographic level steps of the hierarchy are ever-more-precise areas of land, starting at the "State" level and ending at the "Specific Home" level. Within every geographic level, trade-offs

---

13   It is more of a parallelogram or perhaps a trapezoid tilted over and balanced on one of its points.

among your individual "Priorities" (vertical axis) will dictate choice of locations.

For instance, at the state level, you may want to live in Southern California for the weather and ocean scenery, but your family and current job are in Utah, and your need for income and desire to be close to your family motivate your choice to live in Utah.

Within Utah you may want to live in Park City because of the annual Sundance Film Festival and the great ski resorts there, but your job may be on the southwestern side of Salt Lake City (West Valley) and the daily commute from Park City would not be justified by the short-lived film festival each January and the few times each winter when you have time to ski.

And within Salt Lake City and southwestern suburbs you will continue to make choices and trade-offs based on such factors as where the TRAX light rail train runs and stops, the location of varying types of stores and entertainment, the quality of school districts, and so forth.

Your location choice starts at a macro level (state, area of state, county), drills down a local level (city, portion of city, neighborhood, section of neighborhood), and eventually leads to a specific home. Big issues drive choices of macro locations, more rudimentary day-to-day issues drive choices of local location, and individual preferences drive choices of specific homes. Each lower geographic level of choice is dependent on the choice you made at the larger geographic level. All choices made at each geographic level reflect your individual needs, wants, priorities, and budget.

Table 6-1: Location Choice Hierarchy (LCH)

Location Choice Hierarchy (LCH)							
		Increasingly Specific Location ----------->----------->--------->					
	Factor	**State**	**Area within State**	**Cities within Areas**	**Sections of City**	**Neighbor-hoods within City Sections**	**Blocks within Neighbor-hoods**	**Specific Home**
Factors Influencing Decisions / Motivating Priorities	Specific features of home / yard							x
	Overall affordability of home (cost, utilities, commuting, property taxes, HOA, Other)							x
	Quality of neighborhood					x	x	
	Neighborhood design					x	x	
	Convenience to grade schools					x	x	
	Quality of the school district				x	x	x	
	Convenience to entertainment			x	x	x	x	
	Convenience to shopping			x	x	x	x	
	Convenience to leisure activities			x	x	x	x	
	Convenience to jobs:							
	Commuting access		x	x	x	x	x	
	Maximum commuting time		x	x	x	x	x	
	Access to airport for business		x	x	x	x	x	
	Temporary situation (college, military)	x	x	x	x	x	x	
	Closeness to family & friends	x	x	x	x	x	x	
	Closeness to medical care	x	x	x	x	x	x	
	Closeness to special needs services	x	x	x	x	x	x	
	Macro-economic:							
	Income taxes	x		x				
	Sales taxes	x	x	x				
	Cost of living	x	x	x	x	x		
	Existence of job	x	x	x	x			
	Topography-specific leisure activities and scenery	x	x	x	x			
	Climate and weather	x	x	x				
	Laws, government, customs, attitudes	x	x	x				

In this chapter, we will discuss the steps and resources available to help you zero in on geographic locations down to the city level. In the next chapter we will explore neighborhoods and individual houses.

To assist in this discussion, we will walk through a case study of the process with Jack and Eva, identifying priorities, pulling down maps and doing online research along the way. We will jump in and out of the case study as we move back and forth between Jack and Eva and you.

To start, we will examine in detail the components of the couple's Location Choice Hierarchy.

6-2 Deciding Where to Buy – Case Study

6-2-1 Setting Out Your Priorities

Your situation and priorities are as unique as you are. As we work through this case study below, download the respective blank templates from the companion website and fill them in to fit your own priorities.

Eva and Jack live in an apartment in the "Bucktown" neighborhood of Chicago. They just got married last year and are each about four years into their careers. They both grew up in Chicago and are rooted to the area by family and friends, and they enjoy the city life. However, Eva's job as a teacher is in the northwest suburb of Mount Prospect, and she seems to spend half her day driving. Although a commuter train runs to Mount Prospect, her school is not close to the station. Jack works in a building in the downtown Chicago "loop" area, just a five-minute walk from each of two main Chicago commuter train stations, Ogilvie Transportation Center (OTC) and Union Station. The couple has decided to move out of the Bucktown neighborhood to a home closer to Eva's job. They are strongly considering buying a home to gain more living space, a yard, and to start building equity.

6-2-1-1 Finding the Right State and Area of the State

The first part of constructing their LCH, picking the state and area of the state, is easy for Jack and Eva. It is shown in Downloadable Template 6-1.

Jobs, family, and friends are the couple's top priorities and have led the couple to just look in the Chicago area of Illinois. You may be in the same situation, or one of the other factors on the table may be driving your choice of state and area of state. If it is, you may need to do a lot of research to narrow down locations that match your needs.

Downloadable Template 6-1: Location Choice Hierarchy – State and Area of State

Lifestyle Attributes - State and Area of State	Motivating Priorities	Comments	Top Prospects
Temporary situation (college, military, etc.)	N/A		
Closeness to family & friends	High	Jack and Eva grew up in Chicago area: family and friends throughout area	Chicago area, IL
Closeness to medical care	Medium High	Hope to start family, need to be by decent hospital and doctors	
Closeness to special needs services	N/A		
Macroeconomic:			
Income taxes	Medium		
Sales taxes	Low		
Cost of living	Medium		
Existence of jobs	High	Jack works in Chicago loop, Eva works in suburban Mount Prospect	Chicago area, IL
Type / quality of jobs	High	Jack needs area with tech companies	
Topography-specific leisure activities and scenery	Medium	Like nearby lakes or ocean	
Climate and weather	Medium	Both like the change of seasons	
Laws, government, customs, attitudes, etc.			
Same sex marriage, partner rights	Low		
Racial mix and attitudes	Low		
Immigrant community, language, support	Low		
Other	N/A		

6-2-1-2 Finding the Right Counties and Cities

Next, Jack and Eva need to choose counties and cities. Although they already live in Chicago, they know very little about communities and suburbs further out from the downtown city center than they are right now.

They want to make sure they pick the right community in which to buy a home. So they start by examining their lifestyles and what is important to them. The list below covers many lifestyle areas. The list is long to get you thinking. You can download an editable template of this list and tailor the line items and travel times to fit your own lifestyle. You may want to move your most important categories to the top.

Downloadable Template 6-2: Location Choice Hierarchy – Counties and Cities

Lifestyle Attributes - County and City	Notes	Walking Time			Driving Time			Public Transit	
		< 5 min	5 - 15 min	15 - 30 min	< 15 min	15 - 30 min	30 - 60 min	15 - 45 min	45 - 65 min
1. Transportation access:									
a. Freeways & major roads					x				
b. Commuter rail, bus, Amtrak			x						
c. Airports						x			
2. Job:									
a. Primary work site			Jack			Eva			Jack
3. Family and friends:									
a. Parents, siblings, relatives	Parents					Eva	Jack		
b. Friends								x	x
4. Schools:									
a. College / community college						x		x	
b. High school, elementary, middle				x		x		x	
5. Dining:									
a. Casual	Thai		x			x			
b. Formal						x			x
c. Coffee shops			x		x				
d. Take-out (pizza, Chinese, etc.)			x		x				
6. Entertainment:									
a. Bars (sports, pool table, etc.)						Jack			
b. Dance clubs						x			
c. Cinema / theater / comedy							x		
d. Games (bowling, etc.)							x		
7. Outdoor sporting activities:									

Lifestyle Attributes - County and City	Notes	Walking Time			Driving Time			Public Transit	
		< 5 min	5 - 15 min	15 - 30 min	< 15 min	15 - 30 min	30 - 60 min	15 - 45 min	45 - 65 min
a. Running, walking, biking				x					
b. Hiking, climbing				x					
8. Community recreation facilities:									
a. Parks, sports courts and fields				x					
b. Golf courses						x			
c. Pool, gym						x			
9. Shopping nearby:									
a. Groceries, bakery, drugstore				x		x			
b. Clothing, shoes, accessories						x			
c. Eye glasses, medical supply						x			
d. Hardware, lumber						x			
e. Dry cleaners, hair, nails						x			
f. Financial services (banks, brokers, currency exchange, etc.)						x			
10. Services and resources:									
a. Government, courthouse						x			x
b. Doctors, dentists, veterinary						x			
c. Religious (churches, mosques, synagogues, temples, etc.)						x			
d. Cultural (art galleries, museums, orchestra, opera, etc.)						x			
e. Libraries				x					
12. Community attractions:									
a. Natural (beach, rivers, lakes, mountains, desert, etc.)						x			x

Lifestyle Attributes - County and City	Notes	Walking Time			Driving Time			Public Transit	
		< 5 min	5 - 15 min	15 - 30 min	< 15 min	15 - 30 min	30 - 60 min	15 - 45 min	45 - 65 min
b. Racetracks (horses, dogs, cars, etc.)									
c. Amusement parks / waterparks							x		
13. Other									

For Jack and Eva, commuting to jobs and closeness to families and friends are important factors, so they put them right at the top. The county and city in which they live should accommodate these needs and strong desires. As you go down the list you can see a picture of what is important to them and to what they want to be near.

Jack wants to be able to walk to a commuter train station and have no more than a sixty-five minute train ride to downtown Chicago. Eva wants no more than a thirty minute drive to her job in Mount Prospect. Both would also like to be able to take the train downtown to see friends or go to the beach, a dance club, or a sporting event, and they want that train ride to be less than sixty-five minutes.

Jack loves coffee, Thai food, and a good sports bar, so is looking for a community that has all three close enough to residential areas that he can walk to them. Eva wants to be within a thirty minute drive to her parents, and both want to be within thirty minutes to a veterinarian for their dog Oscar. And so on.

We will work with the couple to zero in on counties and cities shortly. But first we need to know more about their housing needs so they can be sure the cities they choose have that type of housing within their price range.

6-2-1-3 Identifying Housing Parameters to Aid in the City Search

Eva and Jack now give some thought to their neighborhood and housing needs and wants. They will examine neighborhoods and homes in greater detail in Chapter 7, but they start with a big picture here. First, they set out some neighborhood wishes.

Downloadable Template 6-3: Location Choice Hierarchy – Neighborhoods

Lifestyle Attributes – Neighborhoods	Choice	Comments
a. Single-family / multifamily / low or high rise	Single-family	
b. Gated / open	Either is fine	
c. Many kids or few kids	Many	Would like to start a family soon
d. Big yards / little yards / no yards	Big yard	For Oscar the Labradoodle, for entertaining, and later for kids
e. School districts / convenience of schools	TBD	Want good school districts
f. Club house	Possibly	
g. Sidewalks	Want sidewalks	For walking Oscar, jogging, and later walking kids to school

The couple has a preference for a single-family home with a yard. They would prefer to live where there are many families with children.

Next, Jack and Eva set out some of their housing needs and wants in a table format so they can clearly see what is important to them. The table is below. You can download a template and edit it to fit your needs and wants.

Downloadable Template 6-4: Housing Needs and Wants Inventory (NWI)

Description	Comment	Needs	Wants		
Housing Needs and Wants Inventory (NWI)					
			Strong	Medium	Weak
Home Type:					
Single-family detached	**Preferred**		Yes		
Condo / townhouse	**Either**			Townhouse	Condo
Twin home / duplex	**Probably not**				
Home Features:					
Number of stories	**2**			x	
Basement	**Yes**		x		
Room numbers / features:					
Bedrooms	**3**	x			
Bathrooms	**2 full baths**		x		
Bath in master bedroom			x		
Eat-in kitchen / dining room	**Both**			x	
Walk-in closet	**In master bedroom**			x	
Location of laundry area	**Not in basement**		x		
Fireplace					x
Game room / media room				x	
Floor plan	**Conducive to entertaining**			x	
Specifics:					
Specific town	**TBD**				
Specific neighborhood	**TBD**				
Specific School district	**TBD**				
Utilities / communications:					
Type of heat (oil, gas, etc.)	**Gas**		x		
City or well water	**City**		x		
Sewage or septic	**Sewage**		x		
Cable or satellite	**Cable**		x		
Outside features:					
Yard	**Prefer fenced**		x		
Deck or Patio	**Either**	x			
Garage- attached / detached	**Prefer attached**			x	

6-2-1-4 Putting All the LCH Parameters Together

Downloadable Template 6-5 on the next page summarizes some of Jack and Eva's most important location hierarchy parameters. Working from this summary of their needs and wants, they can zero in on the right city, neighborhood, and house.

Clearly, proximity to family and jobs is their priority when selecting the state and area within the state. After that, they need a place within one half-hour by car to Eva's job in suburban Mount Prospect. They only have one car and Jack works downtown in Chicago, so they need to be within walking distance of a commuter train line. At least at this stage in their search, commuting access to jobs dictates counties, cities, sections of cities, and neighborhoods. When the couple starts looking for homes available in their price range, they may have to change priorities and make trade-offs.

There is a template of this LCH summary on the companion website for you to download and complete. Take your time and go through the three tables you completed leading up to the summary.

This is your chance to rise above your everyday routine and make some real positive changes in your living situation.

Really do some soul-searching. Think in terms of your current situation and where you see yourself in three years, five years, and ten years. Are you content in your present locale or do you really want to live somewhere else? Are you making a decision to buy a home close to a job you really do not like? Maybe you need to reorder your priorities and live further from the job but closer to the lake or mountains or another amenity in your area. This is your chance to rise above your everyday routine and make some real positive changes in your living situation. Pull down a map of your area and study it. There could be hidden treasures nearby about which you did not previously know.

Downloadable Template 6-5: Housing Needs and Wants Summary

Locations to Consider	Needs and Wants	Reasons
Specific Home	**Want** house with basement and yard. **Need** 3 bedrooms, 2 baths. **Want** floor plan conducive to entertain friends. Would prefer two stories.	Need bedrooms and baths for growth of family. Like to entertain in our home.
Blocks within Neighborhoods	**Want** to be reasonable walking distance from train, park, grocery store, coffee shop, and restaurant(s). **Want** sidewalks.	Enjoy walking to these locations.
Neighborhoods within City Sections	**Want** to be in good school district, and to be near park.	Sidewalks and park for jogging and walking Oscar.
Sections of City	**Need** to live within walking distance of commuter train, want to live on Chicago side of Mount Prospect.	Eva cannot always drop Jack at train. Jack needs to be able to walk. Both enjoy going downtown to hang out with friends and like using train.
Cities within Counties	**Need** to live in a city along commuter train route. **Strongly want** the train ride downtown to be sixty minutes or less.	Only one car; Eva needs to drive it to work in suburbs where there is no public transport; Jack needs to take train.
Counties within Area	**Need** to live in either Lake or Cook county due to trains and proximity to Eva's job.	Eva's job is in Mount Prospect in Cook County. She needs to live within 30 driving minutes of work. Jack can take a train downtown; multiple train lines in Lake and Cook counties. Jack's office is three blocks from station.
Area within State	**Want** to stay in Chicago area for now.	Family and jobs in Chicago area.
State	**Want** to stay in Illinois for now.	Family and jobs in Illinois.

6-2-2 Maps

There are so many types of maps that can help you find the area right for you. Jack and Eva's prioritization of "commuting ease" will dictate some of the maps they access. For you, it might be maps of hiking trails, or comic book store locations, or small airports where you can store your Cessna. There is a map for seemingly anything your priorities encompass. Only your imagination and Internet access can hold you back.

Eva and Jack's search is in the Chicago area. It is a big metropolitan area, so their search includes city and suburbs. You can follow the same procedures in your city or area of search. The concepts are essentially the same everywhere, with some local twists you will find along the way.

Eva and Jack have only one car. The school where Eva teaches is in the Chicago northwest suburb of Mount Prospect and is not located near any public transportation. So Eva will need the car. Jack's office in downtown Chicago is only a five minute walk from the downtown Chicago commuter train station, so taking a commuter train is a great strategy for him. But he needs to be able to walk to a local train station from his new home as well, as Eva cannot always drive him.

So the first map Eva and Jack consult is the Chicago Metra commuter rail line map. If public transportation is important to you, commuter bus and rail maps like the one shown in Exhibit 6-1 on the next page will be essential to you.

Notice on the map, Eva marked an X at the location of her school in Mount Prospect and another at Jack's office in Chicago. Then she draws a circle around Mount Prospect representing her estimate of a thirty minute driving commute time, a "Need" indicated on their LCH summary. By drawing this circle, she identifies an initial selection of viable communities.

Exhibit 6-1 – Commuter Train Route Map

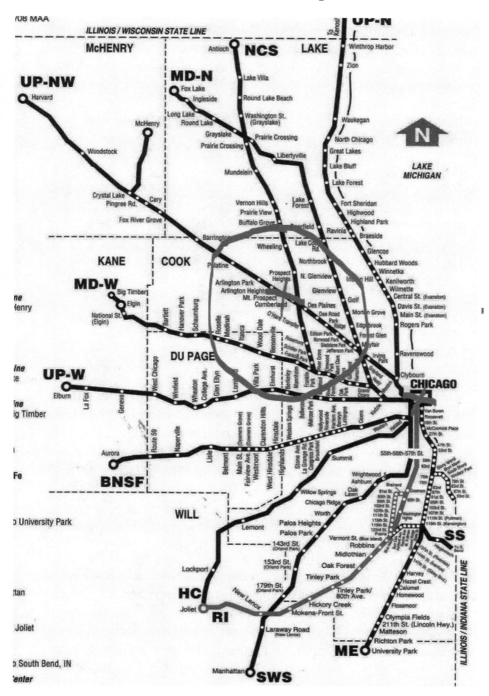

Jack notices that five separate commuter lines have service within the circle, so he creates a list of the communities along each of the lines that have commuter rail stations. That list is presented below. Jack researches and finds that the train ride from every stop listed going to downtown Chicago takes less than sixty-five minutes, a "Strong Want" on their LCH.

Exhibit 6-2 – Commuter Rail Stations Listing by Train Line

Chicago Commuter Rail Stations Within 30 Minute Drive Circle to Mt Prospect				
In Order of Increasing Time and Distance from Downtown Chicago Station				

UP-W	UP-NW	MD-N	MD-W	NC-S
Berkeley	Jefferson Park	Western	Western	Belmont Ave / Franklin Park
Elmhust	Gladstone Park	Healy	Hanson Park	Schiller Park
Villa Par	Norwood Park	Grayland	Galewood	Rosemont
	Edison Park	Mayfair	Mars	O'Hare
	Park Ridge	Florest Glen	Mont Clare	Prospect Heights
	Dee Road	Edgebrook	Elmwood Park	Wheeling
	Des Plaines	Morton Grove	River Grove	
	Cumberland	Golf	Franklin Park	
	Mount Prospect	Glenview	Manheim	
	Arlington Heights	N. Glenview	Bensenville	
	Arlington Park	Northbrook	Wood Dale	
	Palatine		Itasca	
			Medinah	
			Roselle	

Jack and Eva reason that they would prefer to live on the Chicago side of Mount Prospect as it would minimize Jack's commute time, allow Eva to commute "against" the rush hour traffic flowing into the city, and locate them closer to all the downtown Chicago and lakefront amenities, stores, restaurants, and night life they enjoy with their friends. The down side is that real estate is more expensive closer to the city, so they will likely have to accept less house or property for their $250,000 home price budget. Each train stop located on the Chicago side of Mount Prospect is shaded in gray.

Next, Eva does an Internet search for a highway map of Chicago. That map is shown on the next page. She marks a circled X on Mount Prospect. It is clear from this map that there are two Interstate Highways (I-294 and I-90) that run near Mount Prospect, plus three state highways, routes 12, 14, and 45. Eva visually overlays this map on the Metra map. Based on this road analysis, Jack and Eva decide to focus primarily on communities along the UP-NW (Union Pacific / Northwest) and NC-S (North Central Service) train lines identified on the Metra map. Eva notices that the UP-NW line runs parallel to state route 14 which runs right through downtown Mount Prospect, so she decides to give preference to communities along the UP-NW rail line.

Their list is thereby narrowed to Jefferson Park, Gladstone Park, Norwood Park, Edison Park, Park Ridge, Dee Road, Des Plaines, and Cumberland. Jack and Eva decide to add Mount Prospect itself as well since Eva knows it to be a nice community.

Exhibit 6-3 – Highway Map – Chicago Area

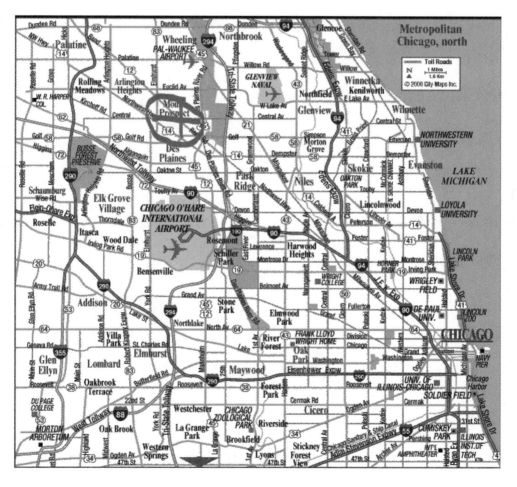

6-2-3 Online Search of Community Information

At first glance, it appears to Eva and Jack that not every train stop is actually a city. For instance, Dee Road sounds to them like a major road and not a town, and they can see on the map that Cumberland is also a road, not a city. So they first decide to research the nature of each train stop, using a combination of maps, Wikipedia.org, City-Data.com, and other community specific websites. They find that Wikpedia.org is a great source for getting both summary statistics and descriptive information.

Table 6-2 summarizes some of the initial information they find.

Table 6-2: Community Information for All Targeted Rail Stop Locations

Train Station Name	Jefferson Park	Gladstone Park	Norwood Park	Edison Park	Dee Road/Park Ridge	Des Plaines	Cumberland/ Mt Prospect
Community Area No.	11	11	10	09			
Community Area Name	Jefferson Park	Jefferson Park	Norwood Park	Edison Park			
County	Cook	Cook	Cook	Cook	Cook	Cook	Cook
City	Chicago	Chicago	Chicago	Chicago	Park Ridge		Mt Prospect
Township					Maine	Maine	Elk Grove, Wheeling
Neighborhoods	Jefferson Park	Gladstone Park	Norwood Park East	Edison Park			
	Gladstone Park		Norwood Park West	Norwood Park West			
	Norwood Park		Old Norwood Park				
			Oriole Park				
			Union Ridge				
			Big Oaks				
School Districts	Chicago Public Schools	Chicago Public Schools	Chicago Public Schools	Chicago Public Schools	Park Ridge-Niles School District 64	District 62 and District 59	Districts 57, 56, 59, 25, 23, 21
					Maine Township HS Ditrict 207	Maine Township HS Ditrict 207	Township HS District 214
Area:							
Total Size	2.35 Sq Mi		4.29 Sq Mi	1.17 sq mi	7.13 sq mi	14.42 sq mi	10.37 sq mi
Land					7.04 sq mi		10.34 sq mi
Water					0.04 sq mi		0.03 sq mi
Population - 2010							
Total		25,448	37,023	11,187	37,480	58,840	54,505
Density	11,000 / sq mi		8,600 / sq mi	9,600 / sq mi	5,286.3 / sq mi	4,087.1 / sq mi	5,310.5 / sq mi
Demographics - 2010							
White	68.67%		81.45%	88.40%	95.40%	77.30%	77.00%
Black	1.04%		0.44%	0.26%	0.02%	1.80%	2.40%
Native American				0.06%	0.06%	0.04%	
Hispanic	19.36%		12.00%	7.79%		17.20%	15.50%
Asian	8.87%		4.58%	2.40%	2.66%	11.40%	11.70%
Other	2.06%		1.52%	1.15%	0.97%	9.40%	2.10%
Zip Codes	Parts of 60630, 60646		Parts of 60631, 60646, 60656	Part of 60631	60068	60016, 60017, 60018, 60019	60056, 60057, 60058
Area Codes					847, 224	847, 224	847
Median Household Income	$ 60,592		$ 64,477	$ 77,678	$ 110,842	$ 65,806	$ 81,574
Per Capital Income							
Median Home Value						$ 250,300	
Website					www.parkridge.us	www.desplaines.org	
Train Station Name	Jefferson Park	Gladstone Park	Norwood Park	Edison Park	Dee Road/Park Ridge	Des Plaines	Cumberland/ Mt Prospect

From this simple search, Eva determines that four of the train stops are actually not towns, but instead are (or within) designated community areas in the city of Chicago. These are Jefferson Park, Gladstone Park (neighborhood within Jefferson Park), Norwood Park, and Edison Park. This means homes in those areas are part of Chicago, so online home searches will have to be done using a combination of the Chicago city and respective neighborhood name. She makes a note that each of these areas receives city of Chicago services and is part of the Chicago Public School system. To get a more accurate visual look at the borders of these communities within Chicago, she does an online search for Chicago neighborhood maps, and finds many, such as the one below.

Exhibit 6-4 Neighborhood Map of Chicago with Hand-Drawn Overlay of Train Route

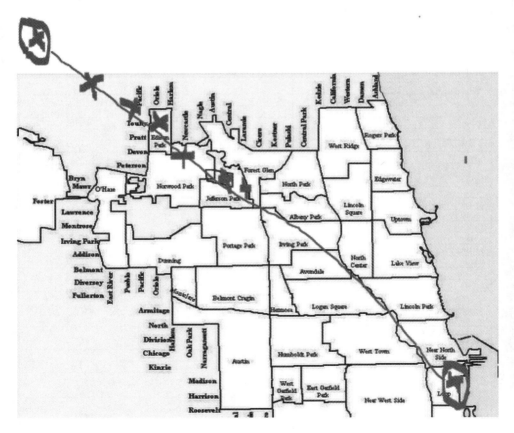

Eva marks each community in which the train stops between Mount Prospect and Chicago Loop on the community map. She draws a rectangle with an x to mark Gladstone Park within Jefferson Park, and draws a circle with an x to mark each end of the train line between Mount Prospect and the Chicago loop. Note the Chicago neighborhoods are outlined and labeled on the map and end with Edison Park. Beyond that lie the suburbs of Park Ridge, Des Plaines and Mount Prospect, which are not neighborhoods of Chicago, but separate suburban cities.

The Dee Road stop is just a second station in the city of Park Ridge, so she combines it into the Park Ridge column on the summary information sheet. Cumberland is a stop in southwestern corner of Mount Prospect in the O'Hare Airport neighborhood, so Eva combines it into Mount Prospect. Both Des Plaines and Mount Prospect are cities with multiple neighborhoods.

You can see that the search also revealed information on area size, population and density, demographics, median income, school districts, local government, zip codes, area codes, and other useful information. Jack and Eva will use this information later as they are narrowing their search.

If you do not live in a major metropolitan area, the nature of information in your initial area search may start out more focused on more condensed geographic levels, such as city areas and neighborhoods. Jack and Eva will drill down to that level of search later.

6-2-4 Online Home Search Sites - Initial Filters and Searches

It is too early to actually start looking at houses, but Jack and Eva need to make sure that homes within their pricing parameters that meet their configuration needs and wants exist in reasonable numbers in each of the target markets before spending time researching each one. Lack of qualifying homes in given markets may cause the couple to either eliminate a market or adjust their search parameters.

To do this, the couple turns to home search sites like Zillow.com, and they start doing filtered searches of houses. The filters they use for searching for homes in each of the remaining target communities are as follows:

Listing type:	All
Price range:	$200,000 - $250,000
Bedrooms:	3+
Home types:	Houses
Baths:	2+
Square feet:	Min 1,000
Lot size	Left blank
Year Built	Left blank
Days of search site	Left blank
Key words	Basement

To start, Eva and Jack focus first on Mount Prospect, Park Ridge, and Jefferson Park since they are the farthest, middle and closest respectively targeted train stop communities on the way to Chicago. Table 6-3 below summarizes the top few properties they find in each suburb.

Table 6-3 - For Sale Home Search Summary – Preliminary Targeted Communities

Community	Price	Home Type	Bed-rooms	Baths	Home Size (sq. ft.)	Price per sq. ft.	Lot Size (sq. ft.)	Base-ment	Year Built	Days on Search Site	Recent Price Change
Mount Prospect	$ 229,900	House	3	2	1,206	$191	8,838	Yes	1962	46	$(10,000)
Mount Prospect	$ 234,500	House	3	2	1,836	$128	7,200	Yes	1971	225	$(500)
Mount Prospect	$ 204,000	House - Foreclosure	5	2	1,128	$181	7,727	Yes	1955	437	$(5,000)
Mount Prospect	$ 209,900	House	3	2	1,040	$202	7,370	Yes	1944	484	$(10,000)
Park Ridge	$ 239,000	Townhouse	3	2	1,500	$159	3,773	Yes	1962	85	
Jefferson Park	$ 237,000	House	4	2	1,196	$198	4,660	Yes	1914	18	
Jefferson Park	$ 224,900	House - Foreclosure	3	2	1,132	$199	3,075	Yes	1957	22	
Jefferson Park	$ 244,900	House	3	2	1,000	$245	3,720	Yes	1947	101	$(4,100)
Jefferson Park	$ 229,000	House	4	2	1,408	$163	4,029	Yes	1911	108	$(20,900)
Jefferson Park	$ 249,000	House	3	2	1,650	$151	4,350	Yes	1918	117	
Jefferson Park	$ 235,000	House	3	2	1,103	$213	3,750	Yes	1921	224	$(5,000)
Jefferson Park	$ 248,000	House	3	2	1,760	$141	3,720	Yes	1949	332	

Without the need to ask, the home search site also shows homes in nearby communities that meet the search filters. Eva finds this helpful and makes notes listing the other communities in which qualifying homes are for sale. Happily, a lot of houses meeting the filter criteria are in Des Plaines, another community on their target list. Therefore, Eva adds Des Plaines to the initial search as well, and finds nine houses meeting the search filter criteria, and appends the following comparative information on their summary table.

Table 6-3 - For Sale Home Search Summary – Additional Homes in Des Plaines

Community	Price	Home Type	Bed-rooms	Baths	Home Size (sq ft)	Price per sq ft	Lot Size (sq ft)	Base-ment	Year Built	Days on Search Site	Recent Price Change
Des Plaines	$ 229,000	House	3	2	1,193	$192	6,255	Finished	1949	4	$ -
Des Plaines	$ 245,000	House	3	2	1,437	$170	6,250	Finished	1950	5	$ -
Des Plaines	$ 249,900	House	3	3	1,238	$202	7,682	Finished	1940	6	$ -
Des Plaines	$ 234,080	House - Foreclosure	3	2	1,388	$169	8,123	Finished	1964	29	$ -
Des Plaines	$ 239,000	House - Foreclosure	3	2	1,134	$211	6,534	Finished	1968	43	$ -
Des Plaines	$ 242,500	House	3	2	1,015	$239	6,599	Finished	1952	46	$(2,500)
Des Plaines	$ 239,900	House	3	3	1,900	$126	6,040	Finished	1914	58	$(5,000)
Des Plaines	$ 249,000	House	4	2	1,236	$201	6,250	Yes	1954	78	$(10,000)
Des Plaines	$ 239,900	House	3	2	1,642	$146	11,761	Yes	1940	106	$(10,000)

Based on their initial search, Jack and Eva are pleased to find several single-family houses meeting their initial search criteria falling within their price range. For Park Ridge, they have to add townhouses and condos to their filters to produce any matches. Given that the median income in Park Ridge is significantly higher than the other committees (see Wikipedia search information in Table 6-2), it is reasonable to expect that average home prices are higher in Park Ridge and fewer will be for sale in their price range. Jack and Eva realize that based on their current savings, income and expenses, Park Ridge may be a stretch community for them to be able to afford, but they will verify this as they go along.

Reviewing their summary lists, Eva and Jack note a few things right away. For instance, the closer to the city, the smaller the lot sizes and the older the homes. You will likely find similar patterns jumping out at you in your area when you do this type of analysis.

They then use the search site's mapping tool to show the location (red dots) of each property that meets their initial filter criteria. The maps are shown on the next page. Jack and Eva repeat this process for each community and build a list of good prospects in each city.

Mount Prospect – Four Homes

Jefferson Park – Seven Homes

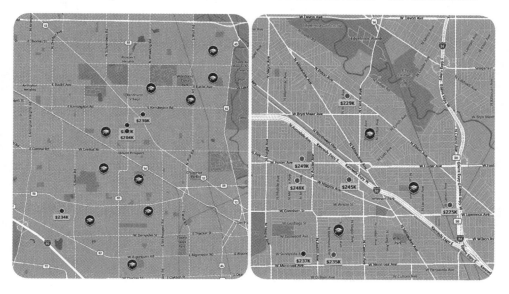

Park Ridge – One Townhouse Only

Des Plaines – Eight Homes

You can follow the same initial mapping and search process in your community or area. Note that schools, parks, forest preserves, roads, and airports are also highlighted on the maps. This information will be useful as you proceed through your own Location Choice Hierarchy (LCH).

Now that Eva and Jack know there are properties in their targeted communities that meet their LCH needs and wants for bedrooms, bathrooms, train access, highway access, and commuting time limits, they are ready to research each community in greater detail to see how each matches up with the couple's lifestyle.

Note locations of schools, parks, forest preserves, roads, and airports as you proceed through your own Location Choice Hierarchy (LCH).

They can learn more online, but they also need to get out and do some firsthand, on-site exploration of each area. Many of the items on their LCH can only be determined by walking or biking through neighborhoods and community downtown areas.

Additional trade-offs will start appearing as they go through the community exploration process. Jack and Eva may have to revisit their LCH and reassess their needs and wants as they learn more through their research. The couple will do this in the next chapter.

6-2-5 Some Key Community Considerations

Some of the top things you need to know about each community before you start looking at neighborhoods and homes are:

1. What is the form of government and who provides various public services?

2. What is the community planning for development, improvements, and zoning changes?

3. Is there a clearly defined downtown area, or just a busy street lined with strip malls?

4. What are the public school districts in the community, as well as non-public schools?

5. What are the statistics on crime rates, and locations of registered sex offenders?

6. What are the locations and names of community parks and recreation facilities?

7. What pubic venues, sports facilities, and local tourist attractions are in the community?

8. Are there any neighborhood associations?

9. What is the community lacking? Are there open borders for expansion or is the community landlocked?

You can learn most of this information online. However, you should visit each town, visit the town hall, and walk, bike, and drive around, getting a sense of the community, its layout, roads, transportation, resources, merchants, schools, and amenities.

6-2-6 Area Amenities

Because Jack and Eva will be within a sixty-five minute train ride to downtown Chicago, they will have a wide area of amenities open to them. Eva decides to search online for Chicago tourist maps and Chicago attraction maps and is rewarded with dozens of maps and descriptive websites.

Local chambers of commerce and visitor centers are also filled with information about the different communities. Some have great websites; others the couple will have to visit in person. Also, Internet searches for restaurants, bars, dance clubs, cinemas, theaters, museums,

> **Do an initial search of amenities at an area level, then as you start to view individual properties, you will want to do a more localized search.**

sports arenas, concert venues, parks, rolling skating rinks, beaches, boat rides, and just about any other form of indoor or outdoor amenity will yield a wealth of area information.

Jack is also interested in restaurants, grocery stores, and coffee shops within walking distance of any home they plan to purchase. He makes a note that once Eva and he have progressed in their search for specific homes, they need to return to the question of amenities at a more localized level.

How close do you want to be to things important to you? Do you want to be near open spaces or parks, or is it more important that you are in the inner city where you are within walking distance to shops, restaurants, coffee, and the farmer's market? Are you the outdoors type? Do you want to be near water where you can kayak or do some boating? Is it important to be near hiking and biking trails?

As with Jack and Eva, you will do an initial search of amenities at an area level, then as you start to view individual properties, you will want to do a more localized search. Amenities are a big part of the quality of life. You may end up sacrificing some nice-to-have home feature to live in a neighborhood or area with your favorite amenities nearby.

6-2-7 Schools

Are you shopping for a home in a good school district? Even if you do not have or plan on having children, owning a home in a sought-after school district can raise your home's value. Schools are a primary concern for lots of people starting a family or with a family already. If you already have children, call the schools in the area to see if you can schedule a visit. Meet with the principal and see if your children can visit with some of the teachers at the school. Children can be anxious about moving and leaving friends, and this may help them feel more comfortable.

GreatSchools.org is a great website offering overviews of districts, parent reviews, test scores, and sometimes homes for sale in the area.

6-2-8 Community Government Plans and Statistics

City-Data.com is one website that gives information on population, crime rates, incomes, neighborhoods, and restaurants. It also has pictures available of the bigger cities and towns, giving you a good idea of what the area has to offer.

Eva also accesses several crime-focused websites to learn about crime in each of their targeted communities. Many show the type and level of each type of crime committed in an area. Some show street maps of the area and pinpoint where the crimes occurred. These sites generally cover bigger cities, so Eva is able to get a pretty good overview. It is best to look at community-by-community statistics, as well as year-to-year statistics for a single community. That way you have some comparison benchmarks.

An uncomfortable but important topic is sex offenders. There are several websites available to research where registered sex offenders live in an area. FamilyWatchdog.com is just one of many where you enter a zip code or home address and a map pops up with all the registered offenders in the area and their addresses.

6-2-9 Flooding

If you are going to be in a flood risk area, check out the government website:

https://www.floodsmart.gov/floodsmart

You can enter the address of any home and see if the home is on a flood plain, and if so, what its elevation and risk is. Depending on your findings, you may need to work the cost of flood insurance into your purchase analysis.

In Jack's review, he noted that Des Plaines, one of their target communities, was named after the Des Plaines River running through it. At this point he does not know for sure, but he speculated that some homes along the river could be at flood risk. He made note that if Eva and he find any desirable homes in Des Plaines, they will need to check out their addresses on the government site or other sites that provide flood zone information.

6-2-10 Other Community Factors

There are many other community factors that may be important to you. Fortunately the Internet is full of resources, and you can pay a visit to local chambers of commerce, city planning commissions, tourist bureaus, county recorders, and other sources can help you research as well.

Pull out the lifestyle forms you completed in this chapter and start going down the pages. Find the community factors most meaningful to you and start researching.

After you do that, it is time to move to selecting specific neighborhoods and homes in the next chapter. This process involves your own online searches, along with enlisting the services of a buyer's agent realtor to accompany you on walkthroughs and to prepare and present offers.

Chapter 7
Looking at Neighborhoods and Homes

"Be he a king or a peasant,
he is happiest who finds peace at home."
—Johann Wolfgang von Goethe

In Chapter 6, we determined counties and cities meeting your needs. The time has come to zero in on neighborhoods and specific homes. We will continue with our case study with Jack and Eva to facilitate the demonstration of concepts, searches, and results. The couple will use the Internet and other resources to start, and then enlist the services of a buyer's agent realtor to help them refine the process and perform walkthroughs of homes.

7-1 Returning to the Home Search Sites

"Thanks for inviting us over, Mom," Jack says as he closes the front door. "We love having Dad over at our house, but I miss seeing you."

"Me too, Mom," adds Eva.

"Let me take your coats. I wish I could have been more involved, but my nurse shift work at the hospital hasn't given me the time to. Another year and I can join your dad in retirement."

She hung their coats up in the hall closet, then the three made their way into the kitchen where Mike was waiting at the table with his computer up and running.

"Hey, it's great to see you two again!" Mike stood up and gave his kids a hug. After everyone had settled at the table, Jayne passed out mugs and poured coffee, then passed out homemade chocolate chip cookies. Then she looked at Mike, her eyebrows furrowed. "Mike, you are only allowed one. We are sticking to our diet."

"Oooh, you're tough on Dad, Mom," Jack says. They all laugh.

"Okay, enough humor at my expense," says Mike. "Let's get down to business. Now that you two have a clear picture of your housing needs and wants, and have selected, researched, and narrowed down your selection of target communities, you will need to return to the home search sites like Zillow.com and Realtor.com to start zeroing in on neighborhoods and specific homes."

"Your previous research was to make sure that there were a sufficient number of homes meeting your basic parameters within your affordable price range and within your target communities. Now you will need to really drill down on features for each specific home."

Eva looks over at Mike. "We have already filtered homes by number of bedrooms and bathrooms, so our most limiting need is for our home to be within walking distance of a commuter train station. We think that ten blocks should be the maximum distance."

"Sounds good, Eva." Mike turns his computer so that everyone can see. He then creates a map on the home search site for each target community, showing a dot for the location of each home meeting Jack and Eva's search criteria. He zooms in on the map for each community until the icon for the commuter train station appears and then identifies which of the dots (houses) are within ten blocks walking distance. For each home meeting the "ten block walk" criteria, he clicks on the "Save this home" button on the search site. For each qualifying house, he also notes the number of stories in the house (the couple prefers two); whether there is a fenced-in yard (for Oscar); if there is an attached or detached garage (they prefer attached); and how many cars it will hold. They all look at the pictures shown on the site for each house to figure out some of these factors. By doing so, everyone is able to get their first look at the homes.

As shown in the table below, Mike found twelve homes in the targeted communities that meet the walking distance parameters. There are no homes in the Jefferson Park neighborhood that satisfy the distance parameters, but every other community has at least one home meeting the couple's filters and within their parameter of reasonable walking distance from the train station.

The last four columns in the table on the next page contain the new fields of information Mike gathered. To make it easier to discuss each home, Mike also numbers each home in column one.

Table 7-1 - For Sale Home Search Summary – Homes within 10 Blocks of Train Station

#	Train Station Near	Price	Home Type	Bed-rooms	Baths	Home Size (sq ft)	Price (per sq ft)	Lot Size (sq ft)	Year Built	Base-ment	Days on Search Site	Recent Price Change	No. Blocks from Train	Garage	Fenced in Yard	No. of Stories
1	Mt Prospect	$204,000	House - Foreclosure	5	2	1,128	$ 181	7,727	1955	Yes	437	$ (5,000)	5.5	Det - 1	Un-certain	1
2	Mt Prospect	$209,900	House	3	1.5	1,040	$ 202	7,370	1944	Yes	484	$(10,000)	6.5	Det - 1	partially	2
3	Mt Prospect	$229,900	House	3	1.5	1,206	$ 191	8,838	1962	Yes	46	$(10,000)	10	Det - 1	No	1
4	Des Plaines	$245,000	House	3	2	1,437	$ 170	6,250	1950	Finished	5	$ -	8	Det - 1	Yes	2
5	Des Plaines	$217,000	House - Foreclosure	3	2	1,134	$ 191	6,534	1968	Finished	43	$ -	10	Det - 2	Yes	1
6	Des Plaines	$239,900	House	3	3	1,900	$ 126	6,040	1914	Finished	58	$ (5,000)	10	Det - 2	Yes	2
7	Park Ridge	$239,000	Townhouse	3	2	1,500	$ 159	3,773	1962	Yes	85		10	3 pkg spc	No	3
8	Edison Park	$219,900	Townhouse	3	1.5	1,280	$ 172	2,260	1956	Finished	162	$ (5,000)	9	Off street parking	No	2
9	Norwood Park	$250,000	House	5	3	1,119	$ 223	4,950	1928		22	$ -	4	No	Yes	2
10	Gadstone Park	$249,750	House	3	1.5	1,000	$ 250	4,760	1952	Yes	26	$ -	4	Det - 2.5	Yes	1 + unf attic
11	Gadstone Park	$249,000	House	3	2	1,650	$ 151	4,350	1918	Yes	121	$ -	5	Det - 2	Yes	1 + unf attic
12	Gadstone Park	$249,900	House	4	2	1,408	$ 177	4,030	1911	Yes	112	$ -	11	Det - 2	Yes	2

The home search site provides interior and exterior photos of each house and its yard. It also provides a description of features and information about prior sales activity of the home, property taxes, nearby schools, and other relevant factors.

Jack and Eva study the photos and information provided for each property carefully.

In looking at each of the twelve homes, Eva and Jack are not happy with any of them.

"Dad," says Jack, "we do not really like any of these. How depressing after all our work."

"Let's try something," said Mike. He increases the price filter on the search site by $50,000 to see what would happen.

The site's home location map practically explodes with new red dots representing additional homes for sale. The number of available homes within ten blocks of the train stations increases by dozens.

"Wow," says Eva. "It looks like we priced ourselves just below the "sweet spot" in the market." Look at the comparable property location maps for Gladstone Park!"

Homes $200,000 to $250,000   **Additional Homes $250,000 to $310,000**

"We need to think about this," said Jack. "We know from our financial analysis that at current interest rates we have enough income to support a larger monthly mortgage payment for a bigger loan than $225,000. The problem is that we may be constrained by the $25,000 we have available for a down payment."

Jayne says, "I am not as swift on computers as you guys, but why are you limiting yourselves to houses priced at $250,000? Chicago is not 'overheated' in a so-called seller's market, so many people will likely sell below their asking price. You guys can actually search for houses listed for a bit more than $250,000 and offer less than the asking price."

"See, she's both smart and good looking," Mike smiles. "And there is something else you two should consider. The lender that preapproved you indicated that you would only need a 10 percent down payment. Using the power of financial leverage, you will need only $1,000 more in down payment for each additional $9,000 you borrow."

◇◇◇◇◇

Jack and Eva think back to their financial foundation analysis. They realize they have excess cash flow of $937.58 per month, even without cutting back on any discretionary expenses. So they reason that with a little sacrifice they could save another $5,000 within the next few months. That would allow them to borrow another $45,000 (up to $270,000), which, when added to the additional $5,000 down payment, would allow them to purchase a house up to $300,000 in value. They realize, however, that when they get to negotiations, they will also have to figure out how to cover their closing costs.

Jack and Eva return to the KHBAN template introduced as Template 2-1 in Chapter 2. Using some trial and error they plug in various Affordable Mortgage Loan Payment Amounts (AMLPA) in Step 1 until they arrive at a $270,000 mortgage showing in the Step 3 output. The AMLPA amount they arrive at is $1,368.05, an increase of only $228.01 over their $1,140.04 projected mortgage loan payment amount for a $225,000 mortgage loan. This increase is far less than their projected $937.58 excess cash flow, and well within their affordability range.

Jack and Eva's updated KHBAN schedule is shown in Table 7-2.

They ask Mike to increase the filter on the home search site and repeat the process of finding houses for sale within ten blocks of the train stations, this time at prices between $250,000 and $310,000 (reasoning they could offer $300,000 for a house listed at $310,000). This yields them dozens of possibilities, many of which possess all or nearly all of their high priority needs and wants attributes. Based on photos and reviews of other information contained on the home search site, they narrow their list of potential target houses to about thirty-five that they think they might really like.

Now it is time for the couple to begin researching and exploring the neighborhoods in which those thirty-five houses are located.

Table 7-2: Update of Key Home Buying Affordability Numbers (KHBAN) Table

Step 1:			
Figure out the Affordable Mortgage Loan Payment Amount you can afford (AMLPA)	$1,368.05		Used trial and error to obtain $270,000 loan amount in Step 3, varying Step 1 amount
Step 2:			
Based on your financial and credit profile, find out from your lender the following three loan terms available to you:			
1. Interest Rate	4.500	%	INPUT
2. Loan to Value (LTV) Percent	90.00	%	INPUT
3. Amortization Term	360	months	INPUT
Step 3:			
This is the Maximum Mortgage Loan Amount (MMLA) for which you will qualify	**$270,000**		Calculated
Step 4:			
This is the Maximum Home Price Amount (MHPA) you can afford to pay, equal to MMLA divided by the LTV percent:			
Maximum Mortgage Loan Amount (MMLA)	$270,000		From Step 3
divided by: LTV Percent	90.00	%	From Step 2
equals: Maximum Home Price Amount (MHPA)	**$300,000**		Calculated
Step 5:			
Savings amount you will need for your down payment:			
Maximum Home Price Amount (MHPA)	$300,000		From Step 4
minus: Maximum Mortgage Loan Amount (MMLA)	$270,000		From Step 3
equals: Down Payment Amount (DPA)	**$30,000**		Calculated
Step 6:			
Savings amount you will need for your Closing Costs:			
Maximum Home Price Amount (MHPA)	$300,000		From Step 4
multiplied by: Approximate Closing Cost Percent	3.00	%	INPUT
equals: Approximate Closing Cost Amount (CCA)	**$9,000**		Calculated
Total Amount Needed for Closing (DPA + CCA)	**$39,000**		Calculated

7-1-1 Neighborhoods

The quality of the neighborhood in which a home is located consistently ranks as the most important consideration when people are choosing a home to buy. That is no surprise. What difference does it make if you have a home with all the features you want if it is situated in an unsuitable area for your needs and lifestyle?

To properly assess a neighborhood, you have to explore it in person.

To properly assess a neighborhood, you have to explore it in person. But you can and should do a tremendous amount of preparatory research on the neighborhoods you are considering before you set foot in them. Some of the pre-visit information you should research online are:

1. Any information describing the history, traditions, development, and growth of the neighborhood;

2. The identity of streets or other officially or customarily designated boundaries of the neighborhood;

On Site Neighborhood Assessment - Checklist

Feel
- What is your first impression?
- What is the curb appeal of the homes?
- Are the homes single-family / multi-family / mixed-use?
- What is the spacing of homes; is there adequate personal space in the front, back, or side yards?
- Are houses well maintained?
- Are the yards well maintained and landscaped?
- Are there gardens and flowerbeds?
- Are there sidewalks?
- Is there on-street parking; is it controlled with neighborhood permits?
- Are nearby shops and restaurants inviting?
- Is the area clean and free of litter?
- Is there a presence or lack of graffiti?
- Do you feel safe walking around?
- Would you feel good calling it home?

Culture / taste / personality
- Is it a historic neighborhood or new development?
- What race / religion / language / heritage is most represented in the neighborhood?
- Where are the nearby churches / synagogues / mosques / temples?
- What is the level and nature of activity?
- What is your feel for the neighbors?

Condition of infrastructure
- What is the condition of:
  o Sidewalks, curbs, and lighting;
  o Public landscaping and buildings;
  o Bridges, roads, traffic control; and
  o Railroad stations and crossings?

3. A large, detailed street map which marks the neighborhood boundaries, or a map on which you can draw them; you will use this map for plotting routes, buildings, and other items of interest you uncover in your research. I am unaware of a service that allows you to electronically draw routes and plot all the items we are going to be plotting, and I am therefore suggesting that you print-out or otherwise acquire a map of the neighborhood on which you can manually plot everything we discuss below;

4. A plot on your neighborhood map of the route you would need to take from various parts of the neighborhood to highways, train stations, and other major transportation routes and services;

5. The identity, location, and ranking of schools and any dividing lines in the neighborhood for children going to one school or the other (plot on map);

6. The nature and location of nearby religious facilities (plot on map);

7. The location of nearby hospitals, police stations, and fire stations (plot on map);

On Site Neighborhood Assessment - Continued

Economic Health of Area
- How active is local merchant business?
- What is the appearance and mix of businesses?
- Is there evidence of public services?

Safety
- Are streets lighted?
- Is police presence visible?

Convenience
- Is access to highways easy and quick?
- Is access to the train nearby?
- What is the overall time, effort and cost of your daily commute?
- Walkability - how far can you safely walk?
- Drivability - is the area congested due to poorly designed or controlled roads?
- Is what you need and want nearby?

Livability
- Is the neighborhood family-friendly?
- Are there nearby parks and playgrounds?
- Are there sufficient nearby amenities?
- Are there sufficient nearby restaurants, services, shops, entertainment spots, and nightlife?
- Are taxes and other expenses too high?

Good Schools
- Are schools in good repair?
- Does activity going on around schools seem appropriate?
- Do you get a good feeling talking with principals and neighbors?

8. Crime statistics for the neighborhood;

9. Addresses of registered sex offenders (plot on map);

10. Identity and location of nearby public venues, sports centers, and tourist attractions (plot on map);

11. Community plans for development and infrastructure changes in and around the neighborhood (notate on map);

12. A history of prices and price changes for homes that sold and are for sale in the neighborhood (notate on map and look for pattern differences within the neighborhood).

Also plot on the map the location of the homes that interest you in the neighborhood. Look at where each is located in the neighborhood in relationship to the other items you have plotted.

The side bars on this page and the previous two list some of the primary on-site assessment factors you will be taking in with all of your senses of sight, sound, smell, taste, and touch. You truly are going to be gaining a feel for the neighborhood. There is a comprehensive On-Site

On-Site Neighborhood Assessment - Continued

Sights
- How attractive are neighborhood home and nearby building designs?
- How do different components of the area visually fit together?
- Do unsightly objects such as high-tension lines and poorly maintained water towers dominate area views?

Sounds
- Stop at various points and various times of day when you are walking around; what do you hear?
  o Children playing?
  o Birds singing?
  o Water lapping the shoreline?
  o Autos and trucks, airplanes, freight trains?
  o Emergency vehicle sirens?
  o Nearby nightclubs and bars?

Smells
- Stop at various points and various times of day when you are walking around; what do you smell?
  o Natural – lakes, forests, flowers?
  o Food – bakeries, restaurants?
  o Industrial – factories, mills, refineries?
  o Sewage or other indefinable, noxious smells?

Neighborhood Assessment Checklist available on the companion website for download (Downloadable Template 7-1).

Traffic patterns, density of people, and services offered in and around neighborhoods can change dramatically during the course of a day. You need to understand the differences before you choose to buy. Some tasks you should perform are as follows:

1. Visit during morning and afternoon rush hours; check out all sides of the neighborhood as significant differences may exist in activity and traffic patterns depending on neighborhood location;

2. Have lunch at nearby restaurants, and check out the night life;

3. Find out about public transportation;

4. Talk to people in the neighborhood, but also talk to people in nearby neighborhoods to get their views as well. What are their likes and dislikes about the area? Determine how opinions about a neighborhood differ among its residents and those of nearby neighborhoods;

5. Visit the nearby grocery stores, cleaners, and merchants; talk with them about the local neighborhoods, schools, and economic vitality of the area;

6. Visit the schools; in most you will not be able to talk with teachers, but you may be able to talk with the principal;

7. Go to the village hall and verify that what you learned in your online research is complete and accurate; while there, ask about neighborhoods as well.

In your research, walk around, bike around, and drive around. You will see things while walking and biking that you will not notice while driving. You can cover ground more quickly on your bike, and still be exposed to more sights and sounds than you would in a car.

In the end, you need to see if you can visualize yourself living in a home in the neighborhood. See yourself at a nearby coffee shop, walking your dog, and jogging. Know you will be comfortable with your commute.

One other thing, be on the lookout for warning signs. These include:

- Graffiti;

- Vandalism;

- Abandoned buildings;

- Excessive "For Sale" signs;

- Excessive "For Rent" signs;

- Homes in foreclosure;

- Evidence of gang activity or crime.

These are all telltale signs of economic distress, crime, and a declining area. On the other hand, look for re-gentrification signs as well. Economic strength may be coming back into a previously distressed area, and the telltale signs may soon become a historical footnote. You might be looking at an opportunity to buy before prices start to take off. But this is a risk, and you may have to endure an extended period of the area being unsuitable before real change occurs.

7-1-2 Jack and Eva Explore Neighborhoods

Jack and Eva spend time over the next few weeks exploring the areas in which the thirty-five homes are located. They initially take their bicycles so they can cover more area, but later do a lot of walking. They walk by each home on their list, as well as around the neighborhoods, taking lots of notes. They look at locations of parks, stores, restaurants, coffee shops, and other priorities. They make sure that there are sidewalks in the neighborhoods so they can walk Oscar. Although they will not need them for a few years, they check out schools at different grade levels in locations within each neighborhood's districts.

At the end of their neighborhood research the couple is very excited and ready to start walking through homes. In preparation for the next stage, the couple watched for business signs and storefronts for realtors while they were exploring neighborhoods. They made notes of some of the realtors' names and phone numbers they saw. They also checked out website sources like Redfin.com, Realtor.com, Zillow.com, and others that provide information about realtors in different markets. They settled on a few of the realtors to call and started setting up appointments for interviews so they could figure with whom they would like to work.

7-2 Working with a Buyer's Agent Realtor

As with Jack and Eva, I recommend that you have a professional real estate agent on your home buying team who will provide expert guidance through the home buying process.[14] Jack and Eva chose not to contact an agent until they completed a lot of research and footwork on their own. You may decide you want to call one sooner to help you with some of the earlier steps in the process. It is up to you dependent on how much time you have and how much you like to do things on your own or work with others. At a minimum though, it makes sense to get a buyer's agent involved before you start doing home walk-throughs.

A good buyer's agent will save you time, money, and headaches. The home buying process is complicated, usually requiring disclosure forms, inspection reports, mortgage documents, insurance policies, deeds, and multi-page settlement statements. A knowledgeable expert will help you through the entire process, negotiate the best deal, provide guidance, and help avoid problems and costly mistakes.

A professional can help you answer two important questions: first, will the property in which I am interested provide the type of environment I want in a home and surrounding community? Second, what will the likely resale value be when I am ready to sell?

14   Websites such as Zillow.com, Realtor.com, and Redfin.com can help you find a qualified realtor in the market in which you are looking.

Your agent will provide objective information and opinions since they are not emotionally attached to the homes you view. If you ever get the sense the agent is more interested in their commission than in your best interests, either talk with them about it, or get a new agent.

An agent can provide local community information on utilities, zoning, schools, taxes, and more. They will also be able to provide information about each property for sale. A professional can help you answer two important questions: first, will the property in which I am interested provide the type of environment I want in a home and surrounding community? Second, what will the likely resale value be when I am ready to sell?

Let us assume you have searched and searched relentlessly, and you finally find the perfect property. You want this home. It is time to prepare an offer and present it to the seller. An experienced real estate agent has the expert knowledge required when drafting and presenting an offer (contract/purchase agreement). Your agent is also experienced in negotiating the best deal by responding to a likely counter-offer from the seller.

There are many negotiating factors to consider, including but not limited to price, financing, terms, date of possession, needed repairs, and whether or not furnishings or equipment are part of the deal. The purchase agreement will provide an agreed upon period of time for you to complete appropriate inspections and investigations of the property before you are obligated to complete the purchase.

After your real estate agent has guided you through the negotiation process, he or she will advise you on which investigations and inspections are recommended or required. These are time sensitive factors, and if not completed by the deadlines, can have serious consequences.

There is no replacement for a professional who is familiar with a particular market and all of its unique attributes.

Of course, you are looking for the best property you can afford that is available on the market. Sometimes the property you are searching for is available, but may not be actively advertised in the market. A professional agent will research and investigate all of their resources in order to find all available properties. Many times a really good deal coming on the market may be sold before it is even openly marketed and advertised. A large share of real estate sales are a result of the agent's network of previous clients, referrals, friends and family, and other agents. This is a big advantage over searching online for your dream home.

Agents have access to the Multiple Listing Service (MLS) through their professional organization memberships. The MLS is a database service provided by a group of real estate brokers that allows each of them to list their houses. Under this arrangement, the listing broker and the selling broker split the commission for each sale. Real estate agents execute over 80 percent of real estate transactions, and their primary tool is the MLS.

Determining the value of real estate is not easy. Home search sites are not the authority on property values. They are a good resource. The value you see attached to a sold property may be the amount recorded at the county, but were there seller concessions? Was the transaction completed entirely using the buyer's cash or financed? Did the buyers pay more than the appraised value because they loved the pink exterior and outdoor shower? The answers to these questions and others are where the Internet falls short. There is no replacement for a professional who is familiar with a particular market and all of its unique attributes.

Real estate agents have done this before. The majority of people buy and sell only a few homes throughout their entire life, often with quite a few years in between each purchase or sale. Even if you have gone through the process before, laws and regulations change over time. Real estate agents are involved in hundreds of transactions over the course of their career and are exposed daily to changes in the market. Having knowledge about the latest developments and housing trends can help streamline the process of finding the perfect place. Having an expert on your side to represent you is paramount.

Buying or selling a home is an emotional undertaking. A home can symbolize the things that you most hold near and dear, like family, rest, and security. It is not just four walls, a roof, and a yard. Homes are associated with memories and sentimental attachments. For most everyone, a home is the biggest purchase they will ever take on. Emotions come up and having an invested, concerned, and objective third party helps you stay focused on the things that most matter to you. Let someone who is not too close to the emotional aspects take on negotiating the purchase. They are competent – it is their profession.

Mike advises Jack and Eva that not everyone assisting with buying and selling homes is an officially registered REALTOR®. Similar to physicians, a REALTOR® takes an oath to follow a Code of Ethics. REALTOR® is a registered trademark identifying professionals who are members of the National Association of Realtors®, or NAR. Not only do they have an obligation to protect their clients, they are held to a high standard to uphold rules and laws governing their practice. Ask your real estate professional if they are a member of the National Association of Realtors®.

7-3 How to Find a REALTOR® that Works for You

Look for an agent who is an expert in the area that interests you. Look at the listings in the area and see who the agents are. Attending open houses is a good way to meet and interview realtors in your chosen location. This gives you an idea of whether or not you will feel comfortable with the agent. How professional are they? What is their area of expertise? Do they know a lot about the community in which they are hosting the open house? If not, they might not be the best choice. Agents you meet at an open house may primarily represent sellers in their practice. If so, they are not what you want. You want to find a "buyer's agent." A buyer's agent's area of expertise is assisting with the purchasing process. Not that they do not have experience selling, but their niche is in working with buyers.

Attending open houses is a good way to meet and interview realtors in your chosen location.

The most important aspect to choosing a real estate professional to work with and represent you is the level of comfort and trust you feel in them. People have different personalities, period. Seek someone who has all of the knowledge and expertise you would expect. But also, make sure you think they will be a good match and will be able to guide and counsel you through the entire home buying process. Their style and frequency of communication is critical and should be easily understood. For example, you do not want to dread calling someone who will talk down to you or worse yet, goes on and on about how great they are every time you call.

The following table contains a list of questions to ask when talking with agents. This will get you started. You will likely add others tailored to your needs, likes, and dislikes.

Exhibit 7-1 Realtor Interview Questions

1. Are you a buyer's agent?

2. How familiar are you with the area in which we are shopping: schools, crime rate, amenities?

3. Can you recommend a reputable mortgage broker?

4. Are you available if I have questions?

5. How can I best get in touch with you?

6. How often will you communicate with me?

7. What tools do you use to help me find a home?

8. How long on average does it take to purchase a home in the area in which I have an interest?

9. Do you have any references I can contact?

10. How long have you been an agent and what is your background pertaining to home buying?

11. Is your real estate license current? Note: the managing broker is required to display all brokers' licenses in the office.

12. Has anyone ever filed a complaint against you? Note: this can be verified online through your state's Department of Finance and Professional Regulation, or equivalent department.

13. Why should I hire you over your competition?

Once you have chosen a buyer's agent, it is time to start working with them.

7-4 Attend Home Walk-Throughs/Showing Appointments

What should you be looking for when walking through a home? Have a list with you for each home and make notes. Print out pages for each home from home search sites. You will be thankful you have a detailed list and printouts if you are looking at multiple homes.

Your agent will usually have an information sheet for each home containing the statistics that Jack and Eva used for their home searches (such as number of bedrooms and bathrooms, garage or parking spaces, square footage, lot size, age of home, etc). To streamline and save yourself from having to print out a bunch of paper, you could write your notes right on your agent's sheets. Just remember your priority items.

Some key items of which you should be aware and make note as you approach and into each home are:

1. Curb appeal – Are the house, yard, shrubbery and gardens, sidewalks, driveway, garage, fences maintained and do they look good together?

2. Look and feel – Does this home require simple cosmetic upgrades that you can do or are you looking at gutting the whole home?

3. Sunlight – How light or dark are the rooms in the house? How much sunlight is coming in when you look at the home? Note the time of day when you view the home, and try to schedule repeat visits at different times. What direction does the home face and what direction do the windows face?

4. Signs of damage, such as cracks in the walls, molding, or tiles, and blotches on the walls or ceilings indicating possible leaks.

5. Smells indicating a mold, rodent, insect, or other problems.

6. Modern or outdated fixtures, cabinets, kitchen and baths, styles, architecture, etc.

7-5 Examine Homeowner Disclosures

Each state has its own laws regarding disclosures as to which forms are required; the forms will vary depending on where you are planning to purchase property. Some states require disclosures regarding items that affect or could affect the property such as:

- Earthquakes, flood zones, and natural hazards;

- Zoning changes;

- Fire hazards;

- Noise pollution, ground pollution, and air pollution; and

- Lead-based paint, mold, and radon.

There are federal disclosures, such as for lead-based paint, required for all transactions for homes built before 1978. The disclosure gives the buyer ten days to conduct inspections for lead-based paint, unless the contingency is waived in writing. The disclosure may be included even though there may not be any lead-based paint. Even though it is prohibited by law, there are still places where lead-based paint is sold. Some sellers will include the disclosure because of a potential lawsuit if lead-based paint were to be found by the buyers.

Sellers are obligated to disclose material facts related to the home. Material facts are commonly defined as anything that would affect the buyer's decision to purchase the home or the price and terms of the buyer's offer. If there is knowledge of a defect, the seller should disclose that information.

Sellers are obligated to disclose material facts related to the home.

For example, there could be a problem with the foundation. In areas with basements, this can be an issue, as are problems causing water to seep into basements. In areas without basements, cement slabs can have defects. A seller whose wood floor shows discoloration may not know it is due to moisture from a leaking pipe, which is an important reason to hire a qualified home inspector.

Some states like California even require sellers to notify buyers if a death has occurred on the property within the last three years. Some buyers are creeped out by the knowledge that someone died in the home. Many buyers are fine with a death occurring in the house as long as it wasn't violent or gruesome. However there are also buyers who believe homes are haunted by former occupants who died in the house. You may be able to obtain specific details of the death.

Most repairs will likely need to be disclosed, but some items are just considered maintenance. For instance, if the homeowner called a plumber to fix a leak under the sink, they state that the pipes once leaked but were repaired. In many cases, home buyers feel a sense of relief if they know certain things have been repaired. It brings a sense of security to buyers if they know a seller has replaced a roof or upgraded the electrical and plumbing system. It shows that the seller cared for and did not neglect the home.

7-6 Peruse Online Sites to Learn about Your Property and Transaction History

As you saw with Jack and Eva, there are several websites that provide an abundance of information about individual homes, as well as the neighborhoods and communities in which they are located. At the date of this writing, Zillow.com and Realtor.com were good examples; FindingHomeBook.com contains up-to-date lists and descriptions of some of the top sites.

The sites contain information such as:

1. Pictures of each home and others on the street by it;

2. Number of rooms and the square footage of the home and lot it is on;

3. Financial information such as property taxes;

4. Satellite views and maps of the neighborhood (so you can quickly see the location of schools, shopping and amenities nearby);

5. A history of purchase and sale transactions and prices;

6. Current estimated market price of the home and neighboring homes;

7. Value of other homes in the neighborhood;

8. New and valuable information continually added.

You can also go to the county assessor's site to get a history of property taxes and see if the taxes are paid up to date. Knowing the amount will assist you with your budgeting, and knowing if the taxes are current may give you useful information about seller motivations.

7-7 Prepare and Compare Your Checklists

As you visit each home, take notes and mark items on your Home Features Checklist. A sample checklist is included at the end of this chapter and is available for you to download from the companion website.

You and your co-purchaser (if you have one) should each perform this task separately. It will take a little longer at each home, but save you lots of time down the road. If you walk into a home and immediately know it is not for you, just write a quick note saying "too dark" or "smells bad" or "tiny living area" or whatever turned you off, and move on. Each time you find one you like, take more time and fill out your checklist in greater detail.

Review your lists and the notes throughout the timeframe you are looking at the different homes. Look at your cumulative notes and lists each day. This helps to keep each home fresh in your mind.

Do your notes and lists match up with those of your significant other or whoever your co-purchaser going to be? You may have loved the home with the big backyard, but completely missed that it only had one bathroom or the floor in the kitchen was sloping. Hopefully you will have one home you agree is the right one overall. Once you have picked out a few favorites, call your real estate agent, and schedule a second showing for those homes so that you can fine-tune your list.

When you find one you like, it is time to submit an offer. The next chapter takes you through the offering, negotiation, signing, and formal inspection process.

Downloadable Template 7-2: Home Features Checklist

Home Features Checklist				
Community Name:				
Neighborhood Name:				
Address:				
Overall Rating:	**Excellent** / **Good** / **OK** / **Bad** / **Awful**			
Overall Observations and Comments				

Quick Disqualifiers	**Comments**
Neighborhood	
Location	
Lot	
Appearance	
Odors	
Noise	
Light	
Disrepair	
Other:	

Home Features Checklist			
Curb appeal:	Excellent	Good	Bad	
Front Yard:	Grass	Dirt	Stone	
Topography:	Trees	Bushes	Gardens	
Driveway:	Asphalt	Concrete	Paving Stone	
	Gravel	Maintained	Disrepair	
Sidewalks:	Yes	No		
		Maintained	Disrepair	
Street lights:	Yes	No		
		Maintained	Disrepair	
Street Parking:	Yes	No		
		Permit Required	No Permit	
Fire Hydrants:	Yes	No		
		Maintained	Disrepair	
Exterior construction:	Brick	Wood	Alum Siding	
	Vinyl Siding	Maintained	Disrepair	
Shutters:	Yes	No		
		Maintained	Disrepair	
Awnings:	Yes	No		
		Maintained	Disrepair	
Roof:	Asphalt	Cedar	Tile	
	Slate	Maintained	Disrepair	

Home Features Checklist

Gutters	Yes	No		
		Maintained	Disrepair	

Walkway to door	Concrete	Asphalt	Stone	
		Maintained	Disrepair	

Front Stoop	Concrete	Wood	Stone	
		Maintained	Disrepair	

Front Porch	Concrete	Wood	Stone	
		Maintained	Disrepair	

Storm doors	None	Aluminum	Wood	
		Maintained	Disrepair	

Exterior doors	Metal	Wood		
	Painted	Stained		
		Maintained	Disrepair	

Front entry / Foyer	Stories:	One	Two		
	Flooring:	Tile	Laminate	Wood	Slate /Stone
	Closets:	None	One	Two	
	Foyer Exit:	Stairway	No doors	Doors	
				Maintained	Disrepair

Bathroom 1	Master Bath?:	Yes	No		
	Bath:	Tub / shower	Tub	Shower	Jacuzzi Tub
	Toilet:	Totally separated		Sep from bath	Not Separate
	Cabinets:	Solid wood	Particle board	Painted	Stained
	Sinks:	One	Two		
	Sink Fixtures:	Brass	Stainless	High end	Low end
	Flooring:	Stone Tile	ceramic Tile	Laminate	Wood
	Walls:	Painted	Wall Paper	Tile	
	Mirrors:				
	Closets	Linen	Clothes	Walk-in(s):	

Home Features Checklist				
Lighting	Overhead	Above Sink(s)	Above Bath	
Windows				

Bathroom 2

Full	Half			
Bath:	Tub / shower	Tub	Shower	Jacuzzi Tub
Toilet:	Totally separated		Sep from bath	Not Separate
Cabinets:	Solid wood	Particle board	Painted	Stained
Sinks:	One	Two		
Sink Fixtures:	Brass	Stainless	High end	Low end
Flooring:	Stone Tile	ceramic Tile	Laminate	Wood
Walls:	Painted	Wall Paper	Tile	
Mirrors:				
Closets	Linen	Clothes	Walk-in(s):	
Lighting	Overhead	Above Sink(s)	Above Bath	
Windows				

Bathroom 3

Full	Half			
Bath:	Tub / shower	Tub	Shower	Jacuzzi Tub
Toilet:	Totally separated		Sep from bath	Not Separate
Cabinets:	Solid wood	Particle board	Painted	Stained
Sinks:	One	Two		
Sink Fixtures:	Brass	Stainless	High end	Low end
Flooring:	Stone Tile	ceramic Tile	Laminate	Wood
Walls:	Painted	Wall Paper	Tile	
Mirrors:				
Closets:	Linen	Clothes	Walk-in(s):	
Lighting:	Overhead	Above Sink(s)	Above Bath	
Windows:				

Bedroom 1

Master BR?	Yes	No		
Extra space for:	Sitting Area	Work-out equip		
Closets	Wall Closets:		Walk-in Closets:	
Attached M Bath	Yes	No		

Home Features Checklist

Bedroom 2	Closets	Wall Closets:		Walk-in Closets:		
	Attached Bath	Yes	No			

Bedroom 3	Closets	Wall Closets:		Walk-in Closets:		
	Attached Bath	Yes	No			

Bedroom 4	Closets	Wall Closets:		Walk-in Closets:		
	Attached Bath	Yes	No			

Kitchen:

Flooring:	Tile	Laminate	Wood		
Pantry	Cabinet	Walk-in			
Sink:	Single	Double	Stainless Steel	Ceramic	Plastic
Cabinets:	Solid wood	Particle board	Painted	Stained	
Number	Overhead				
	Under counter				
	Under sink				
Center Island:	Counter only	Burners			
Counters:	Laminate	Solid			

Appliances:		Microwave	Refrigerator	Dishwasher	Oven / Burners
	Built in:				
	Standalone:				
		Maintained	Disrepair		

Home Features Checklist				
Eating Area:	Yes	No		
Lighting:	Overhead	Under Cabinet	Other	
		Maintained	Disrepair	
Windows	Over sink	By eating area	Other	
Number				
		Maintained	Disrepair	

Living Room

Yes	No	

Dining Room

Yes	No	

Family Room

Yes	No	

Other Rooms:

Den	Exercise Room		Greenhouse	
Sewing Room				
Bonus Room				
Office				

Mud room

Yes	No	

Laundry Room

Location:	Basement	1st floor	2nd floor	

Back Porch

Yes	No			
Enclosed	All Season	Maintained	Disrepair	

Home Features Checklist				
Deck	Yes	No		
	Wood	Plastic Wood	Maintained	Disrepair
Patio	Material:	Concrete	Brick	Stone
	Built ins:	Fire place / pit	Grill	
			Maintained	Disrepair
Back Yard	Grass	Dirt	Stone	
		Maintained	Unkempt	
Back Yard Fence	Wood	Chain Link	Stone	
	Brick	Stucco		
		Maintained	Disrepair	
Back Yard Topography	Trees	Shrubs	Flower Garden	
	Veg Garden	Pond / Waterfall	Parking Spot	
What house backs up to	Neighbor's yard	Alley	Open space	
	School	Business	Other	
Heating system	Gas	Electric	Oil	
	Wood			
	Furnace	Boiler	Stove	
	Base board	Forced Air		
		Maintained	Disrepair	
Air conditioning	Central	Window Unit	Wall Unit	
		Maintained	Disrepair	
Windows	Double Hung	Slider	Crank	
	Single Pane	Double Pane		
		Maintained	Disrepair	

Home Features Checklist					
Basement	Full	Partial	Crawl Space		
	Finished	Unfinished	Drop Ceiling		
	Walk-out	Outside Entry	Window Wells		
	Leakage?	Yes	No		
	Ceiling Height:				
		Maintained	Disrepair		

Insulation	Rolled	Blown In		

Water	City	Common Well	Private Well	
		Maintained	Disrepair	

Sewage	City	Common Septic	Private Septic	
		Maintained	Disrepair	

Chapter 8

I Want That Home! What Comes Next?

"Shut up and take my money!"
—Quote by the character Fry, in the 2010 Futurama
episode entitled "Attack of the Killer App"

8-1 Prepare and Present a Well-Constructed Offer

"I'm sure you have heard the saying, 'everything is negotiable,'" Mike says as he stirs his coffee at Jack and Eva's kitchen table, then fires up his laptop.

"You know me, Dad, I'm always looking for a deal," Jack replies, smiling.

"And he's found us some good ones, too," adds Eva.

"Well, the saying is mostly true when it comes to reaching an agreement between a seller and buyer of a home, but there are practical limits. I'm going to send you some notes later. The first and foremost negotiable item is price, which is the dollar amount you are offering.

But this is just one part of the overall terms of a contract to purchase your home, albeit a very important one. Terms are everything else. Some examples of terms are: amount of deposit, deadlines for inspections, contingencies for the sale of another home, satisfactory home inspection, seller financing, closing date, fixtures and window dressings remaining, et cetera."

The terms of your offer are comprised of much more than the dollar amount you are offering.

Mike glances at the young couple as they nod to each other. Then he continues, "Keep in the forefront of your mind the concept of creating an offer based on the home's value, not the list price. The recent comparable closed sales in the neighborhood give you ammunition and information. If a home is priced at or below market value, you do not have a lot of bargaining room. If the home is priced above market value and has been on the market many days, a lower offer accompanied by a market analysis utilizing comparable sales may get you an accepted offer from the seller. You or your agent should analyze the recent sales and create a market analysis that supports the price and terms of your offer."

"Let's say you have worked up what you think is a fair price offer. What other terms will the seller want to consider?"

Jack and Eva look at each other.

"I can include whether we are offering all our own cash or using financing for a portion of the purchase price," says Eva.

"Correct. If you plan on financing, which you do, what type of loan, FHA, conventional or other are you planning to obtain? What percentage of a down payment are you willing to offer? How much of a deposit (earnest money, escrow, et cetera) are you putting down to show the seller you are committed? When is the closing date? What period of time are you requesting to complete the inspection? Are you paying the closing costs, or are you asking the seller to pay for all or a part of this amount? The more you have in terms of money and flexibility of timeframes, the greater bargaining and negotiating power you have."

"If you can, find out anything about the seller's motivation for selling, as it may assist you in drafting your offer. For instance, the seller might be trying to close as quickly as possible. If so, you may be able to offer a lower amount in return for a better closing date. Or, you may find that adult children are trying to sell their aged parents' home and need time to clear out furnishings. You may be willing to give them extra time to close in exchange for a lower price or other concessions. So ask questions and find out as much as you can before writing your offer. Some sellers believe their home to be worth more than its value. In such cases you may have to walk away from the transactions rather than pay more for a home than it is worth."

8-2 Negotiate

As Mike later told our young couple, contract negotiations require great communication skills and an ability to read the other party. Both parties are trying to get the best price and terms they can, and they often benefit from keeping their emotions and willingness to accept less or offer more to themselves.

Unless you placed high in the most recent "World Series of Poker" tournament, I would suggest that if you are working with an agent, let them do the talking. Do not even attend the offering. Of course, this requires you to trust your agent to behave as you would want and give you the straight scoop on what happened, but it prevents you from giving away more than you need to because your emotions ran wild in the negotiations.

Your goal is to craft a good agreement with price and terms that work for both parties. The outcome and results of a poor agreement have the potential to come back to haunt the parties after closing. What follows in this chapter are some thoughts for you to consider as you prepare to negotiate for the purchase of your home.

8-2-1 Clearly Determine What You Want to Achieve in the Negotiation

Start by figuring out what you want and what you can live with.

As obvious as it may sound, you do not want to start negotiations with an offer with which you are not comfortable. If you do, you can forget your deal. It leaves you no negotiating room, and puts stress on you even if the seller accepts your offer with no changes. So start by figuring out what you want and what you can live with. Consider what you know about the seller's motivations and draft an offer with which you feel comfortable and have wiggle room. It will not be your highest and best offer, but it should be reasonable for the circumstances.

Price may be your primary focus; it is for most people. But as Mike discussed with Jack and Eva, what other key things do you want to achieve? Some examples include:

1. The need to put up the smallest escrow deposit possible to show your commitment to the deal;

2. A closing date early enough to give you enough cushion to leave your current home at the right time;

3. A closing date tailored to meet travel deadlines, school start dates, or work calendar;

It will not be your highest and best offer, but it should be reasonable for the circumstances.

4. Getting the home inspected and having repairs, pest control, mold, radon, lead-based paint, asbestos, or other issues handled;

5. Obtaining a mortgage of a specified size with specified terms or better;

6. Having the seller pay closing costs or provide some of the financing for the home;

7. Making sure the seller leaves the home with no clutter left behind and in a clean condition;

8. Other factors specific to your circumstances.

Write down what you want so you make sure it is included in your offer.

8-2-2 Present Your Offer in a Professional Manner, and Be Prepared to Negotiate

"You catch more flies with honey than with vinegar."
—Unknown

Work to maintain a positive relationship between both parties. Your goal is to achieve an outcome where both your and the seller's needs are met.

Communicate your offer and what you need to the seller directly, or if you are using a broker, then go through your agent who will handle all communications in a clear and reasonable way. The contract negotiation process usually begins with a degree of uncertainty and wariness between buyer and seller. The goal is to move in the direction of trust and honest negotiation as soon as possible.

There is nothing more destructive to the negotiation process than a combative or overly aggressive presentation. Work to maintain a positive relationship between both parties. Your goal is to achieve an outcome where both your and the seller's needs are met, not an impasse where neither party's needs are met, and the deal falls apart. Remember, too, that most sellers have invested time and money in their home and they have established relationships in their neighborhood. They will be unhappy if they feel their former neighbors will be getting a raw deal with a pushy, rude buyer moving into their former home.

Buyers sometimes want to submit a letter to the seller describing why their house is not worth what the list price is by pointing out deficiencies. This is not a good idea and can backfire by immediately putting the seller on the defensive. Homeowners who enjoyed making a home their own by laying the tile and painting the walls will have a negative reaction to a critical buyer. It is best to base your purchase price on the marketplace data, while remaining complimentary of their home. See the bigger picture. Painting over hot pink walls will be rewarding if you are happy with the results of a successful negotiation. It is exciting when the buyer and seller are genuinely happy for each other.

> **It is best to base your purchase price on the marketplace data.**

Sometimes you have no choice but to work with a combative seller or seller's agent. Their strategy can include emotional statements, sarcastic remarks, defensive arguments, threats to terminate, etc., which usually involve their ego. Good solutions and sound logic are not likely to be received openly by this type of negotiator. Working with a combative style negotiator requires good control of your or your agent's emotions, and calm, methodical responses. Strong emotions arouse emotions in others, including fear and anger. Their anger may have a source outside the contract, or it may be a negotiation tactic.

The best approach is to anchor your offered prices, requests for repairs, and other negotiation points to outside data. Show that your proposals are not unreasonable based on the data. Conversations between parties are common, but any agreements should be clearly spelled out in writing.

Be specific. For example, make sure the "wall mounted television" that you like is labeled in the contract complete with brand and model. Oral or unclear written agreements can result in problems at the closing table, and may cause deals to fall apart, especially if the negotiations were contentious.

> **Oral or unclear written agreements can result in problems at the closing table, and may cause deals to fall apart.**

Offering the seller "wins" on some of the terms can be important. Saving face is as important for them as it may be for you. Discuss with your agent or others different ways to get what you want and need while simultaneously making an attractive offer to the seller. Remember, the seller literally holds the keys to the home you are interested in owning.

Technically, every point in the contract is negotiable; however, one of the most effective means of coming to an agreement is to rely on consistent standards when possible. For example, if it is common in your area for the seller to buy the title insurance policy and buyer to pay the survey cost, adhere to these norms. Using accepted standards helps to avoid a situation where there is haggling over every point. On the other hand, if necessary, all the points in an offer can be used to help structure an agreeable deal. These trade-offs may be a way for both parties to get what they want. Your goal is to move in a direction of trust.

Most people are fair-minded and reasonable. They tend to respond well to respectful treatment and to having their concerns heard. If the seller feels that you and your agent are acting with integrity and sincerity, their attitude will be much more cooperative. Contract negotiation

> **It is not proper to discuss your price range, financial details, or urgency to move with the seller.**

is a sensitive area, and anxiety can be high. Both the buyer and seller are under pressure, with their future plans at stake. Acting with integrity does not mean that all cards have to be put on the table. It is not proper to discuss your price range, financial details, or urgency to move with the seller. It is valuable to develop trust because trust raises the level of cooperation between the parties and moves negotiation forward.

Here are some guidelines to follow when dealing with the seller:

1. Listen and understand what the seller has to say;

2. Express appreciation for their home, gardens, and decorating;

3. Respond within a reasonable time to counter offers;

4. Reassure the seller of your ability to close;

5. Reveal some limited personal information about yourselves.

Finding common ground with the seller can be a powerful element in the event of multiple offers. Often, sellers select the buyer to whom they sell for personal reasons. For example, maybe the buyer reminds them of themselves when they moved in with young children. Or, they are of the same religion. Or, the new owners will care for their gardens or feed the birds the way they did.

8-2-3 Understand the Market Climate

"Let's get back to the point your mother was making about how hot the home market is. Knowing the climate of the current real estate market is crucial in determining your strategy for negotiating your offer. You have to know the underlying market conditions."

Jack grins at Mike. "Mom's always had good insights."

"She sure has. One of the many things I love about her. In a typical real estate market, buyers usually offer less than list price. In a hot market, buyers may have to offer more than the list price."

"In a buyer's market you may be presenting an offer on a house that has been for sale for many months. The house may have a small buyer audience due to poor condition or the need for updates. In this case, you have a better negotiating position than you would with a new listing."

Eva stands and stretches, then walks over to grab the coffee pot. "Would you like a fresh cup, Dad?"

"Sure, but let's take a five-minute break. I still have a few things to share with you, and I don't want you two falling asleep on me."

A few minutes later, the three were back at the kitchen table.

"Now, where were we?" Mike mumbles to himself. "Okay, let's pick up here." Setting down his coffee, he says, "If you are in a seller's market, you will need to act quickly and be willing to offer at or near the top of the price range. You may even have to offer over the asking price. This is especially true if the home is in a hot area and has good appeal. If you discover they have multiple offers, you must make your very best offer up front."

"If the seller receives more than one offer, or you happen to be involved in making an offer where multiple offers have been presented, the listing agent and seller will decide how they will handle the situation. They may choose to disclose to all parties, or to disclose to no parties that multiple offers have been received."

> **"Shopping" occurs when the seller discloses the terms of an offer to induce a buyer to submit a better offer.**

"By disclosing that there are multiple offers, the seller is not necessarily 'shopping' your contract. 'Shopping' occurs when the seller discloses the terms of an offer to induce a buyer to submit a better offer. This can result in an environment of distrust and the possibility that the buyers will move on. Usually the procedure is to notify each party that there are multiple offers, and give each party a chance to present their highest and best offer within a certain time. After the deadline, the seller will review all offers and choose a contract with which to work."

"Keep in mind that even though a market overall may be hot or cold, particularly desirable or undesirable areas within the market may be behaving differently. Buyer and seller markets can be localized."

> **Do not let a hot market cause you to jump into a bad situation.**

"Regardless of the heat of the market, make sure you include the contingencies you need in the contract. This is the biggest purchase of your life to date; do not let a hot market cause you to jump into a bad situation. Remember, sellers with problems to unload take advantage of hot markets, and they may try to pressure you into being their free ticket out."

◇◇◇◇◇

8-2-4 Manage Your Contract Contingencies

Make your offer as simple and as straightforward as possible. Contingencies will reduce your leverage for a better price in a buyer's market, or for even being considered in a seller's market. Be proactive about reassuring the seller of your desire and ability to close. But just as Mike told Jack and Eva, do not present a foolish offer missing the contingencies you need.

Here is a reminder list of possible contingencies to include in your offer (the contract).

1. **Must haves,[15] which usually have a specific date by which they need to be done:**

   Contingent on attorney's review[16]

   You may not want to pay to have your attorney review every offer you write prior to submission. Often your offer is on a so-called standard[17] contract form used by your real estate agent. Some paragraphs are crossed out, while other items are written in by hand, and so forth. Including this contingency allows your lawyer to look at the document prior to its becoming enforceable, so any errors, omissions, or troublesome clauses can be addressed. With this clause, you will only have to pay your attorney for reviewing an offer that is accepted by the seller.

   Contingent on inspections

   Usually inspections are defined by a certain period. It is best to keep the time frame within accepted norms.

---

15   Transactions happen all the time without these contingencies, but I highly recommend their inclusion in any contract you sign.

16   If you have your attorney involved in drafting the offer and contract, this contingency is no longer necessary.

17   Be aware that each firm can make up its own "standard" contract form. There is no true industry standard real estate offer document.

2. **Dependent on your circumstances (also usually have a time limit by which they need to be done):**

Contingent on mortgage loan approval

It is always a good plan to be preapproved by a mortgage lender. Include a letter with your offer, improving your leverage. This is critical in a multiple offer situation. If you are making a cash offer, have a proof of funds letter stating that the resources are available.

Contingent on sale of your home

Seller will generally not accept this contingency unless you have a contract on your home. If you can, attach a copy of the contract and status report.

8-3 Sign the Contract

By the time you get to a point of signing the contract, you should have discussed to full comprehension the terms of the offer with your real estate agent, advisors, and/or attorney. They should be able to answer any questions you have regarding the terms such as price, time frames, and negotiable items.

> **Pay close attention to what you are signing, as your e-signature is legally binding.**

More than likely, the seller will want to change some of the terms in the contract as part of the negotiation, so you will need to initial any changes to which you agree. Depending on the extent of the items negotiated, such as price, closing date, and inspection periods, many items can be crossed out and changed. Each time this is done, initials by all parties are required to signify agreement. Using electronic versions of the contract can keep the document looking much cleaner than handwritten modifications.

It has become very common to send documents electronically via email. Signatures and initials for all contracts, addendums, disclosures, etc. can be completed electronically. Lines can be struck and new terms typed in. Initials are required and can be electronic or handwritten. If you are signing electronically, it avoids the need to print out documents and then sign, scan, and return them. This has become an efficient way to conduct business. That said, pay close attention to what you are signing, as your e-signature is legally binding.

If your attorney was not involved in or did not review the offer before it was presented, you should forward a copy of the signed document to him or her as quickly as possible after it is signed. As described above, it is best if you included an attorney's review contingency in the contract if this is the case.

You, your attorney, and your agent need to make sure that you and the seller clear any and all contingencies as quickly as possible. Remember, your escrow deposit is at risk if you do not clear your contingencies in good faith.

8-4 Getting a Formal Inspection

"A house is made of bricks and beams;
a home is made of hopes and dreams."
—Sarah Strassburg

A formal inspection is optional, but, in my view, essential when making a purchase of this magnitude. Even if you did not include an inspection contingency, and even if you plan on purchasing the home "no matter what", you need to get this done so you know what real and potential issues you will be facing when you close on the home. Any potential hazard that could harm you or your family will likely be found.

Do not assume that adverse inspection findings will allow a complete reopening of negotiations. If there is a significant or major problem found during inspection, it is certainly acceptable to ask for a credit from the seller. In a competitive housing market, you may not get it. Sometimes the seller is willing to fix a problem, saving you from extra work when you move in. But this is not always the case.

It is unlikely that a seller will make major repairs. You are better off asking for a credit at closing so you can hire your own repair people and/or contractors.

In some really competitive markets with few homes for sale, prospective buyers will do an inspection before making the offer so they can submit an offer with fewer contingencies. This basically says, "See, we are not asking you to fix things the inspector said should be repaired."

8-4-1 Home Inspection: Finding an Inspector

If you are working with an agent, they will likely have a home inspector that they work with often and trust to do a good job for their client. You could also consult online referral services. Some of them will require a fee to join. Look for an inspector that is part of a professional organization such as the National Association of Home Inspectors, the International Association of Certified Home Inspectors, or the American Society of Home Inspectors. Do not be shy when interviewing potential inspectors about their training and certifications. The inspector's job is extremely important. You are entrusting them with your safety and potentially your life. Making sure you have a well-qualified inspector is worth taking the extra time to verify qualifications.

The following is a list of questions for a potential home inspector.

1. What do you specialize in?

2. How long have you been an inspector?

3. What training and certifications do you have?

4. Do you have "errors and omissions" insurance?

5. Are you familiar with the type of home in which I'm interested: age, construction?

6. Do you belong to any professional organizations?

7. What are your fees?

8. Can I be there during the inspection?

9. Do you offer any guarantees?

10. Do you have experience in the construction field?

11. How long will the inspection take?

12. How soon will a report be generated?

> **Do not be shy when interviewing potential inspectors about their training and certifications.**

8-4-2 What Should Be Included in the Home Inspection?

The cost of an inspection is determined by the size and type of property you are purchasing. An older, larger home may require more time to inspect than a newly constructed townhome, for example. The following is a list of some of the major items that the inspector will cover.

Foundation

Whether you are purchasing a single-family home or a condo in a high-rise, the inspector will make sure the home is on a solid foundation. What supports your home makes or breaks the rest of it. Some signs of foundation problems are uneven floors, or cracks in the walls, floor tiles, moldings, or the foundation itself, and windows and doors that close improperly.

Structure

The structure is the home's skeleton. The inspector will determine what type of framing the home has: wood, concrete, concrete block, or steel?

What type of framing is ideal for the weather conditions in your area? Are you in a snowy region? Do you need to be concerned with hurricane force winds, salty sea air, wind, or flooding? Your

> **Even in a condominium or townhome, where the structure is maintained by an association, it is vital the structure be inspected.**

inspector will consider these questions and assess if the home can withstand the weather conditions of the area. The inspector will also check for damage and signs of infestation of rodents and insects common to your particular location. This includes termites that might attack wood framing, or bats or squirrels that could get into an attic.

Even in a condominium or townhome, where the structure is maintained by an association, it is vital the structure be inspected.

Exterior

The home's siding and trim will be inspected for its integrity. Is the siding stucco, wood, brick, vinyl, or logs?

Does the roof have asphalt shingles, tiles, cedar shakes, or metal? Has a new roof been installed and when? A well-maintained roof protects you from rain, snow, and potentially damaging winds. If you are obtaining an FHA loan, there are restrictions and requirements that must be met.

What material is used for the driveway and walkways: pavers or concrete? Was the material installed properly? Does the driveway and sidewalk drain away from the house? Will the yard drain properly away from the home, preventing moisture, mold, or flooding problems?

Interior

The walls, ceilings, and flooring can reveal water damage, foundation issues, and pest control problems. Kitchen countertops, cabinets, and any built-ins are looked at. Railings are checked for looseness, missing spindles, and proper height.

Plumbing

The inspector examines drainage pipes, faucets, water supply lines, water heaters, irrigation systems, and water softeners for leaks, water pressure, rust, or corrosion that would indicate problems. He will also run the washer and dishwasher to check for proper condition and potential leaks.

Heating and Cooling

The inspector determines if the heating system in the home is a furnace, boiler, or woodstove, and the age of the system. He checks the maintenance records. If there is a chimney, the inspector determines if it is clean, preventing potential chimney fires.

The inspector examines the central air conditioning (AC) system, noting its age and energy rating.[18] He will turn on and run the heating and cooling to make sure that they each are in good repair and operate properly.

Electrical

The inspector checks panels, breakers, and outlets for potential hazards, code violations, and general shortcomings. For example, he will check if there are 220-volt hook ups for the dryer, water heater, and stove; is the home wired with the correct amount of amperage to safely run all electrical systems, and are there dedicated circuits for the AC, water heater, and other high amperage devices?

Radon

Radon is an odorless, colorless, and most importantly, radioactive gas. There is always some naturally occurring radon in any structure. Radon is found in nearly all soil, rock, and water. It enters into buildings through foundation cracks, construction joints, and gaps around pipes. It can also be found in some construction material such as granite used for counter tops. The problem with radon occurs when there is a large concentration. The gas has been linked to lung cancer.

The inspector will use radon test kits to test for high levels of the gas. While he is using the kit, the inspector requires all the doors and windows to remain closed, because the gas escapes easily when either is opened. If there are high levels of radon, there are ways to mitigate the gas. One way is through proper ventilation of the home.

---

18   Energy rating is a designation taking into consideration the approximate efficiency of an appliance, or heating or cooling unit for a home. It is based on an estimate of energy consumption per year (kilowatt hours per year) and typical amount of use per year for the appliance or device.

Other Undesirable Hazards

Lead-based paint and asbestos also pose a health risk. These are usually found in older homes. The inspector will check for these hazards.

Asbestos is a carcinogen found in insulation in older structures. If it is poor condition, such as if it crumbles when handled, it is a hazard to your health. Your risk for lung cancer, asbestosis, and mesothelioma increases in the presence of asbestos. Asbestos poses a lower risk if it is not damaged.

Homes built prior to 1978 may contain lead-based paint. If dust or flakes from the paint are ingested by a child over a long period, it can lead to poisoning and brain damage. This happens over time, and the severity depends on the size of the child, how much is ingested, and the lead content of the paint. Pregnant women are also at risk. It is imperative for the condition of the paint to be checked to make sure that none is flaking and that it does not contain lead. If you love the home, contact your health department for remedies for lead removal or have a list of contractors that do this kind of work.

The list above only touches on what the inspector examines. The inspection report includes pictures, readings, and test results for large appliance, heating and cooling systems, electrical systems, and more. The inspector will check for, and alert you to government and manufacturer recalls. The inspector will also explain what repairs need to be done.

Any defect found is a potential negotiation point. You will then have to determine what could make or break the deal.

Your mortgage broker and lender will be interested in the inspection report. Different loan types, especially FHA loans, have specific requirements. The inspection is a major step toward completing the purchase.

What is not included in the inspection?

Inspectors will check whatever they can see. They are thorough, but will not climb up on your roof, nor will they climb into your attic. If the home has a fenced yard, the fence will likely not be inspected.

Inspectors also will likely not check:

1. Septic tanks;

2. Chimney repairs;

3. Structures separate from the main house such as sheds and greenhouses.

If you want any of these items checked, you will likely have to contract for separate specialized inspections.

Chapter 9
Pre-Closing Preparations

"I run on the road, long before I dance under the lights."
—Muhammad Ali

You have a bunch of people or firms to hire and tasks to complete leading up to your closing, even before the final closing countdown begins. Some of these parties will be dictated by your mortgage lender, some you will choose. This chapter addresses those miscellaneous preparation tasks. The next chapter will take you through the closing countdown checklist and actual closing.

9-1 Escrow Agent / Settlement Agent

After Jack and Eva's offer for a home is accepted, Mike, Jack, and Eva meet once again at the young couple's apartment. With a contract pending, Mike tells them, "Buying a home is a classic situation where both sides have something the other wants, but neither wants to give up their something until the other does so first. Enter the escrow agent. Have you heard of this person?"

"Tell me again, why do we need a scarecrow agent?" asks Jack with a smile.

Eva rolls her eyes. "Please, Jack, don't start with the corny humor – no pun intended, of course."

"If you two keep it up, you will have a time out."

The three laugh, then Mike continues, "An escrow agent serves the purpose of a neutral, trusted third party to transactions. If the seller or buyer is using a realtor, the realtor will act as the initial escrow agent for holding funds, such as your good faith deposit backing up your offer. If no realtor is involved, a law firm or other escrow agent will need to be retained. The escrow agent can be a business or an individual depending on local laws and/or customs."

"Later, the firm through which your closing will occur, such as a title company, will serve as the closing escrow agent (referred to as the settlement agent). Your good faith deposit will be transferred to this agent. Also, any additional funds from you for your down payment or from the seller for a future repair, tax payment, or assessment, et cetera, will be paid to the settlement agent for disbursal to the appropriate party at the appropriate time."

"Okay, I get it," says Jack. "It sounds like a great *field* of work."

Eva rolls her eyes again, and says, "I thought the title company did more than that?"

Mike says, "If you warm up my coffee, I will tell you about title companies."

9-2 Title Insurance Company

Mike sips his coffee. "Hmmm, that's good, Eva. Did you add something?"

"Yes, a little cinnamon. It always makes coffee taste better."

"I'll have to remember that." He takes another sip, then says, "A title insurance company performs two primary functions in your home purchase transaction:

1. It researches the deed to your new home, ensuring that no one else has a claim to the property, and then issues a report with the written analysis of the status of title to the property. The history of the title is called an 'abstract.'

    a. The report includes a legal property description, the names of titleholders, and the manner in which title is held (for example, joint tenancy), tax rate, encumbrances (mortgages, liens, deeds of trusts, recorded judgments), and real property taxes due.

    b. A title report created when the report is initially ordered is called a preliminary report, sometimes referred to as a 'prelim.'

2. It provides two insurance policies, one to your mortgage lender and one to you, under which it will pay for any damages the lender or you incur if it is found later that someone else has a claim to all or a part of your property. The title insurance policy issuer is required to either correct any errors or pay damages resulting from any 'cloud on title', encumbrance, or title flaw in the title that was not reported or recorded correctly."

"Keep in mind that the title insurance company will charge you separately for each of the services it offers. It will charge you a fee for doing the title search and issuing its report, and it will charge you for each insurance policy it issues. Yes, you will have to pay for your lender's title insurance policy as well as your own. Does all of this make sense so far?"

"Yes, we are following you," replies Jack. "Besides, we know you'll be sending us notes to go over."

"That's right. Okay, title companies and their fees can vary greatly. Depending on local practice and customs, a title report is typically prepared by a title company, an abstractor, attorney, or an escrow company. Sometimes your lender will dictate the company used, but sometimes you can choose. You want the best price, but you also want a company that will be around to pay claims if it ever becomes necessary. Do not be penny wise and pound foolish. Pick a reputable, well-established firm that has a strong balance sheet and has been around a long time."

"After you close, ownership of the property will transfer to you. Make sure you know who will be recording this transfer at the local government office (usually the county recorder). After you close, verify with the recorder's office that your interest in the property has been recorded. Failure to record is not common, but sometimes this does not occur and will cause you significant problems later on."

9-3 Get Insurance Lined Up

Mike tells Jack and Eva to ask their real estate agent if they have an insurance agent or broker to whom they like to refer their clients. If they trust their real estate agent, they can likely trust his or her recommendation, or the couple can choose to shop around on their own.

You may want to talk to your friends and family and see if they have ever had to file a homeowner's insurance claim, and if so, how the claim was handled. Steer away from insurance providers who are slow in paying legitimate claims.

If you already have an auto policy, you might get a discount if you keep both policies with the same company. You could also try the company through which you receive renter's insurance.

Are you a veteran? Call USAA (United Services Automobile Association) if you or someone in your family has served in the military. They offer discounts on more than just home and auto insurance. See their website (USAA.com) to see if you qualify.

What is the difference between an insurance agent and a broker?

- Agent: An agent works for an insurance company. They are the intermediary between the company and the client.

- Broker: A broker must have a broker's license, which usually means they have more insurance-specific education than an agent. They may charge an administration fee, because of higher liability.

Agents and brokers fall into two categories: captive or independent.

- Captive: This agent works for one company and only sells policies for a single insurance provider.

- Independent: An agent or broker that compares and offers different policies from several companies, comparing rates and policy details.

You will want to comparison shop when you purchase insurance. Price is not the only factor you will need to consider. Your goal is to get the best coverage you can for the least amount of money.

Some of the factors you should compare in addition to price are:

1. What types of events giving rise to losses does it cover? What types of loss events does it not cover?

2. Are there dollar or time limits on coverage?

3. Will you be compensated based on the market value of your home, or based on its replacement cost?

4. Is there a "deductible", which is the amount you cover out-of-pocket before the insurance kicks in? What are the trade-offs in insurance cost for having a larger or smaller deductible?

5. If your home suffers damage, will your policy cover temporary living expenses for you while your home is being repaired?

6. Will the policy cover the valuables in your home? Will you receive cash for the depreciated value of your belongings or will they be replaced with new items?

The agent or broker will have questions for you as well, including:

1. What is the value of the home you are purchasing?

2. Will you be the sole owner, or will you share ownership with others?

3. Where is the property located:

    a. Is it in a flood prone area?

    b. Are you near a fault line or location known for earthquakes? Are you on a waterfront?

    c. Do you have a retaining wall on a canal?

    d. Is your shoreline susceptible to erosion?

4. Have you had past claims?

5. When are you anticipating to close?

6. Who will be the mortgage lender?

9-3-1 Homeowner's Insurance

In general, a homeowner's or hazard insurance policy covers damage to and theft from your property, including both the structure itself and your personal property. Most policies will cover damage from lightning, hail, wind, and fire. Policies also cover liability and legal responsibilities for any injuries that may happen on your property. If you lose use of your home from a covered event such as fire damage, it may reimburse you for expenses such as renting a home or a temporary stay in a hotel.

You are not required by law to have hazard insurance, but mortgage lenders will require you to do so to obtain a loan. Read your policy thoroughly to see what it covers when natural disasters occur.

You are not required by law to have hazard insurance, but mortgage lenders will require you to do so to obtain a loan.

Policies that cover personal property usually limit payouts to no more than 75 percent of the home's coverage. For instance, if you have a policy with $200,000 coverage on your home, you will be covered for up to $150,000 for your possessions. This may sound like a lot of money, but when you consider all that you have obtained over time, it may not be as much as you think. For instance, do you have antiques that have appreciated with age? Your policy may only cover the depreciated value of an item. If you own collectibles, antiques, or similar items, consider getting a policy that will replace your items, not just give you the money for what the items are worth at the time of your claim.

In some regions, you may be required to obtain flood or earthquake insurance. Most policies will not cover damage from "earth movement", which includes earthquakes, sinkholes, and mudslides. Check to see if the insurance provider will offer a rider to cover disasters unique to the area you want to live.

◇◇◇◇◇

9-3-2 Seller's Home Warranty

"As you know, I'm a firm believer in home warranties," Mike says as Eva once again warms up his coffee and adds a little more cinnamon. "A seller's home warranty is an insurance policy that provides protection against damage, breakage, and disrepair that occurs or is discovered for a predefined period subsequent to your purchase of the home. It is commonplace in some markets, and in others used more as a negotiating tool. Some sellers will offer to pay for a home warranty policy as a means of giving you more comfort with the home purchase."

"Home warranties are desirable for first-time home buyers like you two who are concerned with possible upcoming repairs."

"What is covered with a seller's warranty, Dad?" asks Jack.

"Well, if major home systems fail or malfunction, such as your heating and cooling, the home warranty policy may defray some of the costs of having them replaced or repaired. Also, it may cover some of the costs of appliances if they need to be repaired. If you have a leaky roof, it may cover a repair, but not the cost of a whole new roof. It may cover structural damage. Remember, like any insurance policy, there are always restrictions and conditions."

"Are these home warranty policies only used for old homes?" Eva asks.

"That's a good question, Eva. While you may think that home warranty policies are only used for older homes, if you purchase a new home, the contractor or developer will usually include a warranty. This is to cover the first year of 'working out the kinks' in your new home as new systems and appliances are put into service."

> **A seller's home warranty is an insurance policy that provides protection against damage, breakage, and disrepair that occurs or is discovered for a predefined period subsequent to your purchase of the home.**

"In a seller's market, the seller may not offer a warranty even if it is customary to do so in your area. As the buyer, you could ask if they will include one, or if they will split the cost of purchasing a warranty policy with you, as part of your negotiations."

"You have to be careful. Warranties will not likely cover swimming pools or spas. If you have a plumbing leak, it may cover repair of the leak, but not the surrounding damage to walls or floors. Other exclusions or limits of coverage will be spelled out in the policy. If you can get one, look over the policy so you are not surprised if you have to pay for a repair for which you did not think you would be responsible."

◇◇◇◇◇

9-3-3 Flood Insurance

The home Jack and Eva are buying does not lie in a flood plain. Yours, however, may. If your home is in a flood plain or high-risk, flood-prone area, your mortgage company may require you to purchase flood insurance. If the risk is moderate, you may not have to, but may want to cover your home and belongings for the costs of extensive water damage. If you are unable to work due to high water, you may have problems paying bills and get behind financially. These are all things to consider.

The National Flood Insurance Program (NFIP) is a program managed by the Federal Emergency Management Agency (FEMA). If you plan to live in an area that participates in the NFIP, you will

Just because a home is near water does not mean it is in a flood zone.

be eligible for flood insurance. This means that if an area is deemed to be flood prone, you qualify to purchase insurance through a private company. If you are buying a home that requires flood insurance to obtain a mortgage (such as an FHA mortgage), find out the cost. You may be able to protect or replace your home or valuables due to flooding with this insurance, but that does not mean it is inexpensive. Just because a home is near water does not mean it is in a flood zone. You need to check to be sure.

Floods can be brought on by hurricanes, tropical storms, excessive rain, tidal surge, spring snow melts, clogged storm drains, broken levees, and sometimes earthquakes. Be aware that a homeowner covered by earthquake insurance may not be covered for damage due to flooding caused by the earthquake.

Flood insurance typically only covers damage and loss from water originating outside the home. The water must cover two or more acres, or have affected a nearby property.

If your pipes burst from freezing, losses and damage will likely be covered under homeowner's insurance, but not flood insurance. Mold and mildew from water flowing into your basement that could be prevented by having a sump pump will not be covered.

Once you have purchased the insurance, there may be a waiting period of up to thirty days before the policy goes into effect.

Flood insurance may not cover the full cost of everything you lose. Federal flood insurance policies have caps, currently at $250,000 for the structure and $100,000 for personal belongings. These caps can change, so you should research updated limits. Most policies will compensate you based on the actual depreciated value of your goods, not the replacement cost. For a higher premium cost, you can opt for replacement cost coverage. With this coverage you can replace damaged or lost property with new items without being concerned about depreciation.

Once you have purchased the insurance, there may be a waiting period of up to thirty days before the policy goes into effect. Consider this when negotiating the closing date, especially if you are in the middle of the rainy season in your area or in the area upstream from you.

9-3-4 Earthquake Insurance

Earthquake insurance is designed to cover some of your costs if your home is damaged by an earthquake. The majority of regular homeowner's policies do not cover damage caused by earthquake. Earthquake insurance has high deductibles. It is useful if your home is very severely damaged or destroyed, but not if damage is less than the high deductible.

Rates are dependent on the probability of an earthquake in your area, and each specific home's location and materials and method of construction. For instance, homes built with wood or metal are generally more flexible than those built with brick or concrete, and thereby better withstand the ground shaking. Also, the ground on which your home is built matters. Bedrock or granite is more solid than fill or sandy soil and is less likely to give way.

The majority of regular homeowner's policies do not cover damage caused by earthquake.

If there is an earthquake in the area in which you live, and you are suddenly worried about not having insurance, you may have to wait a few weeks before you have the opportunity to acquire it. Insurance companies will frequently stop selling new policies after a major event due to damage that can be caused by aftershocks.

When you think of earthquakes, you may think of California. However, all the Pacific coastal states are at risk. Alaska has more than 50 percent of all earthquakes in the United States, followed by California and Hawaii.

Other areas of the country are not immune. For instance, states like Oklahoma, Arkansas and Illinois also have earthquakes, though far less frequently. If you refer to the U.S. Geological Survey, you will see the risk to your area or the area to which you are thinking of moving. Unlike hurricanes, which have a season, earthquakes are unpredictable and can happen at any time. Several small earthquakes occur throughout the world daily.

Strengthening your home to decrease damage caused by shaking can save you money on your insurance and decrease your deductible.

If you live in one of the more active earthquake areas and can afford an earthquake policy, you may want to investigate purchasing one. Shop around for the best rate.

Strengthening your home to decrease damage caused by shaking can save you money on your insurance and decrease your deductible.

9-3-5 Life Insurance

Unlike most insurance, claims payments (death benefits) under a life insurance policy go to others rather than you. But that is the purpose of life insurance policies, to make sure others have adequate funds to pay expenses when you are no longer there to provide for them.

Life insurance is important to homeowners with both a mortgage loan and loved ones living in the home. If you die, your loved ones may not be able to continue making the monthly mortgage loan payments on the home. A life insurance policy with coverage equaling at least the remaining balance on your mortgage loan could allow them to pay off the loan at your death, thereby eliminating the monthly mortgage payment.

The cost of life insurance depends on your age and your health history. To obtain a policy, do your research and find a reliable company that has a history of paying out claims without issues.

There are two major categories of life insurance policies, differing in costs and benefits: whole life policies and term policies.

Whole life policies contain both an insurance and savings component. Your premium partially pays for the cost of the insurance and partially goes into a tax-sheltered savings account. Monies in the account earn interest and grow over time, and these earnings are not taxed so they grow more quickly. The savings amount built up in a whole life policy is called its cash surrender value. If you cancel (surrender) the policy, the insurance company will return this amount to you, less some surrender charges.

Subject to certain restrictions, you can borrow funds from your cash surrender value, and pay the funds back, plus an interest charge. The good part is that you are effectively paying yourself back with interest. The bad part is that if you die while a loan is outstanding against your cash surrender value, that amount will be deducted from the death benefit paid out under the policy. So before you borrow against your policy, consider the purpose of having the policy in the first place.

As whole life policies age, often the earnings on the savings component are sufficient to pay all future premiums. At that point, you can decide whether to keep making the premium payments and growing your cash surrender value, or to stop making payments and just let the policy earnings do it for you. If you keep making the payments, the death benefit payout on the policy will also grow, so there is an advantage to your beneficiaries for you to do so.

The annual premiums on a whole life policy will not increase with your age or if you develop health issues. If you stop making premium payments, however, the policy can be cancelled if your cash surrender value account earnings are not sufficient to make the payments for you.

Term policies are less expensive than whole life policies, but have no savings component, build up no cash surrender value, and usually require ever-higher premiums as you age.

Young and healthy people often start with term policies because the policies are more affordable. For the same premium, the insured can obtain a larger payout to his or her beneficiaries than with a whole life policy. The drawback is that term insurance is not intended to be a long-term protection mechanism. At the end of each term (usually annually), you are subject to having to pay a higher premium and perhaps even get a new health examination in order to renew the policy.

Some insurers offer policies combining aspects of whole life and term policies. Often these policies allow the insured to convert the term life portion of the policy to whole life at set points in the life of the policy. Combination policies may offer more affordability in the early years when your earnings are lower, but the advantage of some cash surrender value build-up, stability in year-to-year premiums, and the ability to fully convert to a whole life policy when you can better afford it without having to have a new health examination.

> **Term insurance is not intended to be a long-term protection mechanism.**

9-3-6 Disability Insurance

Disability insurance policies pay claims to insured parties who become unable to work due to an injury or debilitating illness. Most employers offer disability insurance, whether short-term or long-term. You can also purchase policies through private insurers. Having disability insurance can help to make sure you can continue making your monthly mortgage loan and escrow payments if you are unable to work for an extended period.

There are two types of policies:

1. Long-term disability: If you are unable to work, long-term disability policies pay you an amount each month to a defined

percentage of your base pay (usually 50 to 80 percent). Payment will continue for up to a specified number of months or years, depending on your coverage. Some policies pay a fixed monthly amount.

Ask your human resources department or insurance agent about the logistics of payouts for this product. Find out about waiting periods before you can start collecting since this can be up to ninety days. This waiting period is one reason that having three months of living expenses in savings is important.

2. Short-term disability: A short-term disability policy is designed to replace lost wages if you sustain an injury, illness, or have surgery. In some states you can use this benefit for maternity leave. There is a waiting period typically of one to two weeks before the coverage starts.

It is more costly than long-term disability insurance (LTD) because it is more commonly needed. As with LTD you will receive a percentage of your gross income earnings. Depending on the policy you choose, the coverage lasts from 60 to 180 days.

9-4 Title Ownership

Ownership of real estate is evidenced by a legal process referred to as holding title. When you acquire real estate, you take title to the property. Title can be held by one or more individuals, trusts, or legal entities such as corporations or partnerships.

There are significant legal and tax considerations and potential consequences on how you hold title. If more than one individual holds title to a property, problems can occur if issues or events affect the relationship of those individuals. For instance, think divorce, partner breakup, remarriage, step-children, death, inheritance, and other facts of life, and you will begin to get the picture. You should seek advice from an attorney and/or CPA on the legal manner in which you should hold title to your property. Do not skimp on this, or you (or your loved ones) may pay the price later.

The following summaries are a few of the more common ways to hold title to real property and are provided for informational purposes only. This is not a law book: these are layman's descriptions only.

9-4-1 Sole Ownership

A man or woman who is not married.

Example: John Doe, a single man.

An unmarried man/woman.

A man or woman, who having been married, is legally divorced.

Example: John Doe, an unmarried man.

A married man/woman, as his/her sole and separate property:

When a married man or woman wishes to acquire title as their sole and separate property, the spouse must consent and relinquish all right, title, and interest in the property by deed or other written agreement.

Example: John Doe, a married man, as his sole and separate property.

9-4-2 Co-Ownership

Community Property:

Property acquired by husband and wife, or either during marriage, other than by gift, bequest, devise, descent, or as the separate property of either is presumed community property.

Example: John Doe and Mary Doe, husband and wife, as community property.

Example: John Doe and Mary Doe, husband and wife.

Example: John Doe, a married man.

9-4-3 Joint Tenancy

Under joint tenancy, two or more individuals own equal, undivided interests in a designated property. Their joint ownership is created in a single transaction, evidenced by a single legal document. Each individual has the right of survivorship, meaning if one person dies, the other(s) get his interest.

Undivided interests means each owns an interest in the entire property, not just a room or two in the whole property.

> *Example: John Doe and Mary Doe, husband and wife, as joint tenants.*

9-4-4 Tenancy in Common

Under tenancy in common, the co-owners own undivided interests in the real estate property. Unlike joint tenancy, these interests need not be equal and may arise at different times. There is no right of survivorship; each tenant owns an interest, which on his or her death passes to his or her heirs or other designated party.

> *Example: John Doe, a single man, as to an undivided three-fourths interest, and George Smith, a single man as to an undivided one-fourth interest, as tenants in common.*

9-4-5 Trust

Title to real property may be held in trust. The trustee of the trust holds title pursuant to the terms of the trust for the benefit of the trustor/beneficiary.

9-5 Cohabitation Agreement

If you are planning to purchase a home with someone to whom you are not married, you should execute a cohabitation agreement. A cohabitation agreement is not a way to hold title. It is an agreement which sets forth the respective rights and responsibilities of the parties. It addresses issues of ownership and distribution of assets after death. It addresses what happens if the parties split.

Some couples choose to live together without getting married. Some live in states that do not allow same-sex partners to marry. There are many reasons why people buy houses and live together. A cohabitation agreement is an essential document in all of these circumstances.

Do not be naïve and think that this type of agreement reflects on your commitment to the other party. A cohabitation agreement, properly tied into other agreements as discussed below, could help you to insure that your and your partner's wishes and rights are respected in areas where statutes or good case law may not yet be on the books to clearly define what can and should happen in the event of a death of one party or the breakup of unmarried parties.

> **A cohabitation agreement, properly tied into other agreements as discussed below, could help you to insure that your and your partner's wishes and rights are respected.**

Be aware that for a cohabitation agreement to properly work upon death of one of the buyers, it has to be tied in to a combination of each person's will and a "land trust". Otherwise, the heirs can contest it. The issue is that the cohabitation agreement is not a recorded document with regard to the property, and thus a judge may not honor it if a will and land trust do not refer to it. If you plan on using this type of agreement, make sure you consult your attorney and get all aspects set up properly.

On the next page is a simple example of a cohabitation agreement. Depending on assets, liabilities, children, and other circumstances, a cohabitation agreement can be simple or complex. Do not use this form, it is just an example.

_____, Cohabitant No. 1, and _____
_____, Cohabitant No. 2, hereinafter jointly referred to as the Cohabitants, who now live / will live together in the future (circle one) at _____, in the city of _____, county of _____, state of _____, hereby agree on this _____ day of _____, in the year _____, as follows:

1. The Cohabitants wish to establish their respective rights and responsibilities regarding each other's income and property and the income and property that may be acquired, either separately or together, during the period of cohabitation.
2. The Cohabitants have made a full and complete disclosure to each other of all of their financial assets and liabilities.
3. Except as otherwise provided below, the Cohabitants waive the following rights:
    a. To share in each other's estates upon their death.
    b. To "palimony" or other forms of support or maintenance, both temporary and permanent.
    c. To share in the increase in value during the period of cohabitation of the separate property of the parties.
    d. To share in the pension, profit sharing, or other retirement accounts of the other.
    e. To the division of the separate property of the parties, whether currently held or hereafter acquired.
    f. To any other claims based on the period of cohabitation of the parties.
    g. To claim the existence of a common-law marriage.
4. [SET FORTH RELEVANT EXCEPTIONS HERE. For instance, if both Cohabitants are contributing to the debt repayment on the home owned by one party, they might agree that any increase in equity during the period of cohabitation will be fairly divided between them.]
5. The Cohabitants agree to divide the household expenses as follows:
6. [ADDITIONAL PROVISIONS HERE. These can cover just

about any issue, from custody of pets to allocating household chores. The legal obligation to pay child support to any children of the Cohabitants cannot, however, be modified by agreement of the parties.]

7. Each Cohabitant is represented by separate and independent legal counsel of his or her own choosing.

8. The Cohabitants have separate income and assets to independently provide for their own respective financial needs.

9. This agreement constitutes the entire agreement of the parties and may be modified only in a writing executed by both Cohabitants.

10. In the event it is determined that a provision of this agreement is invalid because it is contrary to applicable law, that provision is deemed separable from the rest of the agreement, such that the remainder of the agreement remains valid and enforceable.

11. This agreement is made in accordance with the laws of the state of _____, and any dispute regarding its enforcement will be resolved by reference to the laws of that state.

12. This agreement will become null and void upon the legal marriage of the Cohabitants.

I HAVE READ THE ABOVE AGREEMENT, I HAVE TAKEN TIME TO CONSIDER ITS IMPLICATIONS, I FULLY UNDERSTAND ITS CONTENTS, I AGREE TO ITS TERMS, AND I VOLUNTARILY SUBMIT TO ITS EXECUTION.

_____

Cohabitant No. 1

_____

Cohabitant No. 2

Witnessed by:

_____

(Witness or counsel signature)

_____

(Witness or counsel signature)

Chapter 10

Closing

"If you are prepared, then you are able to feel confident."
—Tom Landry

10-1 Closing Checklist

Like Jack and Eva, you have all your pre-closing tasks completed. Now it is time to get ready for the big day. Below is a checklist for your closing.

Downloadable Template 10-1: Closing Checklist

Closing Checklist	
Checklist Items	**Relevant Information**
1. Determine who will conduct your closing, where it will be, and when.	Who: Where: When:
2. Ask the person who will conduct your closing what to expect at closing.	Notes:
3. Request your closing documents three business days in advance of closing:	
a. By law, the documents must be provided to you three business days before your closing.	Date received: ___/ ___/ 20___ Comments:

Closing Checklist	
4. Identify people you can call if you need help during closing:	
a. Make sure you have their phone numbers with you and they are alert to the fact you may be calling.	Who: _____ _____ Phone: _____ _____ Who: _____ _____ Phone: _____ _____ Who: _____ _____ Phone: _____ _____
5. Schedule time in advance of your closing to review documents:	
a. Make an appointment with yourself.	Day: _____ _____ Date: _____ _____ Time: _____ _____

Closing Checklist

6. Compare your Closing Disclosure to your most recent Loan Estimate:	Item	LE	CD
a. Loan type, interest rate, monthly payment, other key terms?	Loan type:	Fixed /Adj	Fixed /Adj
	Monthly payment:	$ _____	$ _____
	Interest rate:	_____ %	_____ %
	Loan term:	_____ mos	_____ mos
	Balloon term:	_____ mos	_____ mos
	IO period:	_____ mos	_____ mos
	Prepay Penalty:	Yes / No	Yes / No
	_____	_____	_____
	_____	_____	_____
	Item	**LE**	**CD**
b. Are there new fees or have amounts changed?	Underwriting	$ _____	$ _____
	Processing	$ _____	$ _____
	Recording	$ _____	$ _____
	Appraisal	$ _____	$ _____
	Origination	$ _____	$ _____
	Prepaid Interest	$ _____	$ _____
	_____	$ _____	$ _____
	_____	$ _____	$ _____
	_____	$ _____	$ _____
	_____	$ _____	$ _____

Closing Checklist

c. Is there an escrow account for taxes and insurance?		Yes _____ No _____	
	Monthly amounts:		
	Taxes	$ _____	
	Insurance	$ _____	
7. Read the rest of your closing document:			
a. Is your personal informational correct?		Yes _____ No _____	
b. What will happen if you do not pay your loan on time?	Grace period? _____ Late charges? _____ Penalty interest rate? _____		
c. Do all key numbers (e.g., balance, payments, and interest rates) match across all documents?	Balance:	$ _____	Yes / No
	Monthly payment:	$ _____	Yes / No
	Interest rate:	_____%	Yes / No
	Loan term:	_____mos	Yes / No
	Balloon term:	_____mos	Yes / No
	IO period:	_____mos	Yes / No
	Prepay Penalty:	_____mos	Yes / No
	_____	_____mos	Yes / No
	_____	_____	Yes / No

Closing Checklist

8. Arrange your payment for the amount due at closing	
a. You will need a cashier's check or wire transfer.	Amount needed:　　$ _____ How will you pay?　　Cashiers' check/　wire
9. Bring key items and people to closing.	
a. Your cashier's check or proof of wire transfer	
b. Driver's license;	
c. Copy of your purchase contract	
d. Names and phone numbers of your key contact people;	

Closing Checklist

e. Your Closing Disclosure;	
f. Your lawyer or trusted advisor;	
g. Any Co-borrower signing on the loan;	
h. Your check book, in case of last minute changes.	
10. Get answers to key questions at closing.	
a. How will you pay your property taxes and insurance?	
b. Where will you send your monthly payments? Can you set up electronic payments?	
i. Can you set up electronic payments?	Notes:
	Website:www. _____ _____
c. Who should you call if you have questions after closing?	Who: _____ _____ Phone: _____ _____

Closing Checklist	
11. Remember these closing tips:	
a. Take your time. You can have all the time you need to read and understand your closing documents, no matter how long it takes.	
b. Do not sign if your gut tells you something is wrong.	
12. Save your closing packet:	
a. Make sure it includes these important documents:	
i. Closing Disclosure;	
ii. Promissory Note;	
iii. Mortgage / Security Instrument / Deed of Trust;	
iv. Deed, document that transfers property ownership.	

A blank, downloadable version of the closing checklist is on the companion website. You can fill it in on your computer, or print it out, fill it in by hand, and use it. Make sure you fill in key contact information, review documents, arrange funds, and take what you need to the closing. The sections below provide more detailed information on some of the items referenced on the checklist.

10-2 Closing Disclosure

When Mike sits down with Jack and Eva at their kitchen table for their weekly home buying session, he explains the final stages of the process. He starts with the primary document summarizing the terms of a home loan, which is called the Closing Disclosure, or CD.[19] The Closing Disclosure is a five page form designed by the CFPB to help home buyers understand the key features, costs, and risks of your mortgage loan, and lenders must provide it to you before your closing. Beginning October 3, 2015, the Closing Disclosure replaced the HUD-1 Settlement Statement and Final Truth in Lending (TIL) forms that were used up until that point.

Review your Closing Disclosure and make sure you are getting the loan you expect.

As detailed in Chapter 5, to create the Closing Disclosure, the CFPB combined the two federal mortgage disclosures listed above. The CFPB also put in place a rule requiring lenders to give you three business days prior to closing to review your loan terms. The intent of these changes was to make it easier to understand the terms of your mortgage before signing on the dotted line.

As Mike advises our young couple, be sure you go through this document *very* carefully when you receive it. You have done all the work to get this far, do not let up now. Many of the problems people have had in the past with mortgage loans can be traced to not having time to adequately review and consider their loan documents. **Do not make the mistake of thinking that everyone is acting in your best interest**. Review your Closing Disclosure and make sure you are getting the loan you expect.

---

19   The CD is one of two main documents mandated under the TILA-RESPA Integrated Disclosure (TRID) rules. The other is the Loan Estimate or LE form.

Creditor compliance with TRID rules is based on a comparison between the content of the LE and the final executed CD. If you actually pay more on the CD than disclosed on the LE, the creditor must refund the increased amount to you and submit a new (revised) CD you. The timeframe in which the creditor must do a compliance review and issue you a refund if necessary is no later than sixty days after closing.

10-3 Figure Out How Much Money You Have to Take to the Closing

Mike tells Jack and Eva that the Closing Disclosure will show how much money they need to take to closing. "Review it carefully and arrange for a wire transfer or a cashier's check for the correct amount," he said. "You will need to have cleared funds ready for wiring or cashier's check by the day preceding your closing. So plan accordingly."

Mike then explains some of the major items for which they, and you, will need cash, including:

Down payment on the home

This is the initial, upfront portion of the total home cost coming from your own funds, based on the LTV of your loan. These funds are due at closing. It is usually required that the funds be wired, or in some cases a cashier's check will be accepted.

Prepaid interest

At closing, your lender will collect an amount equal to the interest that would accrue on your loan from your closing day up through the first day of the first full month of your mortgage loan. For instance, if you close on May 15, you will pay the lender sixteen days of prepaid interest. Because you do this, you will not have to make a payment on June 1 for a less than one month period; you have prepaid it. The first payment that you will actually have to make will be on July 1, which will cover the full month of June.

The amount of the prepaid interest you will have to pay at closing will be equal to your loan amount multiplied by your interest rate, multiplied by the number of days between your closing date and the first of the next month, and then divided by either 360 or 365 days, depending on the terms of your mortgage loan.

Appraisal fee

This is the fee charged for the appraisal of your home. The lender orders the appraisal and collects the amount of the fee from the buyer. This fee can be paid prior to closing, but it is typically paid at closing, and this makes up part of the total cash due.

Origination fees

Some lenders charge you a fee for the cost of originating your loan. This fee may be a fixed dollar amount or a percent of the loan amount. If the fee is a percentage of the loan, the amount will increase the larger the loan is.

Points

Points are an upfront cash payment you make to your lender in exchange for a lower interest rate on your mortgage loans. Lenders often will offer you trade-offs between the interest rate you pay monthly on the loan and the amount of points you pay upfront at closing on your loan. Points are expressed as a percent of the loan amount; e.g., "2 points" means a charge equal to 2 percent of the loan balance.

A lower interest rate on your loan results in a lower payment. There is a breakeven point at which the cumulative savings you achieve on your monthly payments will equal the amount you paid in points. If you keep your loan outstanding longer than that number of payments, you will benefit from paying the points and receiving the lower interest rate. If you refinance your mortgage loan prior to that number of months, you would have been better off taking a higher rate and not paying the points.

Escrow (Impound) Account

Remember to bring your checkbook to closing just in case small differences arise.

Depending on your down payment amount, you may need to initially fund an escrow account. These funds are used to make payments on your behalf for real estate taxes and premiums for insurance required to protect the property, such as homeowner's insurance.[20] An initial amount is collected at closing to fund the escrow account and additional funds are collected as part of your monthly mortgage payment.

Remember to bring your checkbook to closing just in case small differences arise.

10-4 Documents for Closing

On closing day, expect to sign a considerable number of documents and walk away with a sizeable folder of papers (or electronic files containing images of them). Below is a list of the most important closing documents you will typically see at closing. You should file this paperwork in a safe place for future reference and for your records. Some of the numbers you will need for your tax return will be contained in the Closing Disclosure document, so make a separate copy of it and put it in your tax file.

Some of the documents will vary a little based on the type of loan you are obtaining.

- **Loan Estimate** – This form helps borrowers understand the full cost of the mortgage, including fees and interest.

- **Closing Disclosure** – This form helps borrowers know what to expect on closing day, and how much cash you will owe.

---

20 If you are paying at least 20 percent down, your lender may not require you to escrow funds. If you choose this option, you will be responsible for paying property taxes and premiums for homeowner's insurance when they are due.

A blank Loan Estimate and Closing Disclosure are shown in Appendix D and on the companion website

- **Promissory Note** – This document spells out the legal terms of your loan obligation and the agreed upon repayment terms.

- **Mortgage / Security Instrument / Deed of Trust** – This document legally secures your promissory note with an interest in your home. This means that if you do not pay your note, the lender has the legal right to take your home through a legal process called foreclosure and sell the home in full or partial settlement of the note.

- **Deed** – This document transfers ownership to you (purchase transactions only).

- **Affidavits** – These documents are binding statements by either party attesting to some action or lack of action. For example, the sellers will often sign an affidavit stating that they haven't incurred any liens.

- **Riders / Addendums** – These documents are amendments or additional detailed agreements or disclosures to a base contractual document. For example, you and the sellers may attach a rider to your home purchase agreement whereby you agree that the seller is entitled to continue occupying the home for two weeks after you buy it, but will pay rent to the buyers during that period.

- **Insurance Policies** – These documents provide a record and proof that you have acquired insurance coverage against losses or damages caused by specific hazards or events.

I strongly recommend that you hire an attorney to review all the key documents prepared prior to the closing. You are about to spend a lot of money and you want to make sure all documents are in order and that you are protected legally. I also advise you to have your attorney attend the closing with you to make sure anything that happens at the closing is proper and to review any last minute document changes that may occur.

Regardless of whether or not you hire an attorney, you should review all key terms of the note and the mortgage, review all amounts on the Closing Disclosure (CD) and compare them to the corresponding amounts on the Loan Estimate (LE) to make sure they are the same. Only after you are comfortable with the content of the documents should you sign.

> **Hire an attorney to review all the key documents prepared prior to the closing, and have your attorney attend the closing with you.**

Typically the closing agent will be able to answer any questions you may have. As mentioned prior, you may have already had your attorney review the documents, and may have decided to have your attorney with you at the closing table.

10-5 Get the Keys, the Garage Door Opener, and All Security Codes

If you cannot get in the house, you have a problem. You need to walk away with all keys, garage door openers, and security system codes. You will shortly be changing all these, but you need them to get in your new house.

10-6 Tweet Everyone!

#FindingHomeSuccess

Chapter 11

Packing and Moving

"I'm ready to settle down. Moving away is the first step.
After that, everything will fall into place."
—Unknown

"Congratulations!" Jayne calls out as she enters Jack and Eva's apartment one Friday evening.

"You are ready to move into your new home!" adds Mike as he closes the front door.

"Thanks so much, Mom and Dad. We could never have done this without you," says Eva.

Jack joins them and, after warm hugs are given and pleasantries exchanged, the four sit down at the kitchen table for their final home buying meeting.

"The work isn't done," Mike says and chuckles. "No resting on your laurels. Have you started packing? We have useful tips before you start. Planning out how you pack will help when you unpack. Although this is an exciting milestone in your life, good stress is stress just the same."

"My mom and dad were over yesterday," says Eva. "They brought some empty boxes for us. But we could use all the help and tips we can get."

◇◇◇◇◇

11-1 Cleaning and Painting

Eva and Jack have almost a full month left on the lease of their apartment. They either planned well or are lucky; not everyone gets this kind of time. Some home buyers have to store their belongings and stay in a hotel, with friends, or in a temporary rented residence for a while before their home is "ready" for them to move in, essentially having to move twice. Eva plans on painting before they move in since she is on summer break and has the time. Jack plans to help in the evenings after work.

◇◇◇◇◇

"Do your research and buy good quality paint, brushes and rollers," Mike cautions the young couple. "Do not purchase cheap paint and supplies. You will work harder and the finished product will not be as nice. With the newer paint/primer formulas, you may only need one coat of paint depending on the color of paint you are using. If you are inexperienced, most home improvement stores offer DIY (do-it-yourself) classes. You can also search YouTube for videos on how to paint a room step-by-step."

"Hiring a professional is a good idea if you are not confident about doing a good job or if you have the money but not the time," says Jayne. "However, I know of someone very professional whose services I'll volunteer..." She glances at Mike and smiles. Mike simply shrugs and smiles back.

"It's always best to clean the house top to bottom, prior to moving in, and I'll be there to help," adds Jayne. "I've already booked time off of work. It will feel good to move into a fresh, clean home. We'll wipe out cabinets, mop floors, clean windows, and scrub carpets.

Cleaning an empty home is easier than cleaning a home with furniture and boxes. If you don't clean ahead of time, the floors are dirty when you move, and they will be much harder to clean after all your stuff is moved in."

"My sister said she would help, too," says Eva. "She owes me from when I helped her when she and her husband bought their home."

"That's great!" says Jayne. "We can have a cleaning party."

The two couples debate having a professional come in to deep clean. Deep cleaning costs between $200 and $400 on average, depending on the size of the home and the scope of the cleaning. See Table 11-1 comparing deep cleaning to regular house cleaning.

Table 11-1 General Cleaning versus Deep Cleaning

	General Cleaning	Deep Cleaning	For Both
Kitchen	Top / front of appliances cleaned	Appliances cleaned inside	Drip pans cleaned
	Floors mopped / vacuumed	Cabinets washed down	Sinks disinfected
	Baseboards wiped	Clean behind fridge and stove	Cobwebs swept
	Table and chairs wiped	Surfaces cleaned for dirty spots / fingerprints	Counters cleaned
Bathrooms	Shower / bath cleaned	Shower door gets extra attention	Counter and sink cleaned
	Trash emptied	Garbage cans sanitized	Fixtures shined
	Tile cleaned	Tile grout scrubbed	Mildew treated
	Baseboards wiped	Inside of cabinets cleaned	Mirrors cleaned
			Toilets cleaned
Living areas	Vacuuming	Vacuuming edges of carpet	Closets and stairs vacuumed
	Windowsills wiped down	Mini blinds wiped down	Dusting vents
	Surfaces cleaned	All knick-knacks cleaned	Cobwebs removed
	Mirrors cleaned	Ceiling fans / lamp shades wiped down	Wood floors dust mopped

11-2 Making the Move - Planning and Packing

Depending on how far you are moving and how much stuff you have, you will either hire a company to help you move, do it yourself, or do some combination of both. There is a lot to think about. You have more stuff now than you did when you moved into your dormitory freshman year, including, perhaps, furniture and appliances. Planning is essential. Here are some things to think about that Mike and Jayne discuss with Jack and Eva:

1. ***Budget for your move:*** Moving is expensive. Some moving expenses are obvious: purchasing packing materials, renting a moving truck, hiring movers, and paying for temporary housing or storage if needed. You may have to travel a long distance to purchase your new home. Other expenses include paying deposits for changing utilities and cable.

2. ***Obtain sturdy boxes:*** Start collecting boxes and packing material early. Sturdy boxes of uniform size are best for stacking. If you are not picky, your local grocery store, liquor store, or big box store will usually be glad to have you take their cardboard off their hands. Collecting boxes of all sizes is also helpful. Smaller boxes are good for delicate items. You can put smaller boxes into larger boxes for portability

   If you are not on a tight budget, the large plastic containers from big box stores are nice and usually have handles making it easier for two people to lift one box. Remember though, if you are moving into a home with not a lot of space you might not want to store all those plastic containers. You can give them to the next friend who's moving, sell them online, or see if your local thrift store will take them.

3. ***Pack carefully:*** It is surprising how much moving even a short few miles can jostle your boxes. Speed bumps, sudden stops, and rough handling can make you sad if your favorite wine decanter shatters. Pack that precious cargo in bubble wrap, foam peanuts, or newspaper.

Old newspapers will save you money, but the ink can rub off on your hands or on your items. Use packing tape from a home improvement store or sometimes from the place you rent your moving truck or trailer.

4. **Obtain moving equipment:** You will save your back and those of your helpers by using dollies for moving heavier boxes. You should also get bungee cords to secure items (especially if you have an open pickup truck), and blankets and pillows for packing around items to cushion them. Garbage bags are good to use for packing pillows, stuffed animals, blankets and bedspreads. You can put these bags in between items that might otherwise rub against each other and be damaged.

Get a high quality padlock if you will be leaving your moving truck overnight. A back brace can help with your posture when you are moving and provide support. Forearm lifts are heavy long straps that help you to carry heavy or bulky items without having to lift them too high. Have tools available to dismantle furniture if needed.

5. **Manage box weight:** Be mindful of how much you pack into a box. Books and magazines, tools, pots and pans, and clothes can be surprisingly heavy. You do not want the bottom of the box to break and dump all your stuff out onto the dirty sidewalk. If a box is particularly heavy, mark it as such. The warning will be appreciated by anyone helping you move.

6. **Pack up one room at a time:** This may sound obvious to some, but when you are busy with your job, your commitments, and trying to get ready to move into your new home you may need to think about organization before you jump in to the packing project. Think about how

> **Pack one room at a time. When you start to unpack, you will be happy you did.**

you will be unloading the truck to expedite the process when you arrive at your new home.

7. **Label everything:** And I do mean everything. For example, if you packed up all your favorite party games, label the box

on the top and the side. If you have more than one box, you may want to use more detailed labeling. For example, glow in the dark beer pong game, Cards Against Humanity, Jenga, Monopoly, and Farkle.

Also, put a "Fragile" label on any box containing breakables so those boxes will not have too much piled on top and movers will not toss them around. "This Side Up" is also a great label to keep your items safe. You may not be materialist, but buying and replacing items may not be in your budget after the outlay of expenses for your first home.

Professional movers will use numbered labels to make sure all boxes are accounted for at both ends. You too can use numbered labels and record on a packing list what is in each numbered box. You may prefer this method as you can be more detailed in your descriptions while maintaining privacy. If you do this, you should still use Fragile and This Side Up labels where appropriate.

8. ***Know the layout of your new home:*** Knowing the layout can help you pack your moving truck. Make sure your sectional will fit into your small living room. Measure the wall space in the home. Which direction will you set up your bed? Do you have an office or den you are going to buy a new desk for? Does the desk match the age and décor? Is this even important to you or are you going to continue using your kitchen table as your "mail and bill" space?

9. ***Have cleaning supplies handy:*** Make sure you have your vacuum, mop, broom, and cleaning supplies readily available when you get to your home. Most people moving out are respectful and clean before they leave, but not all are, and your definition of clean may be different. If the house is dirty, you will want to vacuum, sweep, or mop so you are not tracking dirt through your house when you are moving in.

10. ***Hire a moving company or rent a truck:*** Check into this as soon as you know your closing date or when you plan

Ask the rental company if they have any policies regarding possible delays in needing the truck.

on moving. If you want a specific size moving truck, reserve it ahead of time. Ask the rental company if they have any policies regarding possible delays in needing the truck. This may be necessary, for example, if your closing gets delayed. This does happen and you do not want to be out hundreds of dollars or your moving truck as a result.

11. **Recruit help:** It is a safe bet that nobody *wants* to help you move. Well, maybe your parents if you are still living at home, but they probably will not want to lift anything heavy. Bribery may help; pizza and beer. A good rule – no beer until the stuff is moved into the new place. Drinking alcohol on a hot day can lead to dehydration and can increase the chance of accidents. This could even lead to a damaged friendship if someone helping you move gets hurt, for instance with a back injury. Water and soda in a cooler are nice to have as moving can be hot and sweaty work, and are safer than alcohol.

Make sure you are ready before your movers arrive. If you hired movers, it will cost you more money if you are not ready because you will have to pay them just for standing around. If you recruited friends, they will not be happy that you are taking more of their time because you were not ready.

12. **Plan your route, the driver, and parking at the other end:** Avoid rush hour. Plan how much mileage or time you are allowed on a rental truck. Think about unloading at your new home. Is there a driveway? Will a truck fit in it? Will you have to park the truck on the street, and is parking available at various times of the day?

> **Allow yourself plenty of time and overestimate how much time you need.**

Who will be driving the truck? They will have to be allowed to drive under terms of the rental contract. Driving a truck is quite a bit different than driving your Prius. It is big, slow, and you have to use the side mirrors to see behind you. There is a very large blind spot. Make sure you are comfortable doing this or you have someone that is. Otherwise hiring a moving company or getting a movable storage container (e.g., POD) is probably a better way to go.

13. ***Be aware of time constraints:*** Give everyone a time to meet and start loading up. Allow yourself plenty of time and overestimate how much time you need, reducing personal stress, so you do not yell at your helpers for slacking. Make sure to take breaks to avoid injuries.

14. ***Know where to order dinner from to reward your helpers:*** Are you familiar with the restaurants or grocery stores in the area to which you are moving? Be aware if your helpers have food allergies. They have taken the time to help you out, so be cognizant of allergies or food preferences. Having a plan ahead of time is a good idea, because after a heavy moving day everyone is likely to be hungry and tired. This combination is a recipe for disagreements. Make sure you have sufficient cash or that the restaurants and grocery take your credit or debit card. Do not assume.

CHECKLIST OF ITEMS NEEDED FOR MOVING

1. Boxes; all sizes and shapes, cardboard or plastic;

2. Labels (Fragile, This Side Up, etc.);

3. Box number labels, inventory list, and clipboard;

4. Bubble wrap, tissue paper, newspapers, packing paper;

5. Shrink wrap;

6. Packing tape;

7. Utility knife;

8. Blankets, cushions, or pillows;

9. Permanent markers;

10. Trash bags;

11. Mattress bags;

12. Padlock;

13. Tools; hammer, screwdrivers (Phillips-head, straight edge), cordless screwdriver, socket wrenches, hex wrenches;

14. Bungee cords, rope;

15. Dolly;

16. Forearm lifts;

17. Humans: friends and family with strong backs and helpful hearts.

11-3 Hiring a Moving Company

If you have room in your budget, you should hire a moving company. Be aware that you do not have to hire them to move everything. You can just hire them to move the heavy things, like appliances, furniture, your piano, boxes of books, your professional weight lifting machines, and your restored jukebox. It will save time, money, and your back.

Whether you hire a moving company to do some or all of your moving, you need to follow some basic steps.

1. Find out names and contact information of competing companies. You can do this online or using that old Yellow Pages phone book you are using to prop up your computer monitor. You are going to have to call them and ask them a bunch of questions. You need to have a list of questions tailored to your situation. Also, ask friends, family, or your real estate agent who they would recommend.

    Distance matters for the company you hire, as some just do local moves and some will do local and long distance.

    Long-distance moving companies: Examples include Allied Van Lines, American Van Lines, International Van Lines, Mayflower Transit, United Van Lines, Atlas Van

Lines, and PODS. These companies generally have good ratings and reviews.

<u>Shorter distance companies</u>: These are usually smaller companies, but not always.

2. Company address: If you can actually go to the moving company and visit the office, do it. Check out the condition of the trucks. Make sure the trucks are marked with the company name and they do not just use a magnetic sign.

3. Read reviews: Check the Better Business Bureau to see if the company has any complaints.

4. Find out if the company subcontracts out to other companies or if they hire their own crew to do the moving.

5. Obtain references and call them.

6. Make sure they are fully licensed and insured. If there is damage to your valuables, find out if they will cover the damage.

7. How long have they been in business? Try to find a company that has been in business for ten years or more. Likely, they do a good enough job that they have been able to remain in business.

8. Phone numbers (local and toll-free); have these readily available to access.

Eva has a list of phone numbers in her purse and programmed into her phone.

Jack and Eva are excited to start life in their new home. Eva heads to a big box store and buys big plastic containers and packing paper to pack up their apartment. Jack heads to the local liquor store to see if they have free boxes. He subscribes to *The Tribune* and *Sun Times* and has been saving newspapers to wrap up his old baseball trophies. Eva has a big roll of packing paper to pack up all her valuables.

Jack calls all his friends he has helped move over the past few years. "It is time to return the favor," he announces.

11-4 Setting and Hooking Things Up in Your New Home

Set up your bill payments ahead of time: There are a lot of distractions and commotion during a move. Items get misplaced or lost, including important paperwork and outstanding bills. It is best to set up automatic bill pay ahead of time. This will be one more thing not to think about during your move.

Utilities setup and disconnect: Before you start, a good idea is to arrange for the disconnection of utilities at your current address and the setup of your utilities at your new home. You may have to pay deposits to

Set up automatic bill pay ahead of time.

start your service. Make sure not to forget the water, or when you go to take a shower after sweating all day during your move you may be unpleasantly surprised.

Here is a list of the types of companies you may need to contact:

1. Telephone;

2. Electricity;

3. Water and sewer;

4. Natural gas;

5. Heating oil.

Setting up cable: The earlier you set up moving your cable, the more seamless the process will be. Make sure that you know which company services your new home's area. If Internet speed is important to you, be sure to ask if the speed you need is available at your new address. If not, you may need to do some research and determine other options. Especially if you need your Internet for your home business, you will need to be on top of this.

Usually calling the company at least ten days to two weeks ahead of time should be sufficient. Ask if you will be incurring new hookup charges so that you are not surprised when you get the bill. As I said before, moving is expensive, so be ready for your bills to come with additional charges. If you have this planned out ahead of time, you can budget for it.

Major appliances disconnect and set-up: If you own a clothes washer and dryer, you will need to have them disconnected and prepared for moving. You will also need to arrange to have them set up and connected in your new home. If you are buying new appliances, you will need to arrange with the store from which you are buying them to deliver and install them.

> **Make sure you know which type of clothes dryer your home will accommodate.**

Make sure you know which type of clothes dryer your home will accommodate. Many homes have outlets and connections for both electric and gas dryers, but some only accommodate electric.

Change your address at the post office: You can do this online, which is the easiest. You will be charged $1.05. Or you can spend that dollar on gas and drive to your post office and do it in person. You will receive an email confirmation after you have completed the process. The change of address stays in effect for six months. After six months you can extend for another six months, which I would recommend doing, unless you are in a witness protection program.

As said with other moving plans, do this ahead of time. Once you have filed your change of address it takes seven to ten days to take effect. You will get a welcome kit with coupons. You may appreciate the ones for the home improvement stores most.

The USPS (United States Postal Service) has some handy tools and checklists on their sight to help your move.

Miscellaneous: Make sure your keys fit in the doors and the garage door opener works (if you have a garage, that is).

Helpful resources: You can find an up-to-date listing and description of websites devoted to make your move easier on FindingHomeBook.com.

Chapter 12

Become a Homeowner

*"Today I close the door to the past,
open the door to the future, take a deep breath, step on through,
and start a new chapter in my life."*
—Unknown

12-1 Moving In – First Things First

Try not to leave your belongings in boxes too long. It will weigh on your mind and cause unnecessary stress.

You have arrived! Pat yourself on the back, hug your mom, shake your boss' hand, shout for joy, but most of all, feel proud of yourself. You have arrived at the front door of your new home. Put your key in the lock, turn it, open **your** door, and walk into **your** home. Take a moment; take it all in.

While moving can be stressful, try to enjoy this as much as possible. You can arrange things the way you want them. Hang some curtains and pictures wherever you see fit. It is your home; you can put nails in the wall if you want.

Try not to leave your belongings in boxes too long. It will weigh on your mind and cause unnecessary stress. If you can take a little time off work to settle into your new home and add your own personal style, do so.

⬦⬦⬦⬦⬦

"Dad, what do you think we should do first after we settle in?" Jack asks, as he and Mike continue to unload the moving truck.

"Well, you know me, practical to the core," says Mike. "Safety and security are the first order of business, so here are a few suggestions:

1. Change the locks: You may think you have all the keys for your new home, but copies could have been made along the way. Maybe the prior owners gave a copy to the neighbors so they could water the plants or feed the cat during vacations.

2. After changing the locks, put an extra key someplace safe, like in your car. Some people hide a key outside their home. Be careful if you do this. Just like computer login passwords, thieves know the common things people do. Maybe keep a spare key at work in your desk. When you are busy moving you may misplace things, and the last thing you want is for it to be your key.

3. If you have a garage door opener with a security code, change the code.

4. Change the security code on your home security, if you have that, as well. Now your home is secure. Don't you feel better?

> **Take the time to get to know your neighbors. Knowing your neighbors adds security.**

5. Locate your breaker box and main water shut off valve (your home inspector can show you these when you accompany them on the inspection). If you have an electrical problem or major water leak, you will be thankful that you know where and how to turn these off.

6. Take the time to get to know your neighbors. If you prefer to be a recluse, that is fine, but knowing your neighbors adds security. If you know who your neighbors are and what cars they drive, you will be more likely to spot someone who is a stranger to the neighborhood.

12-2 Meet Your Neighbors

Neighbors are human, meaning they have quirks, habits, and characteristics unique to them. As with most groups of people, you will find some neighbors that you like more than others. If you did your neighborhood research well, you should feel comfortable with the location and setting. If you are moving from far away, this may have been more difficult to accomplish ahead of time, so you may have some acclimating to do.

12-3 Notify Friends and Family

If you have moved to a location far from your previous home, where you do not know anyone, make an announcement through social media or perhaps old-fashioned snail mail where you've landed. It is amazing how quickly you can lose touch with people whom you may have seen almost every day.

For security reasons, be careful with social media announcements that you do not notify anyone you do not want knowing to where you have moved or when you are not home.

12-4 Make Your Mortgage Loan Payment

Before moving, find out when your first payment is due. Ask the title agent when you are signing closing papers for a "first payment" letter. This should have the contact information, the amount and

Ask the title agent for a "first payment" letter.

the due date of your payment. Start off right by being on time with your first payment. Timely payments will build your credit score and increase your creditworthiness.

Now take a deep breath. You have prepared for this. Live, enjoy, and take time to relax. This is a big milestone.

12-5 Plan a Housewarming Party

It is late afternoon when everyone finally finishes unloading the moving truck. Eva's parents, Tom and Ann gave the couple a nice starter set of tools, picture hangers, and nails as a moving-in gift, and the tools had already been put to good use assembling a table in the kitchen. Jack, Eva, Mike, and Jayne are still there. Tom and Ann, and Eva's sister Ellie just left, and Jack sent some leftover pizza and beverages home with a small cadre of his friends who helped out.

With the remaining half-finished pizza in front of them, the group sits together in the living room, basking in the glow that only a new home can bring.

"Hey, let's have a housewarming party!" says Eva.

"You read my mind," replies Jayne.

"It's a great way to welcome friends and relatives ... let's celebrate!"

Jack looks over at Mike and winks. "You two can plan it all out. Dad and I are going to rest and finish our pizza."

As the two women chat, they come up with a list for a successful house warming party.

12-5-1 Jayne and Eva's Housewarming Tips

1. Plan the date for two to three weeks after the move. This gives you time to settle in and adds incentive to get unpacked, and to clean.

2. Send out the invitations formally written or informal through social media. Facebook invites or "e-vites" are perfectly acceptable for your techy friends and will save you time during what is usually a busy transition period in your life. Send those who do not have social media written invitations, so as not to exclude anyone.

3. Include an RSVP on the invitation so you can plan a proper amount of food and beverages.

4. Plan your menu. If you have light colored carpeting and lots of children coming, buy drinks that will not stain if spilled, saving you unnecessary stress. Finger foods, chips and dips, and veggie and fruit trays allow for guests to mingle and munch.

5. Give tours of your new home. Show it off. You have earned it.

"Wow, this is some barbeque," Mike says to Jack. "What a perfect evening!"

"Sure is, Dad. And we couldn't have done all of this without you and Mom."

Jack takes the last of the hamburgers off the grill. "Okay everyone, it's time to eat! Eva has everything set out on the picnic table, and there's lots of beverages in the coolers."

A rousing cheer goes up from the group. Eva's dad, Tom, gives a toast and several others follow suit.

"Oscar loves his big backyard," says Mike as he and Jack garnish their burgers.

"He sure does. And I'm sure the kids will too—when Eva and I have them."

"Are you telling me something?" Mike asks.

Jack just smiles, sits down on a lawn chair, and begins to munch on his burger.

◇◇◇◇◇

Jack and Eva love their new home.

Oscar loves his big backyard. Jack and Eva are thinking children, maybe. They love their neighborhood. It is their first home. They had to compromise a little, and make sacrifices, but they accomplished their home buying goal. They found their home, and are thrilled to be settled in.

And they will live happily ever after.

Until they decide to move.

Glossary of Terms[21]

Adjustable Rate Mortgages or ARM: A mortgage loan on which the interest may reset at designated intervals of time (frequency of reset), based on movements in a pre-selected interest rate index and the margin over that index that the lender charges in each interval. The magnitude of rate resets are generally limited by periodic and lifetime caps and floors, establishing the minimum and maximum rate that may be charged in each interval.

Application: The form you will use when applying for a mortgage loan. It is a questionnaire about your income, savings, assets, and debt, and that of the co-borrower.

Appraisal: A written statement of a property's current market value, as determined by a licensed appraiser.

Balloon Payment Mortgage: A mortgage loan which must be paid in full by the borrower after a term that is shorter than the term over which the loan is amortized. For instance, a borrower's payments may be calculated to fully amortize the loan over 30 years. If the loan has a 10 year balloon term, the borrower would have to pay in full the remaining unamortized balance on the loan after the first 120 scheduled monthly payments were made on the mortgage.

Buyer's Agent: A real estate agent that represents a buyer; a representative guiding a buyer throughout the process of purchasing, negotiating, and providing insight and advice exclusively for the buyer.

---

21   For an expanded glossary, please go to the companion website at FindingHomeBook.com.

CMA or Comparative Market Analysis: Evaluation of recently sold homes or properties in an area, referred to as "comparables." The comps or comparables chosen have the same general features as the home being compared. CMAs are most often done by a real estate agent.

Cohabitation Agreement: An agreement between two people who have chosen to live together and are not married. This documentation protects their rights as a couple while protecting individual assets and investments.

Conforming Loans: This is a loan that meets certain guidelines set forth by Freddie Mac and Fannie Mae. There is a limit to how much can be borrowed with a conforming loan.

Conventional Loan: A loan that is not backed or insured by the government.

Correspondent Lender: A lender who initially funds the borrower, but then delivers the loan to a (usually larger) wholesale lender against a prior price commitment the wholesaler has made to the correspondent.

Credit Report: A report from a credit bureau containing detailed information bearing on credit-worthiness, including the individual's credit history, outstanding debts, and a credit score.

Creditworthiness: A lender's view of the amount you are qualified to borrow, mostly based on credit score, your account history of timely payments, assets, and debts.

Debt-to-Income Ratio (DTI): A ratio calculated by adding up your mortgage payment, taxes, insurance, and consumer debt (credit cards, car payment), and dividing by your income.

Deductible (Income Taxes): An expense that you are allowed to take as a deduction from income on your income tax return.

Deductible (Insurance Policy): The amount of money the insured person must pay before the insurance company will pay a claim.

Dual Agent: A dual agent represents both the buyer and the seller in the transaction. This can arise if a buyer calls the selling agent of the home. The agent is obligated to disclose the relationship to both parties as this can cause a conflict of interest.

Earnest Money: The amount the buyer advances to show their intent to complete the transaction. It is also known as a good faith deposit. This money shows that a buyer is willing to sacrifice money to put toward a home's down payment thereby hoping to secure the purchase of a property. It shows the seller that the buyer is serious about purchasing the property.

Errors and Omissions Insurance: Type of insurance that pays claims to parties injured due to errors or omissions committed by a professional providing services.

Escrow for Home Purchase: Earnest money or a deed, bond, or other document held by a third party as insurance toward the purchase of home. The moneys are released only when certain conditions are fulfilled.

Escrow for Taxes and Insurance (Also known as **Impounds**): An agreement whereby the borrower adds a specified amount for taxes and hazard insurance to their regular monthly mortgage payment. The money goes into an escrow account out of which the lender pays the taxes and insurance when they come due.

Federal Emergency Management Agency or FEMA: Part of the Department of Homeland Security, the purpose of the agency is to coordinate during a disaster. There must be a state of emergency declared by the governor of the affected state and a formal request from the President and the federal government to respond to the disaster.

Federal Housing Administration or FHA: A federal government agency established as part of the National Housing Act of 1934. The goals of this institution are to improve housing conditions and standards, help to stabilize the mortgage market, and provide home financing through the insurance of mortgage loans. The organization sets standards for underwriting, insuring loans, and construction.

FICO Score: A single numerical score, based on an individual's credit history that measures the individual's creditworthiness. Credit scores are as good as the algorithm used to derive them. FICO is the most widely used credit score, named for the Fair Isaac Co., which developed it.

Fixed Rate Mortgage: A mortgage loan on which the interest rate and monthly mortgage payment remain unchanged throughout the term of the loan.

Foreclosure: The legal process by which a lender acquires possession of a property securing a mortgage loan when the borrower defaults.

Grace Period: The period after the payment due date during which the borrower can pay without being hit for late fees.

Hazard Insurance: Insurance purchased by the borrower, and required by the lender, to protect the property against loss from fire and other hazards. Also known as "homeowner's insurance."

Home Inspection: Usually associated with the sale of a home. When a professional assesses the condition of a home. These inspections are noninvasive; they do not cause damage to the home.

Hybrid ARM: Type of mortgage loan on which the initial rate holds for an extended period, during which it is a fixed rate loan, after which the loan becomes adjustable rate and its rate periodically resets. Hybrid ARMs typically have an initial fixed rate period of 24, 36, or 60 months.

Interest Only Mortgage: A mortgage on which the monthly mortgage payment consists of interest only for a designated number of months. During those months, the loan principal balance remains unchanged.

Interest Rate: The rate the lender charges the borrower for the loan of money, by custom quoted on an annual basis. This is the cost to borrow money from a lender.

Joint Tenancy: One way two or more owners hold a property together. The share of each holder passes to the others in the event of death. The property holders share equal rights and responsibilities.

Jumbo Loans: A loan that is too large to qualify to be a conforming loan. These loans generally have a higher interest rate as they are harder to sell on the secondary market.

Liquid Assets: Cash and assets that are easily converted into cash with minimal impact. Examples of liquid assets are funds in your savings, checking and money market accounts, certificates of deposit, stocks, bonds, and mutual funds, and of course, any cash you have stuffed in your mattress. Assets are referred to as liquid because they can be transferred quickly, like water moving across a surface.

Loan-to-Value Ratio (LTV): A number that represents the percentage of your home's value financed using a mortgage loan. For example, if your home is worth $250,000 and your mortgage loan is $225,000, then your LTV is 90 percent.

Lock: An option exercised by the borrower, at the time of the loan application or later, to "lock in" the rates and points prevailing in the market at that time. The lender and borrower are committed to those terms, regardless of what happens between that point and the closing date.

Lockbox: A lockbox is generally placed on the front door. If the property is a condominium community, the real estate agent will have instructions as to where to find the lockbox if it is not on the front door of the property. It contains the key to the property and can only be accessed by licensed agents.

Mortgage Broker: An independent contractor who offers the loan products of multiple lenders. A mortgage broker counsels on the loans available from different wholesalers, takes the application, and may do some of the processing of the loan. When the file is complete, but sometimes sooner, the lender underwrites the loan. In contrast to a correspondent, a mortgage broker does not fund a loan.

Mortgage Lender: The party who disburses funds to the borrower at the closing table. The lender receives the note evidencing the borrower's indebtedness and obligation to repay, and the mortgage which is the lien on the subject property.

Mortgage: A written document evidencing the lien on a property taken by a lender as security for the repayment of a loan. The term "mortgage" or "mortgage loan" is used loosely to refer both to the lien and the loan. In most cases, they are defined in two separate documents: a mortgage and a note.

Multiple Listing Service or MLS: A database shared by realtors that enables other realtors, and more recently, potential customers, to view multiple homes. It allows for the sharing of information of multiple property listings and information about the properties.

National Association of Realtors: The largest of the real estate organizations with a membership of over one million. They have both state and local chapters. Members are automatically enrolled in both the state and national organizations when they join a local chapter. Members have access to the local MLS, which is an advantageous benefit. The NAR is one of the largest trade groups.

National Flood Insurance Program or NFIP: This program is managed by FEMA (Federal Emergency Management Agency). If you live in an area that participates in the NFIP, you are eligible for flood insurance. This means if an area is deemed to be flood prone, you qualify to purchase insurance through a private company.

Note: A document that evidences a debt and a promise to repay. A mortgage loan transaction always includes both a note evidencing the debt, and a mortgage evidencing the lien on the property, usually in two documents.

PITI: Shorthand for principal, interest, taxes, and insurance, which are the primary components of the monthly housing expense, before considering homeowner association fees and other direct housing expenses.

Preapproval: An evaluation by a lender to determine whether a prospective buyers qualifies to obtain a loan and the amount the lender is willing to loan.

Prequalification: The process of determining whether a prospective borrower has the ability (meaning sufficient assets and income) to repay a loan. Prequalification is subject to verification of the information provided by the applicant. Qualification is short of approval because it does not take account of the credit history of the borrower. Qualified borrowers may ultimately be turned down because, while they have demonstrated the ability to repay, a poor credit history suggests that they may be not have the willingness to pay.

Principal: The balance owed on a mortgage loan. The term is also used to describe the portion of the borrower's monthly payment that is not interest because that portion pays down the principal owed on the loan.

Real Estate Agent: A licensed person who assists clients with the buying and selling of property. Persons educated in the laws and regulations pertaining to real estate.

Real Estate Attorney: A lawyer that specializes in the practice of real estate transaction law.

REALTOR®: A real estate professional who has decided to pledge a strict code of ethics and standards of practice. To maintain REALTOR® status, they are required to join the National Association of Realtors.

RESPA or Real Estate Settlement Procedures Act: A federal law stating that real estate brokers may not receive compensation from a lender for referring a client. This law is exclusive to residential properties. Commercial properties are exempt from this rule.

Secondary Market: The secondary market is when your mortgage loan is sold to another institution that will then manage your loan. The biggest purchasers in the secondary market are Freddie Mac and Fannie Mae.

Seller's agent: The real estate agent representing the seller of the home or property.

Taxes: The monetary obligation enforced by the government in order to support government activities.

Title Company: A company or institution that examines title for property to make sure that it is a legitimate document.

Trulia: A real estate site that allows users to search for homes and properties. This site also provides information to assist in educating the buyer about various real estate topics.

Rural Development Guaranteed Housing Loan Program or USDA/RHS Loans: A loan for rural property owners issued by the United States Department of Agriculture. The purpose is to meet the needs of ranchers and farmers.

Veterans Affairs Loans or VA Loans: A mortgage backed by the U.S. Department of Veterans Affairs. Designed to assist veterans to purchase homes.

Zillow: A real estate site that allows users to search for homes and properties. This site also provides information to assist in educating the buyer about various real estate topics.

Appendix A
About FindingHomeBook.com

When you access FindingHomeBook.com, you will arrive at the general website home page containing articles and information about finding and buying a home. Although the homepage will likely change many times, at the printing of this book it looked something like this.

FINDING HOME CHAPTERS ▾ FAQS GLOSSARY DOWNLOADS RECOMMENDED SITES

Finding Home

Congratulations! You have taken the first step to finding your home.

Welcome to the companion website for the Finding Home book!

Buying a home is a big step. I am here to help you get started and work all the way through the process.

Buying a home involves *preparation* (research, savings, and soul searching), *tools* (websites, data, forms, checklists, and people) and *processes* (walk-throughs, negotiations, mortgage loan approval, and closing the deal) that will lead you to a home that meets your needs and budget. The Finding Home book will help you navigate the home-buying maze by giving you guidance, answering questions, and helping you feel confident *before* you take your first steps.

In the book, you will find insights and tips for first time home buyers and seasoned investors alike. It is a guide that you can reference any time questions arise, and it incorporates new attitudes, technologies, laws, demographic trends, environmental concerns, and economic realities. Recognizing that changes in these areas are nonstop, I have created this companion website that includes updates, answers to frequently asked questions, an extensive glossary, recommended websites, calculators, downloadable forms, and more.

From the Downloads page of this site, you can download templates for the forms included in this book and customize them for your needs. You can add in your dreams, needs and wants, desired locations, income, budget, family size and everything else related to your home search. Calculators, tracking forms, budget tools, sample documents, and a host of other items are at your disposal.

With that said, let us begin. Together we are going to take the right steps to help you to successfully acquire your first, or next, home.

Here's to your home buying success!

Mike Trickey

From the toolbar at the top of the Finding Home page, you can access the downloadable files referenced in the book by clicking on the Downloads tab. You will be asked for some basic registration information and then given access to the Downloads page. It will look something like this:

Finding Home
What you need to know and do to buy your first (or next) home

FINDING HOME   CHAPTERS ▾   FAQS   GLOSSARY   DOWNLOADS   RECOMMENDED SITES

Protected: Downloads

Chapter 1 Companion Spreadsheet Downloads

Chapter 1 Readiness Checklist

Chapter 2 Companion Spreadsheet Downloads

Chapter 2 KHBAN template

Chapter 2 Balance Sheet

Chapter 2 Quick and Easy Affordability Calculation

Chapter 2 Monthly Revenues and Expenses

Chapter 4 Companion Spreadsheet Downloads

Chapter 4 Daily Expense Tracker

Chapter 4 Budget

Chapter 5 Companion Spreadsheet Downloads

Chapter 5 Lender Comparison

Chapter 6 Companion Spreadsheet Downloads

Chapter 6 Location Choice Hierarchy Tables

Chapter 6 Housing Needs and Wants Inventory

Just find the file you want under the appropriate chapter and double click on it. You will be able to download and open the file. There are a few files in the pdf format, which are sample forms. Most files, however, are in an Excel® format and are fully editable by you. Many have imbedded formulas to perform calculations for you. I imbedded no macros in the files.

The website also provides you access to chapter update information, URL links to other providers of exceptional content to help you in your home buying quest, an expanded glossary, frequently asked questions and answers, and much more.

I welcome your comments and suggestions. You can either access "contact" box on the website, or email me at Comments@ FindingHomeBook.com.

Michael Trickey

Appendix B
Uniform Residential Loan Application

Uniform Residential Loan Application

This application is designed to be completed by the applicant(s) with the Lender's assistance. Applicants should complete this form as "Borrower" or "Co-Borrower," as applicable. Co-Borrower information must also be provided (and the appropriate box checked) when ☐ the income or assets of a person other than the Borrower (including the Borrower's spouse) will be used as a basis for loan qualification or ☐ the income or assets of the Borrower's spouse or other person who has community property rights pursuant to state law will not be used as a basis for loan qualification, but his or her liabilities must be considered because the spouse or other person has community property rights pursuant to applicable law and Borrower resides in a community property state, the security property is located in a community property state, or the Borrower is relying on other property located in a community property state as a basis for repayment of the loan.

If this is an application for joint credit, Borrower and Co-Borrower each agree that we intend to apply for joint credit (sign below):

Borrower _____ Co-Borrower _____

I. TYPE OF MORTGAGE AND TERMS OF LOAN					
Mortgage Applied for:	☐ VA ☐ FHA	☐ Conventional ☐ USDA/Rural Housing Service	☐ Other (explain):	Agency Case Number	Lender Case Number
Amount $	Interest Rate %	No. of Months	Amortization Type:	☐ Fixed Rate ☐ Other (explain): ☐ GPM ☐ ARM (type):	

II. PROPERTY INFORMATION AND PURPOSE OF LOAN		
Subject Property Address (street, city, state & ZIP)		No. of Units
Legal Description of Subject Property (attach description if necessary)		Year Built

Purpose of Loan	☐ Purchase ☐ Construction ☐ Other (explain): ☐ Refinance ☐ Construction-Permanent	Property will be: ☐ Primary Residence ☐ Secondary Residence ☐ Investment

Complete this line if construction or construction-permanent loan.

Year Lot Acquired	Original Cost	Amount Existing Liens	(a) Present Value of Lot	(b) Cost of Improvements	Total (a + b)
	$	$	$	$	$ 0.00

Complete this line if this is a refinance loan.

Year Acquired	Original Cost	Amount Existing Liens	Purpose of Refinance	Describe Improvements ☐ made ☐ to be made	
	$	$		Cost: $	

Title will be held in what Name(s)	Manner in which Title will be held	Estate will be held in: ☐ Fee Simple ☐ Leasehold (show expiration date)
Source of Down Payment, Settlement Charges, and/or Subordinate Financing (explain)		

Borrower	III. BORROWER INFORMATION	Co-Borrower
Borrower's Name (include Jr. or Sr. if applicable)		Co-Borrower's Name (include Jr. or Sr. if applicable)

Social Security Number	Home Phone (incl. area code)	DOB (mm/dd/yyyy)	Yrs. School	Social Security Number	Home Phone (incl. area code)	DOB (mm/dd/yyyy)	Yrs. School
☐ Married ☐ Unmarried (include ☐ Separated single, divorced, widowed)	Dependents (not listed by Co-Borrower) no. ages			☐ Married ☐ Unmarried (include ☐ Separated single, divorced, widowed)	Dependents (not listed by Borrower) no. ages		
Present Address (street, city, state, ZIP) ☐ Own ☐ Rent ___No. Yrs.				Present Address (street, city, state, ZIP) ☐ Own ☐ Rent ___No. Yrs.			
Mailing Address, if different from Present Address				Mailing Address, if different from Present Address			

If residing at present address for less than two years, complete the following:

Former Address (street, city, state, ZIP) ☐ Own ☐ Rent ___No. Yrs.	Former Address (street, city, state, ZIP) ☐ Own ☐ Rent ___No. Yrs.

Borrower	IV. EMPLOYMENT INFORMATION	Co-Borrower

Name & Address of Employer	☐ Self Employed	Yrs. on this job	Name & Address of Employer	☐ Self Employed	Yrs. on this job
		Yrs. employed in this line of work/profession			Yrs. employed in this line of work/profession
Position/Title/Type of Business	Business Phone (incl. area code)		Position/Title/Type of Business	Business Phone (incl. area code)	

If employed in current position for less than two years or if currently employed in more than one position, complete the following:

Uniform Residential Loan Application
Freddie Mac Form 65   7/05 (rev.6/09)   Page 1 of 5   Fannie Mae Form 1003   7/05 (rev.6/09)

292

Borrower			IV. EMPLOYMENT INFORMATION (cont'd)		Co-Borrower		
Name & Address of Employer	☐ Self Employed	Dates (from – to)		Name & Address of Employer	☐ Self Employed	Dates (from – to)	
		Monthly Income $				Monthly Income $	
Position/Title/Type of Business		Business Phone (incl. area code)		Position/Title/Type of Business		Business Phone (incl. area code)	
Name & Address of Employer	☐ Self Employed	Dates (from – to)		Name & Address of Employer	☐ Self Employed	Dates (from – to)	
		Monthly Income $				Monthly Income $	
Position/Title/Type of Business		Business Phone (incl. area code)		Position/Title/Type of Business		Business Phone (incl. area code)	

V. MONTHLY INCOME AND COMBINED HOUSING EXPENSE INFORMATION

Gross Monthly Income	Borrower	Co-Borrower	Total	Combined Monthly Housing Expense	Present	Proposed
Base Empl. Income*	$	$	$ 0.00	Rent	$	
Overtime			0.00	First Mortgage (P&I)		$
Bonuses			0.00	Other Financing (P&I)		
Commissions			0.00	Hazard Insurance		
Dividends/Interest			0.00	Real Estate Taxes		
Net Rental Income			0.00	Mortgage Insurance		
Other (before completing, see the notice in "describe other income," below)			0.00	Homeowner Assn. Dues		
				Other:		
Total	$ 0.00	$ 0.00	$ 0.00	Total	$ 0.00	$ 0.00

* Self Employed Borrower(s) may be required to provide additional documentation such as tax returns and financial statements.

Describe Other Income **Notice:** Alimony, child support, or separate maintenance income need not be revealed if the Borrower (B) or Co-Borrower (C) does not choose to have it considered for repaying this loan.

B/C		Monthly Amount
		$

VI. ASSETS AND LIABILITIES

This Statement and any applicable supporting schedules may be completed jointly by both married and unmarried Co-Borrowers if their assets and liabilities are sufficiently joined so that the Statement can be meaningfully and fairly presented on a combined basis; otherwise, separate Statements and Schedules are required. If the Co-Borrower section was completed about a non-applicant spouse or other person, this Statement and supporting schedules must be completed about that spouse or other person also.

Completed ☐ Jointly ☐ Not Jointly

ASSETS Description	Cash or Market Value	Liabilities and Pledged Assets. List the creditor's name, address, and account number for all outstanding debts, including automobile loans, revolving charge accounts, real estate loans, alimony, child support, stock pledges, etc. Use continuation sheet, if necessary. Indicate by (*) those liabilities, which will be satisfied upon sale of real estate owned or upon refinancing of the subject property.		
Cash deposit toward purchase held by:	$			
List checking and savings accounts below		**LIABILITIES**	**Monthly Payment & Months Left to Pay**	**Unpaid Balance**
Name and address of Bank, S&L, or Credit Union		Name and address of Company	$ Payment/Months	$
Acct. no.	$	Acct. no.		
Name and address of Bank, S&L, or Credit Union		Name and address of Company	$ Payment/Months	$
Acct. no.	$	Acct. no.		
Name and address of Bank, S&L, or Credit Union		Name and address of Company	$ Payment/Months	$
Acct. no.	$	Acct. no.		

Uniform Residential Loan Application
Freddie Mac Form 65 7/05 (rev. 6/09)

Page 2 of 5

Fannie Mae Form 1003 7/05 (rev. 6/09)

VI. ASSETS AND LIABILITIES (cont'd)

Name and address of Bank, S&L, or Credit Union		Name and address of Company	$ Payment/Months	$
Acct. no.	$	Acct. no.		
Stocks & Bonds (Company name/ number & description)	$	Name and address of Company	$ Payment/Months	$
		Acct. no.		
Life insurance net cash value	$	Name and address of Company	$ Payment/Months	$
Face amount: $				
Subtotal Liquid Assets	$ 0.00			
Real estate owned (enter market value from schedule of real estate owned)	$			
Vested interest in retirement fund	$			
Net worth of business(es) owned (attach financial statement)	$	Acct. no.		
Automobiles owned (make and year)	$	Alimony/Child Support/Separate Maintenance Payments Owed to:	$	
Other Assets (itemize)	$	Job-Related Expense (child care, union dues, etc.)	$	
		Total Monthly Payments	$	
Total Assets a.	$ 0.00	Net Worth (a minus b) ▶ $ 0.00	**Total Liabilities b.**	$ 0.00

Schedule of Real Estate Owned (If additional properties are owned, use continuation sheet.)

Property Address (enter S if sold, PS if pending sale or R if rental being held for income) ▼	Type of Property	Present Market Value	Amount of Mortgages & Liens	Gross Rental Income	Mortgage Payments	Insurance, Maintenance, Taxes & Misc.	Net Rental Income
		$	$	$	$	$	$
Totals		$ 0.00	$ 0.00	$ 0.00	$ 0.00	$ 0.00	$

List any additional names under which credit has previously been received and indicate appropriate creditor name(s) and account number(s):

Alternate Name	Creditor Name	Account Number

VII. DETAILS OF TRANSACTION		VIII. DECLARATIONS				
a. Purchase price	$	If you answer "Yes" to any questions a through i, please use continuation sheet for explanation.	**Borrower**		**Co-Borrower**	
			Yes No		Yes No	
b. Alterations, improvements, repairs		a. Are there any outstanding judgments against you?	☐ ☐		☐ ☐	
c. Land (if acquired separately)		b. Have you been declared bankrupt within the past 7 years?	☐ ☐		☐ ☐	
d. Refinance (incl. debts to be paid off)		c. Have you had property foreclosed upon or given title or deed in lieu thereof in the last 7 years?	☐ ☐		☐ ☐	
e. Estimated prepaid items		d. Are you a party to a lawsuit?	☐ ☐		☐ ☐	
f. Estimated closing costs		e. Have you directly or indirectly been obligated on any loan which resulted in foreclosure, transfer of title in lieu of foreclosure, or judgment?	☐ ☐		☐ ☐	
g. PMI, MIP, Funding Fee		(This would include such loans as home mortgage loans, SBA loans, home improvement loans, educational loans, manufactured (mobile) home loans, any mortgage, financial obligation, bond, or loan guarantee. If "Yes," provide details, including date, name, and address of Lender, FHA or VA case number, if any, and reasons for the action.)				
h. Discount (if Borrower will pay)						
i. Total costs (add items a through h)	0.00					

Uniform Residential Loan Application
Freddie Mac Form 65 7/05 (rev.6/09)   Page 3 of 5   Fannie Mae Form 1003 7/05 (rev.6/0)

294

VII. DETAILS OF TRANSACTION		VIII. DECLARATIONS				
			Borrower		Co-Borrower	
		If you answer "Yes" to any question a through i, please use continuation sheet for explanation.	Yes	No	Yes	No
j. Subordinate financing		f. Are you presently delinquent or in default on any Federal debt or any other loan, mortgage, financial obligation, bond, or loan guarantee?	☐	☐	☐	☐
k. Borrower's closing costs paid by Seller		g. Are you obligated to pay alimony, child support, or separate maintenance?	☐	☐	☐	☐
		h. Is any part of the down payment borrowed?	☐	☐	☐	☐
l. Other Credits (explain)		i. Are you a co-maker or endorser on a note?	☐	☐	☐	☐
m. Loan amount (exclude PMI, MIP, Funding Fee financed)		j. Are you a U.S. citizen?	☐	☐	☐	☐
n. PMI, MIP, Funding Fee financed		k. Are you a permanent resident alien?	☐	☐	☐	☐
o. Loan amount (add m & n)	0.00	l. Do you intend to occupy the property as your primary residence?	☐	☐	☐	☐
		If "Yes," complete question m below.				
p. Cash from/to Borrower (subtract j, k, l & o from i)		m. Have you had an ownership interest in a property in the last three years?	☐	☐	☐	☐
		(1) What type of property did you own—principal residence (PR), second home (SH), or investment property (IP)?				
		(2) How did you hold title to the home—by yourself (S), jointly with your spouse (SP), or jointly with another person (O)?				

IX. ACKNOWLEDGEMENT AND AGREEMENT

Each of the undersigned specifically represents to Lender and to Lender's actual or potential agents, brokers, processors, attorneys, insurers, servicers, successors and assigns and agrees and acknowledges that: (1) the information provided in this application is true and correct as of the date set forth opposite my signature and that any intentional or negligent misrepresentation of this information contained in this application may result in civil liability, including monetary damages, to any person who may suffer any loss due to reliance upon any misrepresentation that I have made on this application, and/or in criminal penalties including, but not limited to, fine or imprisonment or both under the provisions of Title 18, United States Code, Sec. 1001, et seq.; (2) the loan requested pursuant to this application (the "Loan") will be secured by a mortgage or deed of trust on the property described in this application; (3) the property will not be used for any illegal or prohibited purpose or use; (4) all statements made in this application are made for the purpose of obtaining a residential mortgage loan; (5) the property will be occupied as indicated in this application; (6) the Lender, its servicers, successors or assigns may retain the original and/or an electronic record of this application, whether or not the Loan is approved; (7) the Lender and its agents, brokers, insurers, servicers, successors, and assigns may continuously rely on the information contained in the application, and I am obligated to amend and/or supplement the information provided in this application if any of the material facts that I have represented herein should change prior to closing of the Loan; (8) in the event that my payments on the Loan become delinquent, the Lender, its servicers, successors or assigns may, in addition to any other rights and remedies that it may have relating to such delinquency, report my name and account information to one or more consumer reporting agencies; (9) ownership of the Loan and/or administration of the Loan account may be transferred with such notice as may be required by law; (10) neither Lender nor its agents, brokers, insurers, servicers, successors or assigns has made any representation or warranty, express or implied, to me regarding the property or the condition or value of the property; and (11) my transmission of this application as an "electronic record" containing my "electronic signature," as those terms are defined in applicable federal and/or state laws (excluding audio and video recordings), or my facsimile transmission of this application containing a facsimile of my signature, shall be as effective, enforceable and valid as if a paper version of this application were delivered containing my original written signature.

Acknowledgement. Each of the undersigned hereby acknowledges that any owner of the Loan, its servicers, successors or assigns, may verify or reverify any information contained in this application or obtain any information or data relating to the Loan, for any legitimate business purpose through any source, including a source named in this application or a consumer reporting agency.

Borrower's Signature X	Date	Co-Borrower's Signature X	Date

X. INFORMATION FOR GOVERNMENT MONITORING PURPOSES

The following information is requested by the Federal Government for certain types of loans related to a dwelling in order to monitor the lender's compliance with equal credit opportunity, fair housing and home mortgage disclosure laws. You are not required to furnish this information, but are encouraged to do so. The law provides that a lender may not discriminate either on the basis of this information, or on whether you choose to furnish it. If you furnish the information, please provide both ethnicity and race. For race, you may check more than one designation. If you do not furnish ethnicity, race, or sex, under Federal regulations, this lender is required to note the information on the basis of visual observation and surname if you have made this application in person. If you do not wish to furnish the information, please check the box below. (Lender must review the above material to assure that the disclosures satisfy all requirements to which the lender is subject under applicable state law for the particular type of loan applied for.)

BORROWER ☐ I do not wish to furnish this information	CO-BORROWER ☐ I do not wish to furnish this information
Ethnicity: ☐ Hispanic or Latino ☐ Not Hispanic or Latino	Ethnicity: ☐ Hispanic or Latino ☐ Not Hispanic or Latino
Race: ☐ American Indian or Alaska Native ☐ Asian ☐ Black or African American ☐ Native Hawaiian or Other Pacific Islander ☐ White	Race: ☐ American Indian or Alaska Native ☐ Asian ☐ Black or African American ☐ Native Hawaiian or Other Pacific Islander ☐ White
Sex: ☐ Female ☐ Male	Sex: ☐ Female ☐ Male

To be Completed by Loan Originator:
This information was provided:
☐ In a face-to-face interview
☐ In a telephone interview
☐ By the applicant and submitted by fax or mail
☐ By the applicant and submitted via e-mail or the Internet

Loan Originator's Signature X		Date
Loan Originator's Name (print or type)	Loan Originator Identifier	Loan Originator's Phone Number (including area code)
Loan Origination Company's Name	Loan Origination Company Identifier	Loan Origination Company's Address

Uniform Residential Loan Application
Freddie Mac Form 65   7/05 (rev.6/09)   Page 4 of 5   Fannie Mae Form 1003   7/05 (rev.6/09)

Michael W. Trickey

<table>
<tr><td colspan="5" align="center">**CONTINUATION SHEET/RESIDENTIAL LOAN APPLICATION**</td></tr>
<tr>
<td>Use this continuation sheet if you need more space to complete the Residential Loan Application. Mark **B** f or Borrower or **C** for Co-Borrower.</td>
<td>Borrower:</td>
<td>Agency Case Number:</td>
</tr>
<tr>
<td></td>
<td>Co-Borrower:</td>
<td>Lender Case Number:</td>
</tr>
</table>

I/We fully understand that it is a Federal crime punishable by fine or imprisonment, or both, to knowingly make any false statements concerning any of the above facts as applicable under the provisions of Title 18, United States Code, Section 1001, et seq.

Borrower's Signature	Date	Co-Borrower's Signature	Date
X		X	

Appendix C
Sample Loan Estimate (LE)

4321 Random Boulevard • Somecity, ST 12340

Save this Loan Estimate to compare with your Closing Disclosure.

Loan Estimate

DATE ISSUED	2/15/2013
APPLICANTS	Michael Jones and Mary Stone
	123 Anywhere Street
	Anytown, ST 12345
PROPERTY	456 Somewhere Avenue
	Anytown, ST 12345
SALE PRICE	$180,000

LOAN TERM	30 years
PURPOSE	Purchase
PRODUCT	Fixed Rate
LOAN TYPE	☒ Conventional ☐ FHA ☐ VA ☐ _____
LOAN ID #	123456789
RATE LOCK	☐ NO ☒ YES, until 4/16/2013 at 5:00 p.m. EDT

Before closing, your interest rate, points, and lender credits can change unless you lock the interest rate. All other estimated closing costs expire on 3/4/2013 at 5:00 p.m. EDT

Loan Terms

		Can this amount increase after closing?
Loan Amount	$162,000	NO
Interest Rate	3.875%	NO
Monthly Principal & Interest *See Projected Payments below for your Estimated Total Monthly Payment*	$761.78	NO

		Does the loan have these features?
Prepayment Penalty	YES	• As high as $3,240 if you pay off the loan during the first 2 years
Balloon Payment	NO	

Projected Payments

Payment Calculation	Years 1-7	Years 8-30
Principal & Interest	$761.78	$761.78
Mortgage Insurance	+ 82	+ —
Estimated Escrow *Amount can increase over time*	+ 206	+ 206
Estimated Total Monthly Payment	**$1,050**	**$968**

		This estimate includes	In escrow?
Estimated Taxes, Insurance & Assessments *Amount can increase over time*	$206 a month	☒ Property Taxes	YES
		☒ Homeowner's Insurance	YES
		☐ Other:	
		See Section G on page 2 for escrowed property costs. You must pay for other property costs separately.	

Costs at Closing

Estimated Closing Costs	$8,054	Includes $5,672 in Loan Costs + $2,382 in Other Costs – $0 in Lender Credits. *See page 2 for details.*
Estimated Cash to Close	$16,054	Includes Closing Costs. *See Calculating Cash to Close on page 2 for details.*

Visit **www.consumerfinance.gov/mortgage-estimate** for general information and tools.

Closing Cost Details

Loan Costs

A. Origination Charges	$1,802
.25 % of Loan Amount (Points)	$405
Application Fee	$300
Underwriting Fee	$1,097

B. Services You Cannot Shop For	$672
Appraisal Fee	$405
Credit Report Fee	$30
Flood Determination Fee	$20
Flood Monitoring Fee	$32
Tax Monitoring Fee	$75
Tax Status Research Fee	$110

C. Services You Can Shop For	$3,198
Pest Inspection Fee	$135
Survey Fee	$65
Title – Insurance Binder	$700
Title – Lender's Title Policy	$535
Title – Settlement Agent Fee	$502
Title – Title Search	$1,261

D. TOTAL LOAN COSTS (A + B + C)	$5,672

Other Costs

E. Taxes and Other Government Fees	$85
Recording Fees and Other Taxes	$85
Transfer Taxes	

F. Prepaids	$867
Homeowner's Insurance Premium (6 months)	$605
Mortgage Insurance Premium (months)	
Prepaid Interest ($17.44 per day for 15 days @ 3.875%)	$262
Property Taxes (months)	

G. Initial Escrow Payment at Closing			$413
Homeowner's Insurance	$100.83 per month for 2 mo.	$202
Mortgage Insurance	per month for mo.	
Property Taxes	$105.30 per month for 2 mo.	$211

H. Other	$1,017
Title – Owner's Title Policy (optional)	$1,017

I. TOTAL OTHER COSTS (E + F + G + H)	$2,382

J. TOTAL CLOSING COSTS	$8,054
D + I	$8,054
Lender Credits	

Calculating Cash to Close

Total Closing Costs (J)	$8,054
Closing Costs Financed (Paid from your Loan Amount)	$0
Down Payment/Funds from Borrower	$18,000
Deposit	– $10,000
Funds for Borrower	$0
Seller Credits	$0
Adjustments and Other Credits	$0
Estimated Cash to Close	$16,054

Additional Information About This Loan

LENDER	Ficus Bank	**MORTGAGE BROKER**	
NMLS/__ LICENSE ID		**NMLS/__ LICENSE ID**	
LOAN OFFICER	Joe Smith	**LOAN OFFICER**	
NMLS/__ LICENSE ID	12345	**NMLS/__ LICENSE ID**	
EMAIL	joesmith@ficusbank.com	**EMAIL**	
PHONE	123-456-7890	**PHONE**	

Comparisons		Use these measures to compare this loan with other loans.
In 5 Years	$56,582	Total you will have paid in principal, interest, mortgage insurance, and loan costs.
	$15,773	Principal you will have paid off.
Annual Percentage Rate (APR)	4.274%	Your costs over the loan term expressed as a rate. This is not your interest rate.
Total Interest Percentage (TIP)	69.45%	The total amount of interest that you will pay over the loan term as a percentage of your loan amount.

Other Considerations

Appraisal	We may order an appraisal to determine the property's value and charge you for this appraisal. We will promptly give you a copy of any appraisal, even if your loan does not close. You can pay for an additional appraisal for your own use at your own cost.
Assumption	If you sell or transfer this property to another person, we ☐ will allow, under certain conditions, this person to assume this loan on the original terms. ☒ will not allow assumption of this loan on the original terms.
Homeowner's Insurance	This loan requires homeowner's insurance on the property, which you may obtain from a company of your choice that we find acceptable.
Late Payment	If your payment is more than 15 days late, we will charge a late fee of 5% of the monthly principal and interest payment.
Refinance	Refinancing this loan will depend on your future financial situation, the property value, and market conditions. You may not be able to refinance this loan.
Servicing	We intend ☐ to service your loan. If so, you will make your payments to us. ☒ to transfer servicing of your loan.

Confirm Receipt

By signing, you are only confirming that you have received this form. You do not have to accept this loan because you have signed or received this form.

_____   _____   _____   _____
Applicant Signature   Date   Co-Applicant Signature   Date

LOAN ESTIMATE   PAGE 3 OF 3 • LOAN ID #123456789

Appendix D

Sample Closing Disclosure (CD)

Closing Disclosure

This form is a statement of final loan terms and closing costs. Compare this document with your Loan Estimate.

Closing Information

Date Issued	4/15/2013
Closing Date	4/15/2013
Disbursement Date	4/15/2013
Settlement Agent	Epsilon Title Co.
File #	12-3456
Property	456 Somewhere Ave
	Anytown, ST 12345
Sale Price	$180,000

Transaction Information

Borrower	Michael Jones and Mary Stone
	123 Anywhere Street
	Anytown, ST 12345
Seller	Steve Cole and Amy Doe
	321 Somewhere Drive
	Anytown, ST 12345
Lender	Ficus Bank

Loan Information

Loan Term	30 years
Purpose	Purchase
Product	Fixed Rate
Loan Type	☒ Conventional ☐ FHA ☐ VA ☐ _____
Loan ID #	123456789
MIC #	000654321

Loan Terms

		Can this amount increase after closing?
Loan Amount	$162,000	NO
Interest Rate	3.875%	NO
Monthly Principal & Interest *See Projected Payments below for your Estimated Total Monthly Payment*	$761.78	NO

		Does the loan have these features?
Prepayment Penalty		YES • As high as $3,240 if you pay off the loan during the first 2 years
Balloon Payment		NO

Projected Payments

Payment Calculation	Years 1-7	Years 8-30
Principal & Interest	$761.78	$761.78
Mortgage Insurance	+ 82.35	+ —
Estimated Escrow *Amount can increase over time*	+ 206.13	+ 206.13
Estimated Total Monthly Payment	$1,050.26	$967.91

Estimated Taxes, Insurance & Assessments *Amount can increase over time* *See page 4 for details*	$356.13 a month	This estimate includes ☒ Property Taxes ☒ Homeowner's Insurance ☒ Other: Homeowner's Association Dues *See Escrow Account on page 4 for details. You must pay for other property costs separately.*	In escrow? YES YES NO

Costs at Closing

Closing Costs	$9,712.10	Includes $4,694.05 in Loan Costs + $5,018.05 in Other Costs – $0 in Lender Credits. *See page 2 for details.*
Cash to Close	$14,147.26	Includes Closing Costs. *See Calculating Cash to Close on page 3 for details.*

Closing Cost Details

Loan Costs		Borrower-Paid		Seller-Paid		Paid by Others
		At Closing	Before Closing	At Closing	Before Closing	
A. Origination Charges		**$1,802.00**				
01 0.25 % of Loan Amount (Points)		$405.00				
02 Application Fee		$300.00				
03 Underwriting Fee		$1,097.00				
04						
05						
06						
07						
08						
B. Services Borrower Did Not Shop For		**$236.55**				
01 Appraisal Fee	to John Smith Appraisers Inc.					$405.00
02 Credit Report Fee	to Information Inc.		$29.80			
03 Flood Determination Fee	to Info Co.	$20.00				
04 Flood Monitoring Fee	to Info Co.	$31.75				
05 Tax Monitoring Fee	to Info Co.	$75.00				
06 Tax Status Research Fee	to Info Co.	$80.00				
07						
08						
09						
10						
C. Services Borrower Did Shop For		**$2,655.50**				
01 Pest Inspection Fee	to Pests Co.	$120.50				
02 Survey Fee	to Surveys Co.	$85.00				
03 Title – Insurance Binder	to Epsilon Title Co.	$650.00				
04 Title – Lender's Title Insurance	to Epsilon Title Co.	$500.00				
05 Title – Settlement Agent Fee	to Epsilon Title Co.	$500.00				
06 Title – Title Search	to Epsilon Title Co.	$800.00				
07						
08						
D. TOTAL LOAN COSTS (Borrower-Paid)		**$4,694.05**				
Loan Costs Subtotals (A + B + C)		$4,664.25	$29.80			

Other Costs						
E. Taxes and Other Government Fees		**$85.00**				
01 Recording Fees	Deed: $40.00 Mortgage: $45.00	$85.00				
02 Transfer Tax	to Any State			$950.00		
F. Prepaids		**$2,120.80**				
01 Homeowner's Insurance Premium (12 mo.) to Insurance Co.		$1,209.96				
02 Mortgage Insurance Premium (mo.)						
03 Prepaid Interest ($17.44 per day from 4/15/13 to 5/1/13)		$279.04				
04 Property Taxes (6 mo.) to Any County USA		$631.80				
05						
G. Initial Escrow Payment at Closing		**$412.25**				
01 Homeowner's Insurance $100.83 per month for 2 mo.		$201.66				
02 Mortgage Insurance per month for mo.						
03 Property Taxes $105.30 per month for 2 mo.		$210.60				
04						
05						
06						
07						
08 Aggregate Adjustment		– 0.01				
H. Other		**$2,400.00**				
01 HOA Capital Contribution	to HOA Acre Inc.	$500.00				
02 HOA Processing Fee	to HOA Acre Inc.	$150.00				
03 Home Inspection Fee	to Engineers Inc.	$750.00			$750.00	
04 Home Warranty Fee	to XYZ Warranty Inc.			$450.00		
05 Real Estate Commission	to Alpha Real Estate Broker			$5,700.00		
06 Real Estate Commission	to Omega Real Estate Broker			$5,700.00		
07 Title – Owner's Title Insurance (optional) to Epsilon Title Co.		$1,000.00				
08						
I. TOTAL OTHER COSTS (Borrower-Paid)		**$5,018.05**				
Other Costs Subtotals (E + F + G + H)		$5,018.05				
J. TOTAL CLOSING COSTS (Borrower-Paid)		**$9,712.10**				
Closing Costs Subtotals (D + I)		$9,682.30	$29.80	$12,800.00	$750.00	$405.00
Lender Credits						

CLOSING DISCLOSURE

Michael W. Trickey

Calculating Cash to Close

Use this table to see what has changed from your Loan Estimate.

	Loan Estimate	Final	Did this change?
Total Closing Costs (J)	$8,054.00	$9,712.10	YES • See Total Loan Costs (D) and Total Other Costs (I)
Closing Costs Paid Before Closing	$0	− $29.80	YES • You paid these Closing Costs before closing
Closing Costs Financed (Paid from your Loan Amount)	$0	$0	NO
Down Payment/Funds from Borrower	$18,000.00	$18,000.00	NO
Deposit	− $10,000.00	− $10,000.00	NO
Funds for Borrower	$0	$0	NO
Seller Credits	$0	− $2,500.00	YES • See Seller Credits in Section L
Adjustments and Other Credits	$0	− $1,035.04	YES • See details in Sections K and L
Cash to Close	$16,054.00	$14,147.26	

Summaries of Transactions

Use this table to see a summary of your transaction.

BORROWER'S TRANSACTION		SELLER'S TRANSACTION	
K. Due from Borrower at Closing	**$189,762.30**	**M. Due to Seller at Closing**	**$180,080.00**
01 Sale Price of Property	$180,000.00	01 Sale Price of Property	$180,000.00
02 Sale Price of Any Personal Property Included in Sale		02 Sale Price of Any Personal Property Included in Sale	
03 Closing Costs Paid at Closing (J)	$9,682.30	03	
04		04	
Adjustments		05	
05		06	
06		07	
07		08	
Adjustments for Items Paid by Seller in Advance		**Adjustments for Items Paid by Seller in Advance**	
08 City/Town Taxes to		09 City/Town Taxes to	
09 County Taxes to		10 County Taxes to	
10 Assessments to		11 Assessments to	
11 HOA Dues 4/15/13 to 4/30/13	$80.00	12 HOA Dues 4/15/13 to 4/30/13	$80.00
12		13	
13		14	
14		15	
15		16	
L. Paid Already by or on Behalf of Borrower at Closing	**$175,615.04**	**N. Due from Seller at Closing**	**$115,665.00**
01 Deposit	$10,000.00	01 Excess Deposit	
02 Loan Amount	$162,000.00	02 Closing Costs Paid at Closing (J)	$12,800.00
03 Existing Loan(s) Assumed or Taken Subject to		03 Existing Loan(s) Assumed or Taken Subject to	
04		04 Payoff of First Mortgage Loan	$100,000.00
05 Seller Credit	$2,500.00	05 Payoff of Second Mortgage Loan	
Other Credits		06	
06 Rebate from Epsilon Title Co.	$750.00	07	
07		08 Seller Credit	$2,500.00
Adjustments		09	
08		10	
09		11	
10		12	
11		13	
Adjustments for Items Unpaid by Seller		**Adjustments for Items Unpaid by Seller**	
12 City/Town Taxes 1/1/13 to 4/14/13	$365.04	14 City/Town Taxes 1/1/13 to 4/14/13	$365.04
13 County Taxes to		15 County Taxes to	
14 Assessments to		16 Assessments to	
15		17	
16		18	
17		19	
CALCULATION		**CALCULATION**	
Total Due from Borrower at Closing (K)	$189,762.30	Total Due to Seller at Closing (M)	$180,080.00
Total Paid Already by or on Behalf of Borrower at Closing (L)	− $175,615.04	Total Due from Seller at Closing (N)	− $115,665.04
Cash to Close ☒ From ☐ To Borrower	**$14,147.26**	**Cash ☐ From ☒ To Seller**	**$64,414.96**

Additional Information About This Loan

Loan Disclosures

Assumption

If you sell or transfer this property to another person, your lender

- ☐ will allow, under certain conditions, this person to assume this loan on the original terms.
- ☒ will not allow assumption of this loan on the original terms.

Demand Feature

Your loan

- ☐ has a demand feature, which permits your lender to require early repayment of the loan. You should review your note for details.
- ☒ does not have a demand feature.

Late Payment

If your payment is more than 15 days late, your lender will charge a late fee of 5% of the monthly principal and interest payment.

Negative Amortization (Increase in Loan Amount)

Under your loan terms, you

- ☐ are scheduled to make monthly payments that do not pay all of the interest due that month. As a result, your loan amount will increase (negatively amortize), and your loan amount will likely become larger than your original loan amount. Increases in your loan amount lower the equity you have in this property.
- ☐ may have monthly payments that do not pay all of the interest due that month. If you do, your loan amount will increase (negatively amortize), and, as a result, your loan amount may become larger than your original loan amount. Increases in your loan amount lower the equity you have in this property.
- ☒ do not have a negative amortization feature.

Partial Payments

Your lender

- ☒ may accept payments that are less than the full amount due (partial payments) and apply them to your loan.
- ☐ may hold them in a separate account until you pay the rest of the payment, and then apply the full payment to your loan.
- ☐ does not accept any partial payments.

If this loan is sold, your new lender may have a different policy.

Security Interest

You are granting a security interest in
456 Somewhere Ave., Anytown, ST 12345

You may lose this property if you do not make your payments or satisfy other obligations for this loan.

Escrow Account

For now, your loan

- ☒ will have an escrow account (also called an "impound" or "trust" account) to pay the property costs listed below. Without an escrow account, you would pay them directly, possibly in one or two large payments a year. Your lender may be liable for penalties and interest for failing to make a payment.

Escrow		
Escrowed Property Costs over Year 1	$2,473.56	Estimated total amount over year 1 for your escrowed property costs: Homeowner's Insurance Property Taxes
Non-Escrowed Property Costs over Year 1	$1,800.00	Estimated total amount over year 1 for your non-escrowed property costs: Homeowner's Association Dues You may have other property costs.
Initial Escrow Payment	$412.25	A cushion for the escrow account you pay at closing. See Section G on page 2.
Monthly Escrow Payment	$206.13	The amount included in your total monthly payment.

- ☐ will not have an escrow account because ☐ you declined it ☐ your lender does not offer one. You must directly pay your property costs, such as taxes and homeowner's insurance. Contact your lender to ask if your loan can have an escrow account.

No Escrow		
Estimated Property Costs over Year 1		Estimated total amount over year 1. You must pay these costs directly, possibly in one or two large payments a year.
Escrow Waiver Fee		

In the future,

Your property costs may change and, as a result, your escrow payment may change. You may be able to cancel your escrow account, but if you do, you must pay your property costs directly. If you fail to pay your property taxes, your state or local government may (1) impose fines and penalties or (2) place a tax lien on this property. If you fail to pay any of your property costs, your lender may (1) add the amounts to your loan balance, (2) add an escrow account to your loan, or (3) require you to pay for property insurance that the lender buys on your behalf, which likely would cost more and provide fewer benefits than what you could buy on your own.

Loan Calculations

Total of Payments. Total you will have paid after you make all payments of principal, interest, mortgage insurance, and loan costs, as scheduled.	$285,803.36
Finance Charge. The dollar amount the loan will cost you.	$118,830.27
Amount Financed. The loan amount available after paying your upfront finance charge.	$162,000.00
Annual Percentage Rate (APR). Your costs over the loan term expressed as a rate. This is not your interest rate.	4.174%
Total Interest Percentage (TIP). The total amount of interest that you will pay over the loan term as a percentage of your loan amount.	69.46%

 Questions? If you have questions about the loan terms or costs on this form, use the contact information below. To get more information or make a complaint, contact the Consumer Financial Protection Bureau at **www.consumerfinance.gov/mortgage-closing**

Other Disclosures

Appraisal
If the property was appraised for your loan, your lender is required to give you a copy at no additional cost at least 3 days before closing. If you have not yet received it, please contact your lender at the information listed below.

Contract Details
See your note and security instrument for information about
- what happens if you fail to make your payments,
- what is a default on the loan,
- situations in which your lender can require early repayment of the loan, and
- the rules for making payments before they are due.

Liability after Foreclosure
If your lender forecloses on this property and the foreclosure does not cover the amount of unpaid balance on this loan,
- ☒ state law may protect you from liability for the unpaid balance. If you refinance or take on any additional debt on this property, you may lose this protection and have to pay any debt remaining even after foreclosure. You may want to consult a lawyer for more information.
- ☐ state law does not protect you from liability for the unpaid balance.

Refinance
Refinancing this loan will depend on your future financial situation, the property value, and market conditions. You may not be able to refinance this loan.

Tax Deductions
If you borrow more than this property is worth, the interest on the loan amount above this property's fair market value is not deductible from your federal income taxes. You should consult a tax advisor for more information.

Contact Information

	Lender	Mortgage Broker	Real Estate Broker (B)	Real Estate Broker (S)	Settlement Agent
Name	Ficus Bank		Omega Real Estate Broker Inc.	Alpha Real Estate Broker Co.	Epsilon Title Co.
Address	4321 Random Blvd. Somecity, ST 12340		789 Local Lane Sometown, ST 12345	987 Suburb Ct. Someplace, ST 12340	123 Commerce Pl. Somecity, ST 12344
NMLS ID					
ST License ID			Z765416	Z61456	Z61616
Contact	Joe Smith		Samuel Green	Joseph Cain	Sarah Arnold
Contact NMLS ID	12345				
Contact ST License ID			P16415	PS1461	PT1234
Email	joesmith@ ficusbank.com		sam@omegare.biz	joe@alphare.biz	sarah@ epsilontitle.com
Phone	123-456-7890		123-555-1717	321-555-7171	987-555-4321

Confirm Receipt

By signing, you are only confirming that you have received this form. You do not have to accept this loan because you have signed or received this form.

_____ _____ _____ _____
Applicant Signature   Date   Co-Applicant Signature   Date

CLOSING DISCLOSURE

PAGE 5 OF 5 • LOAN ID # 123456789

Index

D

E

F

G

H

I

J

K

L

M

N

O

P

Q

R

RESPA (Real Estate Settlement Procedures Act) ... 97, 100, 288

Restrictions ... 34, 144, 145, 226, 236, 241

Retail lender ... 34

Rider ... 236, 261

Risk(s) ... 19, 31, 35, 71, 98, 117, 123, 124, 131, 147, 179, 193, 223, 228, 237, 240, 257

Rural Development Guaranteed Housing Loan Program ... 289

S

Savings accounts ... 25, 26, 41, 48, 49, 80-83, 87, 90, 147, 241

Savings plan ... 81, 84-86

Secondary market ... 286, 289

Security (financial) ... 18, 68

Security (physical) ... 47, 62, 92, 137, 197, 202, 262, 277, 278, 284

Security instrument ... 256, 261

Security interest ... 115, 287

Self-assessment ... 41, 94

Seller(s) (the) ... 32, 33, 37, 41, 95, 101, 106, 144, 195, 197, 201-203, 212-224, 231, 236, 237, 261, 284

Seller concessions ... 196

Seller's agent ... 217, 289

Seller's market... 186, 219, 221 237

Separate property ... 244, 247

Septic tanks ... 229

Settlement agent ... 35, 97, 230, 231

Shopping (your contract) ... 220

Social Security number ... 65, 67, 109, 135

Sole ownership ... 244

Special assessments ... 35

Starting interest rate ... 131

Status of title ... 232

Structure (contract) ... 218

Structure (investment) ... 131

Structure (property)... 35, 225-229, 235, 238

Student loan ... 19, 24, 43, 58, 72, 73, 87, 91

Sweet spot (home price range) ... 185

T

Tax advisor ... 36

Tax deduction(s) ... 30, 42, 47, 83

Tax liens ... 20, 65

Tax-sheltered savings account ... 241

Temporary living expenses ... 234

Tenancy in common ... 245

U

V

W

Z